DATE DUE

OC 29 '01		
MR 25 02		
AP 15 02		
SEPT 15		
NO 1 0 '09		
FE 1 1 '10		

DEMCO 38-296

Chocolate

Recent Titles in
Contributions in Intercultural
and Comparative Studies

Chocolate
Food of the Gods

EDITED BY

Alex Szogyi

Foreword by Herman A. Berliner

Prepared under the auspices of Hofstra University

**Contributions in Intercultural and Comparative Studies,
Number 14**

GREENWOOD PRESS
Westport, Connecticut • London

Library of Congress Cataloging-in-Publication Data

Chocolate : food of the gods / edited by Alex Szogyi ;
    foreword by Herman A. Berliner.
        p.   cm.—(Contributions in intercultural and comparative
    studies, ISSN 0147–1031 ; no. 14)
        Prepared under the auspices of Hofstra University.
        Includes bibliographical references (p.   ) and index.
        ISBN 0–313–30506–4 (alk. paper)
        1. Chocolate.   2. Cocoa.   I. Szogyi, Alex.   II. Hofstra
    University.   III. Series.
    TX415.C43   1997
    641.3′374—dc21   97–12772

British Library Cataloguing in Publication Data is available.

Library of Congress Catalog Card Number: 97–12772
ISBN: 0–313–30506–4
ISSN: 0147–1031

First published in 1997

Greenwood Press, 88 Post Road West, Westport, CT 06881
An imprint of Greenwood Publishing Group, Inc.

Printed in the United States of America

Every reasonable effort has been made to trace the owners of copyright materials in this book, but in some instances this has proven
impossible. The editor and publisher will be glad to receive information leading to more complete acknowledgments in subsequent print-
ings of the book and in the meantime extend their apologies for any
omissions.

Contents

II.   CHOCOLATE AND LITERATURE   45

III.   CHOCOLATE COMMERCE AND HEALTH   109

Foreword

Herman A. Berliner

I have a long-standing passion for learning and an appreciation of the best in scholarship. I also have a long-standing passion for good chocolate. And I must admit that chocolate has had an influence on some of the decisions I have made. For example, in international travel, I first visited those countries that were known for their chocolate. Now, there are lots of reasons to visit Switzerland, Germany, and Austria and an enormous number of things to see and do and people to interact with, but the availability of chocolate was for me not an insignificant part of the decision process. As proof, I note that during a two-week trip to Switzerland, I managed to eat 14 different chocolate mousses, and I enjoyed them all. It is, therefore, not surprising that I just got around to visiting China recently, although I had always wanted to visit. And although I love Chinese food, I still packed a good supply of chocolate. However, at the first place we stopped, I found Swiss-style chocolate made in China, and later that day at the hotel, I found chocolate mousse on the menu. And both the chocolate bar and the mousse were delicious.

Chocolate knows no boundaries; speaks all languages; comes in all sizes; is woven through many cultures and disciplines; and like China, it has a long history. It impacts mood, health, and economics, and it is part of our lives from early childhood through the elderly years. There are costs associated with chocolate, and there is magic. One can love chocolate, and one can study chocolate. I do both. As an economist, I study the economic and business impact of chocolate—and it is significant. But so is its psychological impact and its impact on health. Chocolate is both an industry and a sensation. And a delight.

I was pleased to direct Hofstra's scholarly conference "Chocolate: Food of the Gods," and I am especially pleased that Alex Szogyi, who was an important presenter at the conference, has edited the conference papers and prepared this impressive volume. I thank him and everyone else who participated in the conference, and I thank Hofstra University's president Dr. James M. Shuart and the Hofstra Cultural Center for making this conference possible.

This conference volume will give the reader the scholarly flavor of the conference. But every detail of the chocolate conference also supported the conference theme, including "chocolate" breaks between sessions, an all-chocolate banquet (recipes included in this volume), and a performance of *The Chocolate Soldier* operetta. I know you will enjoy reading this volume, and I hope you continue to enjoy chocolate in all its facets.

Herman A. Berliner
Provost and Dean of Faculties
Hofstra University

Introduction

Alex Szogyi

For quite a few centuries now, chocolate has been one of humankind's primary obsessions. It exerts a pristine power over those who are passionately addicted to its intensities. In these last years of the twentieth century, it is surely one of the few addictions and obsessions that are no danger to life or limb. Although sugar has been found to be a noxious peril, it may very well be that diabetics, cholesterol counters, and sex maniacs could most profitably substitute chocolate for their other vagaries and lapses. Since this is an age of subtraction and substitution, megalomaniac anxieties, and fears for the end of our world, it may very well be that chocolate could become one of the safe panaceas, although we hardly dare mention this for fear that its price may egregiously escalate upon the morrow. As it is, the price of candy bars in movie houses has become danger-ously prohibitive—worse than popcorn!

The history of chocolate and cacao takes us from the New World, Mexico, and tributaries to Spain and then France, Austria, Switzerland, and its present Eldorado, Belgium (one of the world's authentic culinary meccas). Its impor-tance in the philosophical scheme of things to French culinary philosopher Brillat-Savarin remains most impressive. The celebrated gastronomical dictionary of Alexandre Dumas glorifies chocolate as well. American teachers and eminent gastronomes such as Judith Olney and Maida Heatter glorified chocolate. Judith Olney once entered a cooking class, placed her hands on her hips, and stated that she had never met a man as impressive as a piece of chocolate! The aphro-disiac qualities of chocolate are on a par with its inspirational elements. As may readily be intuited, chocolate is a subject worthy of the most serious contempla-tion and the highest levels of visceral serendipity. To paraphrase one of the provocative economic indicators of the moment, Don't be at home without it.

Hofstra University's noted colloquium "Chocolate: Food of the Gods" devoted three days of serious study to the subject and even provided a banquet menu entirely composed of dishes made with chocolate—from chocolate pasta, chocolate mint ice, and the celebrated Mexican gourmet dish chicken mole, to numbers of chocolate desserts such as a Black Swan gâteau and fruit dipped in chocolate, ending with truffles containing chocolate liqueur. Everyone survived nicely and was in good humor for some time afterward. For in truth and essence, chocolate makes people feel good.

The subjects studied were chocolate and children, chocolate and psychology, chocolate and literature, chocolate lore, chocolate and your health, and chocolate and business. There was a chocolate film festival as well as provocative chocolate breaks. Nineteen of the 29 presentations were submitted for publication, often revised over the years. If anything, now that the end of the twentieth century approaches, there have been even more realizations about the value of chocolate. Recently, the late news on television revealed that it is quite possible that chocolate may be beneficial to good health and helpful to those who suffer from cholesterol problems. We may be returning to Brillat-Savarin's realization in the early 1800s that chocolate was, indeed, the perfect digestible food. Even nonchocoholics may realize that chocolate has beneficial values beyond the giving of energy and loving feelings in a dangerous, dark world.

And so, here we go, exploring the world of chocolate, which began as a highly intoxicating drink prized by Montezuma and later became as valuable as money, appearing in literature, music, art, and psychology. Professors and professional chocolate purveyors are equally interested in elucidating the meaning of chocolate consumption.

On to *Theobroma cacao*, the food of the gods.

Deepest thanks to Professor Alexej Ugrinsky of the Hofstra Cultural Center, who has been so supportive of this chocolate adventure and without whose encouragement it would have been difficult to get it all together.

Profound thanks, also, to Judy D'Angio, who prepared the text and helped with a thousand important details. Her hard work and fine sense of humor made the difficult task manageable.

PART I

Chocolate and Psychology

CHAPTER 1

Chocolate and Loneliness among the Elderly

William Alex McIntosh
Karen S. Kubena
Wendall A. Landmann

Chocolate is a consuming passion in the United States. The intake of chocolate in the form of chocolate candy was assessed from data from the U.S. Department of Agriculture's *Nationwide Food Consumption Survey 1987–1988* (Seligson, Krummel, and Apgar, 1994). The intake per capita was 4.6 kilograms per year. In this study, males had chocolate candy intakes of 50 to 55 grams per day, while those of females were around 40 grams per day. Since the early 1980s, Americans have increased their chocolate intake by nearly two pounds per capita per year (Adler et al., 1983; Current Health, 1985). Part of this increase is due to the changing image of chocolate; for many, expensive chocolate is as appealing as a good wine (Adler et al., 1983).

Researchers have speculated a great deal over chocolate's popularity. Some have noted its "addictive" properties (Hirsh, 1984), while others argue that the attraction occurs because of innate preferences that humans have for sweet foods, intensified by cultural changes in what constitutes "good" food (Rozin, 1982, 1987; Mintz, 1985; Barthes, 1979; Greene, Desor, and Maller, 1976). Also important are chocolate's sensory attributes, including its characteristic flavor and unique "mouth feel," which is attributable to a melting point near body temperature.

An interesting hypothesis advanced by several researchers—but never tested specifically with chocolate—suggests that some individuals who are threatened by stressful events eat more (Guthries, 1979; Logue, 1986). It is said this occurs because the perception of the "internal stimuli associated with anxiety and those associated with hunger" becomes confused (Logue, 1986, 174). Others suggest that eating reduces anxiety (Robbins and Fray, 1980).

Nutritionists have long felt that the elderly are particularly vulnerable to nutritional disorders because of the social isolation and loneliness associated with old age (Exton-Smith, 1980; McIntosh, Shifflett, and Picov, 1989). The elderly are more likely to be widowed as well as to have lost many of their cohorts. Such losses are said to lead to despondency and lack of concern for nutritional health. Meals are skipped, and convenience foods are substituted for those that require much preparation. Foods with high levels of refined carbohydrates may enter the elderly's diets because of the little or no preparation time they involve. Few have investigated whether social isolation and loneliness affect the diet in any particular way.

This study examines the possible relationship between (1) stressful events and social isolation and (2) the intake of chocolate by elderly individuals. We expect that those elderly who experience a greater number of stressful events and are socially isolated will eat more chocolate than those who have experienced fewer events and are not isolated.

METHODOLOGY

The data utilized in this study are drawn from the "Social Support, Stress, and the Aged's Diet and Nutrition" project.[1] The sample is composed of 424 elderly Houstonians, age 65 or more, who were selected randomly through two approaches. The first approach was random-digit dialing; 355 of the respondents were located in this way. Membership lists of the American Association of Retired Persons (AARP) and churches constitute the second approach. This part of the sample was gathered by random sampling from membership lists of these organizations.

The sample drew respondents from the Houston Standard Metropolitan Statistical Area (SMSA) (Texas), which includes a six-county area. The respondents were located in 32 communities, including Houston, which ranged in distance from Houston from 2 to 50 miles. Approximately 25 percent of the sample lived in small towns or rural areas.

The data on chocolate consumption are derived from dietary records, which produced approximately 22,000 food items. These data were drawn from 24-hour recall and dietary record data. A 24-hour dietary recall was obtained at the beginning of the interview, followed by a diet history. Booklets of two-dimensional (2d) food models, which were developed from photographic mechanical transfers (PMTs) of foods and plastic food models, were provided to each subject for estimation of portion size. The 2d models were good representations of the texture and depth of the food items. Data from the dietary records were obtained by telephone interviews two days after the face-to-face interview. During the telephone interview, the respondents read entries they had made in dietary record forms left with them during the face-to-face interview.

All of those items containing chocolate were extracted from the food file and recorded as chocolate. Each individual in the sample was assigned a score from 0 to 17, based on the number of items containing chocolate that he or she had consumed during the three-day period of data collection. A second chocolate consumption was formed by assigning a "0" to those who consumed no choco-late and a "1" to those who consumed any chocolate during the 3-day period.

The experience of stressful events is based on a "life events" inventory developed by Blazer (1980) for studies of the elderly. Using a Holmes-Rahe (1967) approach, this scale determines how many stressful events (e.g., family illnesses, financial difficulties, problems with family members, victimization by crime, etc.) the respondent has suffered in the last 12 months. The number of events ranges from 0 to 12 events among our respondents. In addition to stressful events, the respondents were asked how far away their friends lived and if they argued frequently with their friends.

Loneliness was examined from the standpoint of social isolation. Fischer and Phillips (1982) have argued that loneliness is essentially a subjective pheno-menon, which, while important, neglects the objective condition of being alone. The objective approach examines "particular types of social relations a person must lack in order to be considered isolated" (22). Those with either few or nonexistent social relationships are considered socially isolated. We derived social network and social support variables from items similar to those of Claude Fischer (1982) and Eugene Litwak (1985) to ascertain social isolation.

Specifically, the respondents were asked to indicate whether they received any of 17 kinds of help (with everyday living needs such as cooking, companionship, comfort, home repairs, loans of money or household items, advice about food, finances, or government programs, etc.). The names of all those individuals providing such help were obtained. The number of names generated by each of these questions represents the degree to which the respondent is connected to other persons. Those with no or few names associated with most forms of help are considered socially isolated. We used this information to determine the amount of companionship and other forms of social support received by the respondents; we also obtained an indication of network size by summing up the number of nonredundant names across each type of help received.

We also used these lists of names to generate information about the respond-ents' "intimate" networks. After Fischer (1982), the five names (or less) that appeared most frequently were identified as the respondents' intimate networks. A series of questions about each of the five individuals was asked to determine the homogeneity (gender, ethnic, religious, church membership) and density. Density is the extent to which the five individuals mentioned most frequently knew or were acquainted with one another. We elected to include size, density, and homogeneity in our analysis because prior research indicates that small, dense, homogeneous networks are more supportive than larger, less dense, heterogeneous networks (McIntosh, Shifflett, and Picou, 1989). Finally, we determined whether the respondents generally ate alone and cooked for them-selves.

Social isolation indicators were obtained from this intimate network data by focusing on network size, density, and the lack of aid from the social support network (e.g., lack of companionship, comfort, help with activities of everyday living). Density measures the degree to which network members are interconnected.

Specifically, we argue that networks characterized by small size, low density, heterogeneity, or the provision of little aid are more socially isolating than large, dense, homogeneous, or more helpful networks. Also, we hypothesize that individuals who eat or cook alone or who get along poorly with members of their intimate networks can be viewed as more isolated.

FINDINGS

Table 1.1 contains statistics describing the frequency of chocolate intake, some sample characteristics (e.g., sex, age, education), stressful life events and situations (e.g., frequency of arguing with close friends), and social isolation. Nearly 60 percent of the elderly sample ate no food items containing chocolate during the three-day period, 20 percent ate 1 item, and 12 percent 2 two items. The remaining 8 percent accounted for the consumption of between 3 and 17 chocolate items.

The elderly's ages average roughly 72 years, with educational and income achievements of 13 years and $10,500 respectively. Over the past 12 months, the elderly in the sample experienced 2.1 life events. Fewer than 40 percent of the sample have the majority of their closest friends living five miles away or farther. On average, the elderly argue with their friends infrequently.

Turning to social isolation, the average network size is 12.5 persons, meaning that, on average, the elderly can rely on 12 people for such things as companionship, advice, intimacy, loans of small amounts of money and other things, rides to the grocery store, and so on. The standard deviation for this variable average is 15.2, indicating that 68 percent of the sample have between 7 and 17 individuals in their network. In addition, not all of the smaller networks are particularly intimate; about 25 percent of these networks are not particularly high in density (that is, fewer than 50 percent of the network members know one another). In addition, some contain no more than casual acquaintances and neighbors.

The elderly's networks are heterogeneous in terms of gender but more homogeneous in terms of religion, ethnicity, and church attendance. That is, the elderly, like other age groups, gravitate toward persons similar in religious and ethnic background and who attend the same church. Approximately 52 percent of the elderly's networks are composed of kin, 38 percent of friends, and 13 percent of neighbors.

The elderly have, on average, four individuals whom they can visit, go out with, have over to their homes, and so on. Sixty-four percent prepare their meals alone while 35 percent eat alone.

Table 1.1
Descriptive Statistics for Chocolate Intake

A. No. of Chocolate Items Eaten

	N	(%)
0	249	58.80
1	85	20.00
2	50	11.80
3	15	3.60
4	11	2.60
5	8	1.20
6	4	.94
10	1	.23
17	1	.23

B. Description of Sample

	Mean
Age	71.94 years
Years of Education	13.0 years
Income	$10,500.00
Sex (% Female)	60.1

C. Stressful Events and Situations

Number of Life Events	2.100
% Friends Who Live Far Away	37.31
Frequency Argue with Friends	1.89

D. Social Isolation (Social Network - Social Support)

Network Size	12.50 persons
Density	0.687
Heterogeneity:	
Gender	0.725
Religion	0.3992
Ethnicity	0.259
Church Attendance	0.347
% Kin	51.5
% Friends	37.6
% Neighbors	12.7
% Former Coworkers	4.2
% Voluntary Organization Members	4.18
Companionship in Everyday Activities	4.27 persons
Mealtime Companionship (eat alone)	35.40
Prepare Meals with Others (prepare alone)	63.80

Table 1.2
Chocolate Intake Variables Correlated
with Indicators of Stressful Events and
Situations and Social Isolation

	Chocolate Intake (yes = 1; no = 0)	Amount of Chocolate (number of items)
Stressful Events and Situations		
Life Events	.114**	.135***
Friends Live Far Away	.088*	.095*
Argue with Friends	.080*	.012
Social Isolation		
Network Size	.068	.082*
Network Density	.027	− .012
Companionship in Everyday Activities	.054	.144***
Mealtime Companionship	.096*	.052
Help with Meals	.085*	.024

*Significant at the .10 level.
**Significant at the .05 level.
***Significant at the .01 level.

Next, the Pearson's Product-Moment correlations in Table 1.2 indicate that chocolate intake is indeed related to indicators of stress. The dichotomous indicator of intake and the amount indicator of intake are correlated with the life events scale. This indicates that those who have experienced stress-producing events in their lives in the past 12 months are more likely to eat chocolate and eat more of it than those who have had fewer experiences. Arguing with friends and having one's closest friends or relatives live beyond the immediate neighborhood are also associated with eating chocolate.

Turning to correlates of chocolate consumption with social isolation, the findings are less consistent with our hypotheses. Chocolate consumption *increases* as the size of the elderly's social network and the amount of companionship received increase. Similarly, those who have mealtime companionship or someone who helps them prepare meals are more likely to eat chocolate.

CONCLUSIONS

The consumption of chocolate by the elderly appears to be affected by stressful events and situations but not by social isolation. These findings lend support to the notion that stressful events produce stimuli in those experiencing the stress not unlike hunger. A possible explanation for these findings is that depression is frequently associated with stressful events and situations but not necessarily with social isolation. Depression, in turn, has been said to adversely affect the diet (McIntosh, Shifflett, and Picov, 1989). Thus, depression may serve as an intervening variable here. Those who suffer stressful life events and situations develop depression, and this leads to eating chocolate or, if they are regular chocolate eaters, eating more of it.

The findings also suggest that *less* isolated elderly either eat chocolate or more of it, depending on the indicators examined. These findings dispute the original contention that the socially isolated would take refuge in chocolate. It appears instead that connections to the outside world may lead to the use of chocolate to entertain. In other words, it may be used as a means of maintaining social ties as opposed to a substitute for a lack of such ties.

NOTES

The authors would like to thank the help provided by Juliann Walker for assistance with data analysis and literature searches in the preparation of this paper. We would also like to express our gratitude for her assistance during the entire project. She also graduated with a Master of Science degree in Dietetics in 1989, and has served as a registered dietitian in the United States Air Force.

1. This work was supported by Grant #AG04043-03 from the National Institute on Aging.

REFERENCES

Adler, Jerry, Diane Weathers, Don Shirley, Deborah Prager, Holly Morrison, and Ray Wilkinson. 1983. America's chocolate binge. *Newsweek* (April 4): 50–54.

Barthes, Roland. 1979. Toward a psychosociology of contemporary food consumption. In *Food and Drink in History*, edited by Robert Forester and Orest Ranum. Baltimore: Johns Hopkins University Press. 166–73.

Blazer, Dan. 1980. Life events, mental health functioning, and the use of health care services by the elderly. *American Journal of Public Health* 70: 1174–79.

Current Health. 1985. The all-consuming passion. *Current Health* (December): 6–19.

Exton-Smith, Anthony N. 1980. Nutritional status: Diagnosis and prevention of malnutrition. In *Metabolic and Nutritional Disorders in the Elderly*, edited by Anthony N. Exton-Smith and I. F. Caird. Bristol: Wright. 66–76.

Fischer, Claude. 1982. *To Dwell Among Friends*. Chicago: University of Chicago Press.

Fischer, Claude S., and Susan L. Phillips. 1982. Who is alone?: Social characteristics of people with small networks. In *Loneliness: A Sourcebook of Current Theory, Research and Theory*, edited by Lettitia Anne Peplau and Daniel Perlman. New York: John Wiley. 21–39.

Guthrie, Helen Andrews. 1979. *Introductory Nutrition*. 4th ed. St. Louis: C. V. Mosby.

Hirsh, Kenneth. 1984. Central nervous system pharmacology of the dietary methoxanthines. In *The Methoxanthine Beverages and Foods: Chemistry, Consumption and Health Effects*, edited by Robert Johnson. New York: Methuen. 235–301.

Holmes, T. H., and R. H. Rahe. 1967. The social readjustment rating scale. *Journal of Psychosomatic Research* 11: 213–18.

Hoskin, Jonathan C. 1994. Sensory properties of chocolate and their development. *American Journal of Clinical Nutrition* 60 (supp.): 106S–107S.

Litwak, Eugene. 1985. *Helping the Elderly: The Complementary Roles of Informal Networks and Formal Systems*. New York: Guilford Press.

Loque, A. W. 1986. *The Psychology of Eating and Drinking*. New York: W. H. Freeman. McIntosh, William Alex, Peggy A. Shifflett, and J. Steven Picou. 1989. Social support, stressful events, strain, dietary intake, and the elderly. *Medical Care* 27: 140–53.

Mintz, Sidney W. 1985. *Sweetness and Power: The Place of Sugar in Modern History*. New York: Viking.

Robbins, T. W., and D. J. Fray. 1980. Stress induced eating: Fact, fiction, or misunderstanding. *Appetite* 1: 203–33.

Rozin, Paul. 1982. Human food selection: The interplay of biology, culture, and individual experience. In *The Psychobiology of Human Food Selection*, edited by Lewis M. Barker. Westport, Conn.: Avi. 225–54.

Rozin, Paul. 1987. Psychobiological perspectives on food preferences and avoidances. In *Food and Evolution: Toward a Theory of Human Food Habits*, edited by Marvin Harris and Eric B. Ross. Philadelphia: Temple University Press. 181–205.

Seligson, F. H., D. A. Krummel, and J. L. Apgar. 1994. Patterns of chocolate consumption. *American Journal of Clinical Nutrition* 60 (supp.): 1060S–64S.

CHAPTER 2

Locus of Control
and Chocolate Perceptions

Larry M. Starr
Elana Rose Starr

The seminal research by Heider (1958) laid the groundwork for most of the research dealing with attributional motivation theory. Within this rubric of ascribing causes for behavior were Heider's four elements: ability, effort, task difficulty, and luck. Ability and effort are considered to be qualities of a person, that is, internal forces. Task difficulty and luck are considered to be qualities outside a person's direct control, that is, external forces.

In a similar analysis, De Charms (1968) differentiated between Origins, individuals who feel that they choose their own behavior, and Pawns, those who believe their actions are determined by forces beyond their control. Origins rely mainly on cues within themselves when trying to accomplish a task or negotiating the conflicts of the environment, while Pawns depend primarily on cues external to themselves.

While these differentiations are of interest in a theoretic and heuristic sense, the direct application to practical and behavioral issues was made by Rotter (1966). According to Rotter, those people with stable expectancy patterns, characterized by a belief that reinforcement and success are contingent on previous experience, may be designated as Internal (I). When one is characterized by a relative neglect of previous experience and an expectation that future outcomes and reinforcement depend on forces beyond themselves, a designation of External (E) is applied.

Extensive research has been performed to distinguish between the characteristics of Is and Es. Various performance measures indicate some of the attributes of Is to be high self-esteem (Fitch, 1970); high need achievement (McClelland, et al., 1953); more reliance on self regardless of task (Julian and Katz, 1968); and less amenability to the influence of others (Crowne and Liverant, 1963; Strickland, 1970). Qualities of Es, on the other hand, tend to be low self-esteem

(Fitch, 1970); low need achievement (McClelland, et al., 1953); greater field dependency (Strickland, 1970); and more passiveness (Rotter, 1966).

Most research on I-E, often termed "Locus of Control," is performed in a similar manner. Subjects are administered a written questionnaire (Rotter, 1966) and then divided on the basis of their score, following a median split. Those scoring in the Internal or External direction are presented with a task or other performance or choice measure, and responses are gathered.

While well-organized surveys of the research literature have documented the reliability and validity of the scale and its underlying assumptions in a variety of natural and field studies, correlational studies of the I-E scale and other personological variables have often yielded disappointing results. It may be, as noted by Rotter (1966, 21), that this is due to influences of situation-specific attitudes within the domains of the behavior investigated.

The present study focused not so much on a personologic variable as on a deep and powerful underlying preference for one category of food—namely, chocolate. Used as a reinforcement in many social and child-rearing circumstances across all social strata and subcultures, chocolate has become more than a simple food and may take on secondary reinforcement characteristics in a variety of situations. Of particular interest to the authors was whether social learning theory, as acknowledged by Rotter and others, could be used to define and discriminate between those who prefer chocolate and those whose food preferences run in other directions. Indeed, such information could be of interest both in a theoretical sense and also in a more practical sense. Whether chocolate is preferred more by Internals or Externals could have an impact on marketing and other sales efforts since attention to advertising copy and descriptions would be expected to differ for these personality types.

The present study was designed to investigate the following questions: First, following measurement of Internals and Externals on a standardized I-E scale, could scores be used to distinguish those who preferred chocolate over non-chocolate foods? Second, what kinds of foods, if any, were listed by chocolate and nonchocolate lovers?

METHOD

Subjects

During April 1988, students in three classes of psychology and in the school of engineering at Villanova University were given an opportunity to participate in a brief questionnaire survey. During regular classes, their professors indicated that a study was being done on the topic of "chocolate" and asked for volunteers to complete a personality test and short follow-up questionnaire.

Procedure and Text Instruments

Students who agreed to participate were administered a questionnaire booklet containing four pages. The first three pages included a 25-item version of the Internal-External (I-E) Locus of Control scale (Schopler, 1971) and an answer page. This version differed from Rotter's (1966) original in that responses were made to a five-point interval scale and included fewer items. Statistically, Schopler's revision balanced out the bimodality that generally occurs with the original two-alternative forced-choice scale.

Following the I-E test in the questionnaire booklet was a single-page "Food Attitude Survey." This consisted of a request for age and sex data and 17 attitudinal questions. The first 13 involved rating the degree to which one liked foods such as "chocolate ice cream," "ice cream (other than chocolate)," "cookies other than chocolate," and "cookies containing chocolate" according to a five-point interval scale ranging from 1 (not at all) to 5 (very much). Of the 13 items, 6 designated chocolate as a component, while the remainder either discounted chocolate "donuts not containing chocolate") or described a non-chocolate food ("fresh fruit," "fruit pie").

Question 14 (Do you enjoy making your own desserts?) and Question 15 (Do you consider yourself to be a good cook when it comes to desserts?) also required a five-point interval response scale. Question 16 (What is your favorite dessert?) and Question 17 (Describe the taste of chocolate) were open-ended items requiring response coding for categories.

Results

Sixty-five students ranging between 18 and 45 years of age and with a mean of 21.5 years participated in this study. Males and females were relatively even in distribution (36 males; 27 females; 2 no responses).

The mean responses to Questions 1 through 13 are presented in Table 2.1. As noted, while some variability was found among the chocolate and chocolate-absent pastries, the highest-rated food and the choice with the smallest standard deviation was fresh fruit ($\bar{X}$ = 4.31; SD = .789). The lowest-rated food, and the only item shown to be less than 3 on the five-point scale, was chocolate cheesecake ($\bar{X}$ = 2.92). A "chocolate score" was also computed for each respondent by summing the values selected in the six chocolate foods found in the list. The mean for this score with a possible range of 6 to 30 was 20.92. A slight majority of the students (53 percent) enjoyed making their own desserts ($\bar{X}$ = 3.20) and considered themselves (52 percent) to be good cooks ($\bar{X}$ = 3.03).

Selections of a "favorite dessert" produced a wide variey of items that were coded into 10 categories (cake; ice cream; pie; cheesecake; cookies and candy; fruit/jello; donuts/éclairs; soufflés; drinks/milkshakes/cappuccino; and trifles). Consistent with earlier data, "pies" were noted as the favorite food by the most

Table 2.1
Mean Preferences for Foods

Question Description	Mean Response
Chocolate ice cream	3.65
Ice cream (other than chocolate)	3.89
Chocolate cake/brownies	3.89
Cake (other than chocolate)	3.55
Fruit pie	3.22
Fresh fruit	4.31
Cookies containing chocolate	3.88
Cookies other than chocolate	3.55
Candy bars	3.37
Chocolate donuts	3.20
Donuts not containing chocolate	3.57
Cheesecake	3.78
Chocolate cheesecake	2.92

Note: Scale ranged from 1 (low preference) to 5 (high preference).

respondents (28 percent). When asked to "describe the taste of chocolate," some variability also occurred and was coded into two categories. First, each response was noted to be positive or negative by the coders. Second, the descriptions were rated as either perceptual Physical Sensations, such as "refreshing," "reviving," and "satisfying"; Simple, Evaluative, such as "sweet," "chalky," "creamy," and "gooey"; or Other, such as "unique" and "long-lasting."

Seventy-four percent of the students rated chocolate positively, 9 percent rated it negatively, and the remainder expressed no evaluative direction in their descriptions. The majority of the respondents described chocolate with Perceptual labels (52 percent), followed by Simple Evaluative (15 percent), Physical Sensations (11 percent), and Other (6 percent). Fifteen percent of students made no attempt to describe the taste of chocolate. Of those who did list their favorite dessert, however, 53 percent noted that chocolate was a component, while 47 percent listed a food without chocolate.

Analysis of the I-E scale revealed that scores ranged from 52 to 112, with a mean of 82.22. Since the possible range (25 to 125) would have the mean fall at 75, the present sample is only slightly above the mean and reflects a tendency of these students to be more External than Internal in their orientation.

Correlation analysis produced a number of interesting relationships. The item of initial interest, I-E, was significantly correlated with subject sex ($r = -.21$, $p = .04$), indicating that more men than women scored in the External direction. Externals were also more likely to prefer fresh fruit (Question 6) than Internals ($r = -.26$, $p = .02$). There was no significant correlation between I-E score and any of the individual chocolate foods. Using I-E score as criterion and the food preferences as predictors in a stepwise multiple regression indicated that total chocolate score (consisting of six chocolate foods) was the strongest predictor, followed by preference for ice cream (other than chocolate) and cheesecake (other than chocolate). Examination of the means for these values showed that Externals were less interested in chocolate (lower chocolate scores) and had stronger preferences for ice cream and cheesecake than Internals.

Total chocolate score also correlated with a number of items in this survey. Those with stronger chocolate preferences were more likely to state that they enjoyed making their own desserts ($r = .39$, $p = .001$); were more likely to consider themselves to be good cooks ($r = .37$, $p = .001$); and were more likely to list chocolate with positive labels in their description of a favorite dessert ($r = -.52$, $p = .001$).

CONCLUSIONS

The relationship between I-E and chocolate preference seems to run in the Internal direction. Externals tended not to prefer chocolate and to list fruit and other nonchocolate foods higher. Apparently, being External (neglect of previous experience as the basis for future expectations) may be less related to chocolate choices because of a general belief in lack of one's personal control over outcomes. Chocolate lovers, in this survey, not only enjoyed and described their foods but also tended to make chocolate desserts and felt they were good at such activities. Possibly, this kind of direct experience of working with chocolate is characteristic of Internals in general and chocolate-preferring Internals in particular.

While it would be simplistic and erroneous to state that all Externals hate chocolate, of the 74 percent of students who rated chocolate positively and 9 percent who rated it negatively, most of the positives came from Internals, and all of the negatives came from Externals. Indeed, Externals used labels such as "chalky," "boring," and "too intense," and one listed the favorite dessert as "diet jello."

Use of labels in describing the taste of chocolate proved to be interesting. Of particular enjoyment to the researchers were the comments made by respondents during the questionnaire responding. Various "oohs" and "aahs" as well as "This is making me hungry" were emitted by respondents. One subject, in an effort to be quite clear about her preferences, not only gave a description of her favorite dessert but also listed the ingredients (flour, sugar, condensed milk, etc.). Other interesting labels included: "It tastes like sex feels," "orgasmic," and "awesome."

As a follow-up to this study and for possible use by those in the marketing of chocolate, it may be of interest to know the apparent audience. If most chocolate lovers, that is, chocolate buyers/chocolate attenders to advertising, are Internal, perhaps more direct selling to those with this personality characteristic could be attempted. Merely showing people eating and enjoying chocolate is certainly a persuasive message, but a stronger focus on mechanisms of personal control could also be applied. As one coauthor noted, "I wouldn't trust something really important to someone who didn't like chocolate."

REFERENCES

Crowne, D., and S. Liverant. 1963. Conformity under varying conditions of personal commitment. *Journal of Abnormal and Social Psychology* 66: 547–55.

De Charms, R. 1968. *Personal Causation*. New York: Academic Press.

Fitch, G. 1970. Effects of self-esteem, perceived performance and choice of causal atttribution. *Journal of Personality and Social Psychology* 16: 311–15.

Heider, F. 1958. *The Psychology of Interpersonal Relations*. New York: Wiley and Sons.

Julian, J., and S. Katz. 1968. Internal vs. external control and the value of reinforcement. *Journal of Personality and Social Psychology* 8: 89–94.

McClelland, D., J. Atkinson, R. Clark, and E. Lowell, 1953. *The Achievement Motive*. New York: Appleton-Century-Crofts.

Rotter, J. 1966. Generalized expectancies for internal vs. external control of reinforcement. *Psychological Monographs*, vol. 80.

Schopler, J. 1971. Personal orientation scale. Personal communication. [See Balik, B. and Starr, L. (1973). Investigations of internal vs. external control and volunteering behavior, unpublished manuscript, Villanova University.]

Strickland, B. 1970. Individual differences in verbal conditioning, extinction and aware-ness. *Journal of Personality* 38: 364–87.

CHAPTER 3

Curing Irrationality with Chocolate Addiction

Catherine S. Elliott

There are those who claim that chocolate "seems above choice and without alternatives." If true, chocolate would be what an economist terms a *pure lexicographic commodity*. It is ranked highest in an individual's ordering of preferences over different market baskets. This implies that, regardless of the level of other goods or income, the individual always chooses a market basket on the basis of which one has the greatest amount of chocolate. Moreover, the presence of chocolate is required before decisions can be made on other choice alternatives. Thus, all remaining choices must be postponed until after the individual acquires chocolate. Hence, the term *lexicographic*: When looking up a word in a dictionary, the first letter must be found before it is possible even to attempt to find the second.

Identifying chocolate as a lexicographic good helps economists understand some of the behavior of chocolate lovers, but it doesn't explain why chocolate is elevated to this station by these individuals. The premise of this chapter is that chocolate ranks first in a lexicographical ordering because it can cure irrationality. Most people suffer from moments of lack of willpower. When faced with a conflict between short-run desires and what they know is "best in the long run," they often choose to follow temptation—only to regret it later. Fortunately, the use of chocolate as an enticement for long-run optimal behavior can prevent the irrational choices made when willpower is low. In addition, because the effectiveness of chocolate in this role will increase, it may be optimal for imperfectly rational individuals to create in themselves a psychological addiction to chocolate.[1]

This chapter is organized in the following way. The second section explains the concept of imperfect rationality, including how it differs from the assumptions of traditional economic models of individual decision making. The third section is a nontechnical discussion both of the nature of the dilemma faced by people when willpower is low and of the solution provided by enticements such as chocolate. In the fourth section, economic theory is applied to illustrate and analyze more fully the conclusions of the previous section. (Each element of the microeconomic graphical analysis is defined before being used. However, readers do not need to understand the techniques of this section in order to understand the results.) And the fifth section argues the case for rational psychological addiction to chocolate.

IMPERFECT RATIONALITY

Economists traditionally have used a very simple model of decision making— essentially one wherein each individual possesses perfect information and is incapable of error. Under all circumstances, individuals do what is best for themselves. Such behavior is called rational. By implication, individuals are irrational whenever they knowingly choose an action that is not best for them.

Theories based on economic rationality assumptions are straightforward and tractable. Mathematical formulas summarize the desires and constraints of the rational decision maker, and the mathematics of optimization determine an exact maximum, that is, the dominant strategy or optimal set of choices. For these reasons, most economic analysis utilizes the perfectly informed and infallible decision maker even though the existence of such a person is at odds with theories of human behavior in other disciplines and more important, with the results of experimental studies performed by both psychologists and economists.[2]

Because of the increasing amount of contradictory evidence, however, a new field called *behavioral economics* has developed in the last decade. Behavioral economics reflects an interdisciplinary approach to the study of decision making and focuses on investigations of actual behavior as opposed to the implications of mathematical models of presupposed optimal behavior. This implies that irrationality is not ruled out *a priori*. Thus, research in this area is leading to the creation of more descriptive and realistic (i.e., behavior-based) assumptions and theories of human decision making.

In general, it is hard to convince most economists that people do not or are not always able to act in their own best interest. John Kenneth Galbraith reportedly once said that economists have an "irrational passion for dispassionate rationality." However, in his book *Ulysses and the Sirens*, Jon Elster (1986) put forth an argument that even economists find difficult to refute. Elster asserts that the existence of binding behavior is proof of human irrationality. Binding behavior occurs when people know what action is optimal or best for them yet also know they are incapable of completing it without some type of precommitment or tie to that action. Hence, Elster's reference to the story of Ulysses being bound to his ship's mast in order to hear (and survive) the song of the Sirens. Elster concludes that human rationality is imperfect because people need to use bindings frequently in everyday life to prevent irrational or suboptimal actions:

Man often is not rational, and rather exhibits *weakness of will*. Even when not rational, man knows that he is irrational and can *bind himself* to protect himself against the irrationality. This second-best or imperfect rationality takes care both of reason and of passion. (111)

Most examples of binding behavior center on withdrawal from substances to which an individual has become addicted, such as tobacco, alcohol, drugs, or food. To precommit to the optimal strategy of breaking a harmful addiction, an individual could enter a hospital with the consent of a physician or pay large fees to a specialty clinic. Extreme cases of binding behavior to prevent over-eating have included submitting to operations that seal off sections of the stomach or to wearing face braces, which wire the mouth virtually shut.

By introducing constraints that eliminate alternatives from the individual's set of choices, the above binding strategies alter the environment within which the decision to use the addictive substance is made. Other, less drastic means of altering a decision environment are used, however, when the consequences of the suboptimal action are not as severe as in the previous examples. Instead of constructing immovable barriers to prevent certain behaviors, individuals can set up self-administered systems of inducements or positive reinforcers.

The use of positive reinforcers to guarantee what Elster terms second-best rationality (but first-best or optimal behavior) is a common, everyday occurrence—students bribing themselves to study with the promise of a favorite television program later in the evening, researchers planning to take a vacation after the completion of a difficult project, or diners promising themselves dessert in order to eat a meal with vegetables. For most readers, it probably takes little or no effort to think of other examples where weakness of will is overcome in a similar fashion. A positive reinforcer is linked to the optimal action to make it more attractive than the suboptimal action, even when willpower is low.[3] Individuals learn through experience the type and amount of reinforcer needed to bribe themselves into doing "what is best" in different choice situations.

SHORT-RUN VERSUS LONG-RUN OPTIMALITY

I claim that chocolate may be the perfect binding or positive reinforcer to entice individuals into behaving rationally in their everyday lives. It is a harmless substance,[4] yet a substance that possesses the ability to cure the irrationality of weakness of will. Chocolate can create lasting devotion in its users, who assert it yields an unusually high level of satisfaction per unit consumed. It is a unique commodity, with no exact substitutes—impossible to duplicate because it is composed of more than 300 different chemical elements (Adler, 1983). One of those chemicals, phenylethylamine, is the same created by the brain when an individual becomes infatuated or falls in love (Robinson, 1984). Little wonder chocolate is referred to by the cocoa plant's scientific name. *Theobroma cacao*, or "the food of the gods." Indeed, Ruth Galvin (1986) reports that the Aztecs were convinced chocolate came from their god Quetzalcoatl as a "consolation to Man for having to live on Earth," and "after life, it was expected to be served perpetually" (57). Perhaps Quetzalcoatl also sent chocolate to help humans overcome moments of weakness of will and thus to constrain suboptimal behavior.

How is chocolate able to cure irrationality? Simply stated, the promised reward of chocolate yields a present value to the individual that is high enough to counter the temptations of the moment. Essentially, a present value is the current worth of a future activity. The concept is borrowed from the theory of managerial finance, where it is used to evaluate investment opportunities that normally involve an initial outlay of cash in the expectation that future receipts will yield a profitable return.

Even without taking inflation into account, a future dollar is not worth the same as a present dollar simply because the present dollar could, at the very least, earn interest in a savings account. This implies that the current value of a promised future dollar is less than a dollar. The actual present value is determined by the selection of a rate at which to discount the future dollar. Business firms choose the highest interest rate the future dollar would have earned if it had been possible to invest that dollar at the present time.

Individuals, like businesses, make choices in the present that determine returns in the future, but unlike businesses, neither the current choices nor the future returns always have a cash equivalent. Economists term the total value to an individual of any activity the *utility* of that activity. Utility is synonymous with satisfaction or happiness and is necessarily subjective because it can be based on nonpecuniary considerations. In the same way the utility of any present-day activity varies from individual to individual, the present value of the utility derived from future activities also varies. However, for any given individual, the utility of a desirable event occurring in the future is less than the utility of the same event occurring in the present.[5] Similarly, disutility is discounted—the possibility of a detrimental event does not seem nearly so bad if scheduled for the future instead of the present.

In order for chocolate to work as a positive reinforcer for second-best rationality, the present value of chocolate must be high enough to entice individuals into following long-run optimal behavior. The need for the positive reinforcer to have a high present value in order to be effective can be induced from the work of C. C. von Weiszacker (1971). Von Weiszacker identified a decision paradox similar to Elster's imperfect rationality: The dilemma faced by someone who should stop making decisions based on short-run desires or preferences because an alternative set of preferences will result in greater utility in the long run. The decision maker is aware of the long-run gains yet is unable to switch to the long-run preferences.

Von Weiszacker concluded that the only way to guarantee an optimal solution to this dilemma is social engineering, that is, contracting with a government organization to enforce behavior consistent with the individual's long-run preferences. However, as Elster points out, it is unrealistic (and unpalatable) to give an outside agent the power to solve every irrationality of this type by forcibly engineering the optimal behavior. Fortunately, we do not have to.

After experiencing the regret of following short-run strategies, we become aware of our imperfect rationality. We then can contract privately with ourselves to use positive reinforcers to bind us to our long-run preferences. Although it will be too late to undo the damage of having followed short-run strategies in the past, the binding will limit any further losses in utility in the future.

The key to successful private engineering lies in the answer to the following question: If the dominant strategy yields the highest satisfaction in the long run, why don't we simply switch to the long-run preferences?

The answer is: Because choices are based on the present value of future utility and not on the value that would be realized in the long run. Thus, when a suboptimal strategy is chosen, the present value of the utility of the optimal behavior is too low to overcome the current utility of the short-run behavior. In the absence of positive reinforcers, this leads to the continuation of suboptimal actions. Therefore, the present value of the utility of the long-run optimal behavior must be increased. Mental persuasion or willpower works for the perfectly rational, but for those of us who are imperfectly rational: Chocolate.

It is well known that the promise of chocolate can entice children through a dinner of lima beans and liver, and adults through the most difficult and tedious projects. Students seem very familiar with binding tricks such as one "M&M" per page read of Tolstoy's *War and Peace*.[6] The thought of chocolate, that is, its present value, has enough utility to overcome the current disutility of the task at hand and thus to bribe individuals into acting optimally. The next point at issue is how chocolate actually changes a decision maker's choice set.

Recall that imperfectly rational individuals are aware of the consequences of both the short-run and the long-run optimal choices; and in particular, they are aware that when the long-run becomes the present, they will regret choices based on short-run preferences. In order to avoid the disutility of future regret, the imperfectly rational voluntarily institute binding mechanisms to guarantee what Elster terms second-best rationality. What must be explained, then, is how short-run strategies can be seen as optimal without binding and yet suboptimal with binding.

The answer lies in the definition of *short run*. The pleasure of short-run temptation is experienced immediately—or at least sooner than the additional satisfaction or utility derived from following optimal long-run strategy. To illustrate how this time difference leads to suboptimal choices, consider the age-old dilemma faced by college students every weekend—how much to study versus how much to party (or not study). Table 3.1 shows possible values[7] for the daily utility of a suboptimal study strategy for a Monday exam (resulting in failing the exam) and for an optimal study strategy (resulting in doing well on the exam). The utility values for Saturday and Sunday derive directly from the different times spent studying and partying. The values for Monday represent

Table 3.1
Utility Study Plans

	Sat.	Sun.	Mon.
Utility of suboptimal study plan	10	10	−50
Utility of optimal study plan	6	6	25

the student's utility from the actual exam performance. If time were collapsed into a single moment, the student would face the choice of immediately experiencing total utility equal to −30 or total utility equal to +37. There would be no conflict between short-run and long-run optimization. Even without binding behavior, the imperfectly rational student of Table 3.1 would choose the optimal study plan to obtain the utility level +37.

Time is not an instant, however; it is a continuum. When willpower is low, short-run "temptation" exists because the present value of the optimal (dominant) study strategy becomes lower than the present value of the suboptimal study plan. In the extreme case, moments of low willpower can result in individuals shortening their time horizons.

Assume that on Saturday our student ignores the utility of Monday completely. If the remaining utility is not discounted, the choice set becomes the option of experiencing the total utility of +20 or the option of experiencing the total utility of +12. The student goes to the party. Thus, behavior seems "irrational" in the short run only if the impact of time on the decision process is ignored.

It is clear that choices made when willpower is low are still utility-maximizing choices, but they are also choices made with present value calculations that significantly devalue or ignore altogether both long-run benefits and costs. To ensure long-run optimality, the results of the utility-maximizing calculations must be changed so that even when willpower is low, the dominant strategy is followed. Thus, second-best rationality does not require changes in an individual's discount rate[8] or preferences but requires changes in the components of the choice set. Specifically, the decision maker must attach enough positive reinforcers to appropriate units of the activity yielding the long-run benefits so that the discounted or immediate utility of the optimal strategy becomes greater than the utility of the suboptimal strategy.

Consider how an enticement of chocolate can change the decision-making environment to guarantee second-best rationality. For one hour of studying, for example, the reward could be one Belgian dark chocolate truffle. Based on the author's personal values, the utility rankings for truffles when used for recreation, when used as a reward, and when abused could be represented as shown in Table 3.2.

Table 3.2
Utility of Belgian Chocolate Truffles

Recreational Use	5
Use as a Reward	9
Chocolate Abuse	−2

Thus, the reward value of chocolate is separate from the value of the chocolate itself. Similarly, if the truffle is eaten *and* the suboptimal strategy is followed, the guilt of chocolate abuse will cause the total utility of the truffle experience to be negative.

Based on the values for Belgian truffles in Table 3.2, then, the total utility rankings in Table 3.1 for the two study plans would change to become those shown in Table 3.3.

Table 3.3
Utility Rankings Based on Belgian Truffles

	Sat.	*Sun.*	*Mon.*
Utility of suboptimal study plan with chocolate abuse	8	8	−50
Utility of optimal study plan with chocolate rewards	15	15	25

No matter what discount rate is used by an individual with the new utility values in Table 3.3, the dominant long-run study strategy will be followed each day. The key is to promise a reward that is realized (i.e., eaten) in the future but in a closer future than the time when the long-run utility of the investment activity, studying, is realized.

AN ECONOMIC ANALYSIS OF SECOND-BEST RATIONALITY

In Figures 3.1 and 3.2, the economic framework of constraints and indifference curves is used to illustrate both the von Weiszacker irrationality paradox and how the promise of chocolate can bind an individual to the optimal long-run strategy. The analysis is based on the example in the previous section. Hours spent studying are measured on the vertical axes, while hours spent partying (or not studying) are measured on the horizontal axes. For simplicity, assume the relevant time frame is a single day, less 8 hours for sleep. The constraint line then represents a choice situation in which the student has 16 hours to allocate between the two activities.[9] The constraint line has a slope of −1 because an hour of studying is an hour that cannot be spent partying, and vice versa.

The indifference curves, labeled U_1, U_2, and U_3, for example, each illustrate combinations of studying and partying that would give the student equal utility or satisfaction. Thus, points on the same indifference curve represent all combinations of the two activities between which the student would be indifferent and could not make a choice. If U is defined as the level of utility associated with each respective indifference curve, then in Figure 3.1: $U_3^* > U_2^* > U_1^*$.

A series of indifference curves is termed a *preference mapping* and is the tool used by economists to illustrate both a summary of the complete preference structure of a representative consumer and the specific welfare accessible to that consumer within a given set of constraints.[10] Shapes of indifference curves can change to reflect the varied personalities of different consumers or the different preferences the same consumer might have over various commodity bundles.

Figure 3.1 is drawn to illustrate the optimal combination of studying and partying. Although three levels of welfare are graphed, the constraint line prevents the student from reaching the utility level U_3^*. Both U_2^* and U_1^* are possible, but the rational student will always choose a strategy consistent with the highest level of utility attainable. Because U_2^* is the highest indifference curve the student in Figure 3.1 can reach, the optimal strategy is to study s^* hours and party p^* hours, where $s^* + p^* - = 16$. (It is assumed that all work and no play makes students dull.)

A perfectly rational consumer has a single preference mapping, as in Figure 3.1, and is better off only when a higher indifference curve is reached. However, because an imperfectly rational individual suffers from "weakness of will," two indifference mappings exist. One mapping represents the preferences an individual would have if always perfectly rational (the so-called long-run preferences). The second mapping represents the preferences the imperfectly rational individual actually has when willpower is low (the so-called short-run preferences).

Given that the two mappings must necessarily overlap, increases in welfare can now be judged only by comparing the utility levels attached to the specific indifference curves. It is important to note that each separate mapping fulfills the requirements for economic consistency—the indifference curves within a specific mapping do not intersect. This implies, for instance, that if the consumer is operating with the short-run mapping, all choices will be rational with respect to that particular mapping.

Figure 3.1
Long-run Optimal Strategy (s*, p*)

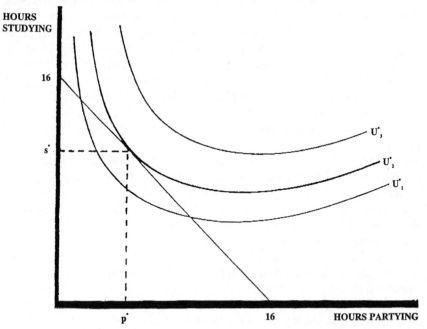

Figure 3.2
Short-run Preferences and Suboptimal Strategy (s†, p†)

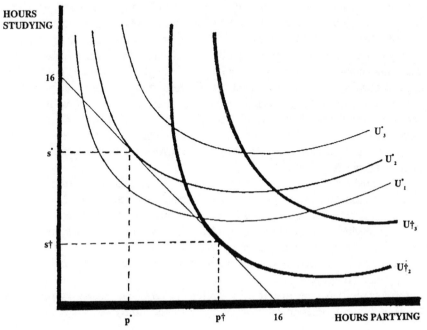

The two mappings are drawn in Figure 3.2. The three thin indifference curves labeled U^*_1, U^*_2, and U^*_3 are identical to those of Figure 3.1, representing long-run preferences. The two thick curves, $U\dagger_2$ and $U\dagger_3$, illustrate the von Weiszacker dilemma—the short-run preferences brought on by the temptations of the moment. As stated above, the short-run and long-run preference mappings intersect each other because they represent completely different, yet internally consistent, attitude toward the activity combinations summarized by the graph of the consumer's choice set. With respect to Tables 3.1 and 3.3 in the previous section, the thin indifference curves reflect the utility of long-run optimal study plans, while the thick indifference curves reflect the utility of long-run optimal study plans.

Consider the strategy that would maximize utility if the thick indifference curves in Figure 3.2 were the individual's only preference mapping. $U\dagger_3$ is the highest utility level of the graphed curves, but again, it is unattainable because of the constraint line. Therefore, this student would choose to study $s\dagger$ hours and party $p\dagger$ hours in order to reach utility level $U\dagger_2$.

Imperfectly rational students, however, have both the long-run and short-run sets of preferences. Once again, if faced with the choice between immediately experiencing $U\dagger_2$ or immediately experiencing U^*_2, the student would not need binding to choose (s^*, p^*) to obtain utility level U^*_2. However, the future is not the same as the present. Define PV to be the present value or utility of any given study/party strategy. Then the short-run strategy of $(s\dagger, p\dagger)$ is followed because when that decision is made, $PV(U\dagger_2) > PV(U^*_2)$, even though the returns to studying are realized, $U^*_2 > U\dagger_2$.

When suffering from lack of will power, the individual chooses the strategy $(s\dagger, p\dagger)$ even though in the *long run* U^*_2 is greater than $U\dagger_2$. Again, the question is why? Von Weiszacker believed it could be explained by inertia or force of habit—hence, his solution of an outside government agency simply forcing the individual to act in a way consistent with long-run optimal behavior. After some experience with the utility associated with the long-run preference mapping, von Weiszacker asserted the individual would then come to recognize that the move had been "for the best" and even be grateful for the intervention. (This agrees with a favorite scenario of parents: The son or daughter finally realizing that the parents were right each time a rule had been justified with the phrase "You'll understand when you're older.")

As pointed out in the previous section, von Weiszacker's explanation does not allow for voluntary action to bring about second-best rationality. Yet binding mechanisms are used successfully by many people. The dilemma is solved because individuals intuitively understand that utility gains or losses are valued differently if promised for the future than if received in the present and that enticements can be used to increase the daily utility value of following the long-run optimal strategy.

Of course, it is true that if a benevolent government agency enforced the strategy (s^*, p^*), then in comparison *only* to the utility associated with the suboptimal strategy (s†, p†), the person would be better off in the long-run (i.e., the student would be better off on *Monday* if forced to study optimally all weekend). However, it is likely that the person will experience enough disutility from the interference with voluntary choice to outweigh any utility gained from the long-run strategy.

Consider again how a voluntarily instituted reward system of chocolate guarantees second-best rationality and first-best behavior. The student attaches the chocolate enticement to the activity of studying. The present values of alternative activity mixes are recalculated to determine the optimal short-run strategy. The correct bribe guarantees that $PV(U_2 + C^*) > PV(U_2)$, where C^* represents the amount of chocolate needed to tip the scales in favor of the dominant, long-run strategy.[11] (Note that chocolate consumption is complementary to the optimal activity level; thus, there is no need to change the time constraint on studying and partying. The necessary amount of C^* will vary among individuals, depending on their personal valuation of chocolate. The important point is, however, for those fortunate enough to appreciate its qualities, chocolate, the food of the gods, can solve the von Weiszacker irrationality paradox.

RATIONAL CHOCOLATE ADDICTION

In this section, it is argued that choosing to become psychologically addicted to chocolate can be rational. Those who succeed might be termed *rational chocoholics*. Psychological addiction will both guarantee the future success of chocolate as a binding mechanism for second-best rationality and minimize the amount needed as a bribe in any given choice situation.

Before proceeding, a distinction between psychological and physical addiction must be made. Physical addictions lead to diminished utility per unit of the substance consumed. For example, the effectiveness of a sleeping pill or pain killer lessens over time as more is needed to perform the same function. An economist would say that the additional or marginal utility of a given unit of the substance declines as the individual becomes physically addicted.

In contrast, psychological addiction (which is counseled here) *increases* the marginal utility per unit of the substance. Chocolate becomes more valuable to the psychologically addicted because the same amount of chocolate gives more satisfaction than before. As opposed to needing more and more to reach the same euphoric state, the rational chocoholic can reach it with less. Thus, once psychologically addicted, the increase in the marginal utility of a unit of chocolate actually decreases the amount needed as a binding to overcome short-run temptations. Of course, this does not imply that the psychologically addicted won't eat more chocolate than before their addiction; it just implies that chocolate has become more desirable relative to other commodities. Further, the previous chocolate "high" is less expensive in the sense that less chocolate is now required to produce the positive feelings. Thus, psychological addiction can decrease the cost of the binding mechanism.[12]

Psychological addiction also minimizes the probability of a possible significant negative side effect: Weight gain. For example, triple-chocolate brownies, with chocolate frosting and chocolate chunks, have been correlated with increases in the average weight of certain known chocolate lovers. Fortunately, psychological addiction increases the present value of chocolate by increasing the marginal utility per unit of chocolate. If the present value of a chocolate enticement goes up, the amount needed for binding goes down, and this side effect can be minimized or eliminated entirely.

Even without psychological addiction, promises of chocolate yield substantial present values—recall the joy chocolate brings to its users and in particular, the lovelike euphoria it creates even in nonaddicts. Once past consumption of chocolate has created the addiction, any additional chocolate gives greater satisfaction per unit. This increase in the inherent utility of chocolate also increases its effectiveness as a positive reinforcer for optimal activity. The higher the present value of the enticement, the more likely the optimal strategy will be followed in order to secure the enticement.

In order to complete the argument that it can be rational to addict oneself to chocolate in order to guarantee long-run optimality, we must consider whether or not addictions prevent rational behavior. In other words, can addicts optimize? Gary Becker and Kevin Murphy (1988) proposed a theory of rational addiction. A rational addict (or nonaddict) maximizes utility consistently across all time periods by accounting for how past consumption of an addictive substance can change current and future consumption patterns. Given this framework, Becker and Murphy were able to demonstrate that even the behavior of an addict can be explained by a model of a utility-maximizing individual.

Becker and Murphy do not claim it is rational to plan an addiction to drugs, alcohol, or cigarettes. However, their model does allow for beneficial addictions if future productivity and income are increased. Becker and Murphy's work thus allows us to claim that addicts can still optimize and that not all addictions are harmful. Therefore, because side effects are minimized, and binding effectiveness is maximized, creating a psychological addiction to chocolate can be rational.

CONCLUDING REMARKS

As pointed out in the introductory section to this chapter, the typical economist employs models based on assumptions of optimizing behavior. The model presented herein has been no different. However, the typical economist also assumes individuals are capable of making decisions consistently across time by taking into account not only current costs and benefits but all future costs and benefits. This is how the model in this chapter is different.

Individuals can suffer from moments of weakness of will. Weakness of will shortens time horizons. Although an optimal choice is made with respect to the shortened time span, it is suboptimal with respect to all relevant time periods. This causes regret when the future becomes the present. However, as Elster points out, individuals know this and can use positive reinforcers to bind themselves to following dominant long-run strategies. Elster calls this second-best or imperfect rationality. Although irrationality is possible, binding behavior limits its occurrence. Short-run temptations can seem optimal to an individual without binding yet can become suboptimal with binding.

For many, chocolate is the most effective binding mechanism because even the promise of future chocolate is valued highly in the present. Thus, the present value of future chocolate consumption is great enough to outweigh the utility derived from actions normally followed when willpower is low. In addition, chocolate can become more successful as a positive reinforcer for long-run optimal behavior if individuals are psychologically addicted to it. Chocolate then increases in utility value, and the same binding effect is achieved at less expense.

Because psychological addiction aids in its subsequent ability to cure irrationality, chocolate may be one of the only substances for which it is rational to create such an addiction. Furthermore, rational chocolate addiction can justify the careful process by which parents addict their children to sweets. If we admit that our children are also imperfectly rational, then we must admit their need for effective means of binding. Thus, if parents want their children to maximize successfully as adults, children should be introduced to chocolate as early in life as possible. People who seem immune to chocolate, unable to benefit from its unique qualities, were probably deprived of it during childhood.

Certainly, rational chocolate addiction helps explain why chocolate is "above choice and without alternatives." If chocolate can bind us to what is best for us, it can be argued that chocolate should be ranked first in a lexicographical ordering. Moreover, although chocolate is not the only available binding mechanism, no rational chocoholic could ever be persuaded to use any other.

NOTES

1. It must be stated at the outset that the analysis in this chapter is not intended to explain recreational chocolate use or chocolate abuse.

2. See, for example, psychologists Amos Tversky and Daniel Kahneman (1986) and economist Richard Thaler (1980).

3. Of course, reinforcers can be negative as well as positive. Effective negative reinforcers would lower the total satisfaction gained from a suboptimal action below the total satisfaction gained from the optimal action.

4. Contrary to what many people believe, pure chocolate does not cause or aggravate acne; it contains no cholesterol and little caffeine; and if eaten in the form of a milk chocolate bar, is less likely to cause tooth decay than other sugar snacks (or carob) and "has eleven times more protein, ten times more calcium, seven times more phosphorous, five times more riboflavin (vitamin B), and eight percent more potassium" than a medium-size apple (Robinson, 1984).

5. One exception is when anticipation of the event gives utility. When the event itself occurs, individuals lose the utility of the anticipation and thus may see themselves as worse off.

6. In Australia, Mars candy bars are advertised with the jingle: "A Mars a day helps you work, rest, and play."

7. The numbers used in Tables 3.1, 3.2, and 3.3 are theoretical utility values chosen to be consistent with the case under discussion.

8. If people could simply change the rate at which they discount the future gains or losses, there would be no need for binding. These individuals would be capable of producing the willpower needed for perfect rationality.

9. The relevant time frame is determined by the particular individual's shortsightedness. In this case, when the student's willpower is low, only the benefits and costs realized within a 16-hour period are considered. Depending on the individual and the circumstances, the relevant time constraint could be shorter or longer than 16 hours.

10. The economic framework of constraints and indifference curves is used instead of the familiar demand and supply curve models because it allows us to judge the effect on consumer welfare of trade-offs between different activities or commodity bundles. Demand and supply curves focus on solely the market for a single activity or commodity. In order to analyze the von Weiszacker paradox, however, we need to describe the decision to pursue an optimal mix of activities versus a suboptimal mix.

11. Graphically, the addition of the bribe to the choice set would be incorporated in two ways: (1) the axes relabeled to reflect the possibility of joint activities (e.g., studying with chocolate consumption at appropriate intervals) and (2) the long-run indifference (I) curves relabeled $U^*_I + C^*_I$ where $I = 1, 2, 3$.

12. This becomes important if searching for a least-cost binding mechanism. However, the statement must be qualified. It is only true when comparing the same brand of chocolate before and after addiction. Obviously, if the rational chocoholic discovers Belgian chocolates are better than Hershey's, the dollar amount spent per ounce of chocolate is likely to rise. The utility values for Saturday and Sunday derive directly from the different times spent studying and partying. The values for Monday represent the student's utility from the actual exam performances.

REFERENCES

Adler, Jerry. "America's Chocolate Binge." *Newsweek*, April 4, 1983.

Becker, Gary S., and Kevin M. Murphy. "A Theory of Rational Addiction." *Journal of Political Theory, 96*, (1988).

Elster, Jon. *Ulysses and the Sirens: Studies in Rationality and Irrationality*. Cambridge: University Press, 1986.

Galvin, Ruth Mehrtens. "Sybaritic to Some, Sinful to Others, But How Sweet It Is!" *Smithsonian*, (1986).

Robinson, Dick. "The Temptation of Chocolate: Need We Resist Any Longer?" *Health Magazine, 16*, (1984).

Thaler, Richard. "Toward a Positive Theory of Consumer Choice." *Journal of Economic Behavior and Organization, 1*, (1980).

Tversky, Amos and Daniel Kahneman. "Rational Choice and the Framing of Decisions." *Journal of Business, 59*, (1986).

Weiszacker, C.C. von. "Notes on Endogenous Changes in Preferences." *Journal of Economic Theory, 3*, (1971).

CHAPTER 4

Perceived Attributes of Chocolate
Harold E. Yuker

There have been a number of studies on the perceived attributes of chocolate. One study indicated that giving adults free samples of chocolate-flavored peanut butter led to acceptance by adults and a change from an image that chocolate was only for children.[1] Another study reported that presenting the phrase "Hershey's Chocolate" at subliminal levels had no effect on college students.[2]

Although chocolate is sometimes identified as a cause of headaches,[3] carefully controlled studies indicate "chocolate on its own is rarely a precipitator of migraine headaches."[4]

QUESTIONNAIRE

The first step in my research was to develop a questionnaire. In final form, it contained 24 items in two parts. *Part I* asked respondents to indicate how they perceive chocolate by choosing from among 15 different pairs of adjectives. For example:

Good	__	__	__	__	__	Bad
Unhealthy	__	__	__	__	__	Healthy
Harmless	__	__	__	__	__	Harmful
Dietetic	__	__	__	__	__	Fattening

Each pair of adjectives was separated by five columns so that the individual could rate chocolate as, for example, very good, good, neutral, bad, or very bad—or very healthy, somewhat healthy, neutral, somewhat unhealthy, or very unhealthy.

Then the respondent was asked to list some other words he or she would use to describe chocolate.

Part II of the questionnaire contained eight questions.

1. How much do you like chocolate?
2. How much chocolate do you eat?
3. How many days would it take you to eat a pound of chocolate?
4. How often do you diet?
5. How much "junk food" do you eat?
6. How many cigarettes do you smoke per day?
7. How old are you?
8. What is your gender?

The questionnaire was filled out by 325 people, mostly undergraduate students at Hofstra University. They constitute what is called a *haphazard sample*—and are *NOT* representative of all people in the United States or even all college students.

Most of the sample respondents (74 percent) were 18 to 21 years old; 58 percent were female, and 42 percent were male. Questionnaire responses are given in Table 4.1, and responses by gender are presented in Table 4.2. Table 4.3 summarizes some of the responses of individuals who like chocolate versus the responses of those who don't. And Table 4.4 presents adjectival perceptions of chocolate based on like versus dislike.

RESULTS

In this sample, 33 percent said they like chocolate very much, and 27 percent quite a bit; this compares to only 4 percent who said not very much and 2 percent who said not at all (see Table 4.2). Even though they like chocolate, only 7 percent said they eat a lot of chocolate, and 16 percent eat more than average; this compares to 35 percent who do not eat much and a mere 2 percent who do not eat any. Apparently, some individuals have a lot of self-discipline. It is important to remember that we measured perception rather than the actual amount eaten. We do not know how the students in the sample defined "a lot" or an average amount.

About 60 percent of the students said they would eat a pound of chocolate in a week or less; 12 percent, in a day or less. It would take 9 percent about a month and 4 percent a year or more.

These students eat junk food. Some 31 percent said they eat more than average. This compares to 32 percent who said they do not eat much and 2 percent who said they eat no junk food.

Even though about two out of every three respondents in our sample eat at least an average amount of both chocolate and junk food, they do not diet much. Thirty-seven percent never diet, 37 percent diet once in a while, and 25 percent of the people in our sample said they diet either continually or very often. I wonder how many of the 37 percent of college students who now say they never diet will still say the same when they are 45 years old!

They do not smoke much. Some 81 percent said they never smoke cigarettes, while 3 percent smoke at least a pack a day. We did not ask about other vices.

Responses of the total sample indicated that 91 percent perceived chocolate as sweet; 81 percent as fattening; 80 percent as pleasant; 63 percent as attractive; 60 percent as energizing; 57 percent as heavy; 57 percent as interesting; 56 percent as happy; 54 percent as unhealthy; 50 percent as good; 49 percent as exciting; 36 percent as addictive; and 35 percent as harmful. (see Table 4.1).

Persons who like chocolate perceived it as sweet (93 percent), pleasant (92 percent), attractive (75 percent), addictive (70 percent), interesting (70 percent), happy (69 percent), good (61 percent), energizing (55 percent), and exciting (51 percent). Those who do not like chocolate perceived it as unhealthy (87 percent), harmful (58 percent), and bad (55 percent). Both those who like it and those who do not perceived chocolate as fattening, sweet, and heavy. (see Table 4.4).

There were several gender differences. Women like chocolate more than men. Women eat more chocolate than men; about one of every three women, compared to one out of eight men, said they eat more than an average amount of chocolate. There are no differences in the amount of junk food eaten by men and women. Men diet less; 54 percent of the men and 25 percent of the women said they never diet. And more women than men smoke cigarettes—26 percent compared to 10 percent (see Table 4.2).

One question asked, "What other words would you use to describe chocolate?" Some of the answers demonstrate creative imagination.

The following is an alphabetic sample:

acne causing	awesome	calming	dangerous
deadly	delectable	deeeelicious	disgusting
erotic	guilt producing	heavenly	intoxicating
irresistible	luscious	messy	mysterious
nonnutritious	rich	satiating	satisfying
scrumptious	sexy	sickening	sinful
sticky	tranquilizing	yuk!	yummy

Many more words were listed by those who like chocolate than by those who do not particularly like it, and more by women than by men.

Table 4.1
Percentage Responses to Questionnaire Items

Respondents' perception of chocolate in terms of opposite adjectives.
The middle category represents neutrality or bipolarity.

Attractive	31	32	31	3	3	Ugly
Dietetic	0	0	10	27	54	Fattening
Dull	3	3	37	36	21	Interesting
Addictive	26	10	29	13	23	Nonaddictive
Energizing	23	37	28	6	6	Weakening
Expensive	8	26	46	15	5	Cheap
Bad	9	11	31	23	27	Good
Harmless	9	16	40	23	12	Harmful
Heavy	18	39	37	6	3	Light
Not Sweet	0	1	8	35	56	Sweet
Unhealthy	18	36	39	9	2	Healthy
Pleasant	44	36	13	4	2	Unpleasant
Exciting	18	31	40	8	4	Unexciting
Happy	24	32	38	4	2	Sad
Masculine	2	4	80	10	4	Feminine

Note: Percentages may not add to 100 because of rounding-out errors.

Table 4.2
Responses to Questions by Males, Females, and Total Group

	Female		Male		Total	
	N	%	N	%	N	%

1. How much do you like chocolate?

	N	%	N	%	N	%
Very much	75	40	31	23	106	33
Quite a bit	54	29	34	25	88	27
Average amount	50	26	61	45	111	34
Not much	9	5	4	3	13	4
Not at all	1	0	6	4	7	2
N	189		136		325	

2. How much chocolate do you eat?

	N	%	N	%	N	%
A lot	20	11	3	2	23	7
Above average	37	20	15	11	52	16
Average amount	69	37	59	43	128	40
Not much	59	31	55	40	114	35
None	4	2	4	3	8	2
N	189		136		325	

3. How many days would it take you to eat a pound of chocolate?

	N	%	N	%	N	%
Less than 1	3	2	2	2	5	2
1	20	12	11	9	31	10
2	13	8	9	7	22	7
3-6	34	20	19	15	53	18
A week	41	22	24	19	65	22
8-15	29	17	20	16	49	16
16-29	12	7	6	5	18	6
A month	13	8	14	11	27	9
32-350	6	4	10	8	16	5
A year or more	1	0	10	8	11	4
N	172		125		297	

Table 4.2 continued

	Female		Male		Total	
	N	%	N	%	N	%

4. *How often do you diet?*

Always	32	17	8	6	40	12
Very often	35	18	9	7	44	14
Once in a while	75	40	46	34	121	37
Never	47	25	73	54	120	37
N	189		136		325	

5. *How much "junk food" do you eat?*

A lot	21	11	10	7	31	10
Above average	37	20	30	22	67	21
Average amount	67	35	48	35	115	35
Not much	60	32	45	33	105	32
None	4	2	3	2	7	2
N	189		136		325	

6. *How many cigarettes do you smoke per day?*

None	140	74	123	90	263	81
1-9	22	12	3	2	25	8
10-19	19	10	7	5	26	8
20 or more	8	4	3	2	11	3
N	189		136		325	

7. *How old are you?*

17	1	1	1	0		
18-19	50	26	30	22	80	25
20-21	96	52	62	46	158	49
22-29	31	16	31	23	62	19
30-49	10	5	9	7	19	6
50-	1	1	2	2	3	1
N	188		135		323	

Note: Percentages may not add up to 100 because of rounding-out errors.

Table 4.3
Responses of Persons Who Like Versus Don't Like Chocolate

Like	Don't Like	
38%	0%	Eat more chocolate than average
21%	100%	Eat less chocolate than average
31%	13%	Often diet
32%	55%	Never diet
36%	9%	Eat junk food
30%	62%	Eat little or no junk food
81%	90%	Don't smoke

Table 4.4
Perceptions of Chocolate

Like	Don't Like		Like	Don't Like	
		Positive			
92	39	pleasant	2	26	unpleasant
65	42	energizing	11	26	weakening
70	26	interesting	2	32	dull
69	19	happy	2	19	sad
75	32	attractive	1	36	ugly
61	6	good	11	55	bad
51	13	exciting	3	45	unexciting
		Negative			
89	100	fattening	0	0	dietetic
70	36	addictive	9	36	nonaddictive
50	68	heavy	10	6	light
42	87	unhealthy	15	0	healthy
29	58	harmful	28	16	harmless
		Neutral			
93	84	sweet	0	3	not sweet
34	29	expensive	20	19	cheap
14	6	feminine	6	9	masculine

NOTES

1. Bettinger, Charles, O., et al. *The impact of free-sample advertising.* Journal of Advertising Research; 1979 June vol. 19(3) 35–39.

2. Stephen, George, G. and Jennings, Luther B. *Effect of subliminal stimuli on consumer behavior: Negative evidence. Perceptual and Motor Skills*; 1975 December vol. 41(3) 847–854.

3. Paulin, Judith M., et al. *The prevalence of headache in a small New Zealand town. Headache*; 1985 May vol. 25(3) 147–151

4. Moffett, A. M., et al. *Effect of chocolate in migraine: A double-blind study. Journal of Neurology, Neurosurgery and Psychiatry*; 1974 April vol. 37(4) 445–448.

PART II

Chocolate and Literature

CHAPTER 5

Conventions of Chocolate as Weapons of War and Peace in Shaw's *Arms and the Man*, Straus's *The Chocolate Soldier* and in the MGM Film Version, *The Chocolate Soldier*

Anne K. Kaler

Wise soldiers substitute chocolates for cartridges, gumdrops for guns, sweets for swords. Shakespeare's Falstaff armed himself with sack, the sweetened Spanish wine, instead of pistols; American soldiers won the hearts of the world's children by sharing enriched chocolate bars with them. When George Bernard Shaw illustrated his antiwar polemics in his play *Arms and the Man* (1951), he had his Swiss mercenary Bluntschli confess that "you can always tell an old soldier by the inside of his holsters and cartridge boxes. The young ones carry pistols and cartridges: The old ones, grub" (136). The "grub" to which Bluntschli refers is that divine "food of the gods": Chocolate. A study of the literary conventions about chocolate shows that chocolate has become, in literature at least, a tasty weapon in the arsenals both of war and of love. How could Professor Higgins coax Eliza Dolittle into her vowels without her reward of chocolate candies? How could Horace Vandergelder in *Hello Dolly* woo Irene Malloy without his chocolate-covered unshelled peanuts? The legendary power of chocolate to strengthen soldiers in love and in war and in literature was solidified by Shaw's play, the 1909 operetta *The Chocolate Soldier* and the 1941 film adaptation of the same title starring Nelson Eddy and Rise Stevens.

First used as a sacred stimulant by the Aztec ruler Montezuma, chocolate entered European culture through the Spanish conquistador Cortes who claimed that *xocoatl* (pronounced *sho quatl*) was a "divine drink which builds up resistance and fights fatigue. A cup of this precious drink permits a man to walk for a whole day without food" (Morton and Morton, 1986, 6). However, for the first few centuries of its popularity, chocolate was a drink rather than a food, as Spanish monks crushed and then whipped bitter cocoa beans into a breakfast drink. The Spanish court even used chocolate as dowry for its princesses, and when the French popularized cocoa for the breakfast delicacy of the aristocrats, chocolate soon became a sign of masculine virility and feminine willingness. In England, chocolate shops vied with coffee houses and tea shops as centers of political debate. The Dutch extracted cocoa butter and added sugar; the Germans lauded it as a health cure. The Americans introduced baking chocolate, and the Austrians incorporated it in their Sacher tortes. The English added sugar to the cocoa butter to make the first candy bar, and the Swiss perfected milk chocolate to lighten the bitter taste of the candy. Thus, the truly international nature of chocolate represents in literature the sum of chocolate's many tastes; it mirrors the bitter taste of war and the sweet flavor of love.

When Shaw wanted to create his antiheroic soldier, he found ready ammunition in the convenient Balkan war between Serbia and Bulgaria in 1894, which provides the setting for his play *Arms and the Man*.[1] Into the household of a Bulgarian major near the Dragoman Pass in 1885, the starving Swiss soldier Bluntschli stumbles into the bedroom of the romantic Raina and consumes her chocolates. When she taunts him as being only a "chocolate-cream soldier," Raina defines a new term for a soldier, one who is more interested in his own survival than in heroism—the "chocolate soldier."

The appeal of this title of the "chocolate soldier" was so great that the 1909 operetta and the 1941 film version used it, because it immediately identified its subject—a chocolate soldier—as the hero of a romantic comedy. By subtitling his play as "an antiromantic comedy," Shaw warned that his plays do not easily transfer from one genre into another: "If any gentleman is simple enough to think that even a good comic opera can be produced by it [his play], I invite him to try his hand, and see whether anything resembling one of my plays will reward him" (Preface, 119). In the early 1900s, Oscar Straus, a Viennese composer, accepted the challenge. The German librettists Rudolf Bernauer and Leopold Jacobson took full liberties with Shaw's script, all the while protesting that their "comic opera in three acts . . . closely follows the incidents, situations, and structure of the original story" (*Soldier*, 1925, Argument 5). By the time that the *Der Tapfere Soldat* opened as *The Chocolate Soldier* in the 1909 English version by Stanislaus Stange, the producers acknowledged that the comic opera was an "unauthorized parody" of Shaw's comedy. So incensed was Shaw with the liberties taken that he never permitted another musical production of his plays during his lifetime.[2]

Shaw had no objection to the nature of a comic opera: He admits that *Arms and the Man* is cast in an "ordinary practical comedy form . . . for fun, fashionable dresses, a little music" (Preface, 113). As an experienced music critic, Shaw knew the appeal of the European comic opera form, which concentrated on comic elements, sentimental subjects, and happy endings. Developed from eighteenth-century musical interludes set between the acts of serious drama, the opéra bouffe was the musical equivalent of Viennese pastry—airy, frothy, sweetly satisfying, and served up *mit Schlag*. Later in the century, however, the *opéra bouffe* shifted its terminology, if not its content, to the word *operetta*, a word that defined that generation of musical comic operas that preceded the musical comedy. For example, the earliest editions of *The Choco-late Soldier* classify it as an *opéra bouffe*, but by the frontispiece of the 1925 version of *Der Tapfere Soldat*, the word *operetta* appears in the English version done by Grace I. Colbron and copyrighted by Hans Bartsch.[3]

All comedy depends on commonly understood signals or conventions accepted by the audience. The linking of chocolate and soldiering telegraphs to the audience that the production is a comedy. Shaw and his subsequent writers use familiar conventions of chocolate, soldiers, name changes, and antimilitarism to create their comedies. The first of these is the combined term of the *chocolate soldier*, who takes his place among the ranks of an illustrious army of stereo-typed characters. His history actually stretches back through Falstaff to *il capitano* of the improvisational Italian theater of the *commedia dell'arte* all the way back to the *miles gloriosus*, or braggart soldier, of Greco-Roman theater. Shaw knew the appeal of delating such a military character by ridiculing the romanticism that popular culture attaches to the uniformed hero. As a skilled playwright, Shaw deflates the character by breaking the concept of the heroic soldier into four separate characters—Bluntschli, Sergius, Major Petkoff (the father of the heroine Raina), and a Russian officer in the Bulgarian army (sometimes called Massakroff). Shaw assigns the dimension of the young lover (the *inamorati*) to his real hero Bluntschli, who, at 34, is rather old and set in his ways to be the young lover. Nonetheless, Bluntschli claims to have "an incurably romantic disposition" that appeals to his *inamorata*, the overly romantic Raina.

In contrast, the pseudohero Sergius becomes "a bombastic fellow and vastly tedious in his speech [and] his braggadocio was, therefore, never too outrageous to please" (Duchartre, 1966, 227–29). He resembles the *condottiere* that Machiavelli describes as a "type which becomes much more plausible when one recalls the blood-curdling combats . . . the unexpected wheeling of a horse [which] was sometimes enough to decide the issue of the struggle" (227). And indeed it is Sergius's horse bolting beneath him that causes him to lead the charge for which he is wrongly declared a hero. As the braggart soldier and the swaggering lover like Falstaff, Sergius's comic posturing sets him up for the satiric deflation needed for comedy. Instead of winning Raina's heart, Sergius is trapped by the upwardly mobile maidservant Louka, the conniving soubrette. Like *il capitano*'s mask, Sergius's personality is "intended to emphasize the contrast between a brave appearance and a craven nature" (227).

Although the third spin-off from the hero, Raina's father, Major Petkoff, represents a blustering commander, his origins are lodged in his role as the comically deceived father, the *panteleone*, while his wife Catherine plays the flutter-brained dowager. The last division of the *il capitano* figure is that of the overly polite Russian officer who searches for the fugitive Bluntschli. In the operetta, this character is called Massakroff and serves as a comic character with his inefficient gallantry, which permits the fugitive to go unnoticed; in the film, the character is unnamed but has a major dance number in which he and his men are dressed in the costumes of the farcical *commedia dell'arte*: Turkish pantaloons and pointed shoes, vests and sashed waists, "splendid uniforms embellished with the turbans of infidels . . . with fierce, bristling moustaches" (228–89).

Shaw's drama also follows the satiric bent of the *commedia dell'arte* as it uses the tensions between classes as vibrant subject matter. Take, for example, the character of Louka, written for Shaw's actress-friend Florence Farr. Louka would seem to be a second lead, but it is her rise from her servant status to wife of a military officer that makes the play such a social satire. As he does in *Pygmalian*, where Eliza marries the weak Freddy Eynsford-Hill rather than Henry Higgins or Colonel Pickering, Shaw embodies the theme that a strong woman can manage a weaker man; Louka will survive her marriage with Sergius in the same way that Bluntschli will survive the war. While Raina and her family may be trapped in the worries over social status, Bluntschli and Louka worry about the essentials of food and survival. These two are "arch-realists . . . who follow a familiar Shavian dialectic: From idealism to disillusioned cynicism to a state containing something of both, a realistic view of the world untied with a knowledge that it could be better" (Whitman, 1977, 195, 249).

Although Straus's *opéra bouffe* and MGM's 1941 film use the same title of *The Chocolate Soldier*, the stories differ widely from Shaw's and from each other. Straus's operetta revamps Shaw's plot in order to romanticize militarism, but the major story still revolves around the chocolate soldier-hero and Bulgarian heroine. The 1941 film, however, borrows the classic convention of the play-within-a-play in the manner of Shakespeare's *The Taming of the Shrew*, where a drunken Christopher Sly watches a play of the same title. Cole Porter's *Kiss Me Kate* has Fred and Lily Graham play their story out within their Broadway revival of Shakespeare's *The Taming of the Shrew*. Such devices permit the themes of the better-known original to mirror those of the invented couple. The film embeds into an extravagant Broadway production of Straus's operetta *The Chocolate Soldier*, the major story of Ferenc Molnar's *The Guardsman*. Molnar's hero and heroine—Karl Lang and Maria Lanyi—appear as the leads in the staged operetta production, but their marital plight mirrors that of hero and heroine in the operetta.

Another convention is the significant and symbolic changes of names from the play to the operetta. The operetta chooses names that suggest the characters' personalities. For example, when Shaw's Major Petkoff is elevated to Colonel Popoff, the name suggests that he does "pop off" when he is angry. When Bluntschli is reduced to Bumerli, elements of farce and satire are implied in the comic name. Other name changes are not as easily justified: Shaw's Raina becomes Nadina, Sergius becomes Alexius, Catherine is changed to Aurelia, Nicolia to Stephan—for no apparent reason. An interesting link among the genres is the fact that in the movie the friend of the hero Karl is called Bernard, perhaps a backhanded tribute to Shaw. Some conventions violate the intent and structure of Shaw's play: In Straus's operetta, the librettists elevate the character of maidservant Louka to the status of Raina's cousin and rename her Mascha. Thus, in the operetta, when Alexius (Sergius) is rejected by Nadina (Raina), he can be matched and mated with a woman of equal value in her newly invented cousin Mascha.

Shaw's antiwar intentions were further violated by the switch in emphasis from antimilitarism in the play to a romanticizing of the military in the operetta and the movie. Stating in his preface why he wrote the play, Shaw protests that he "can no longer be satisfied with fictitious morals and fictitious good conduct, shedding fictitious glory on . . . war, cruelty, cupidity" (Shaw, 1951, 120). His character of Sergius is the most altered.   While Shaw has him as a comic character "ridiculous through the breakdown of his ideals," he does not condemn Sergius "for his falling short of them" (Whitman, 1977, 39). Sergius is a "hero" because he led a charge against the enemy, although he admits he "won the battle the wrong way" (Whitman, 1977, 151). The play's professional soldiers recognize that he is a bombastic fool: Major Petkoff opposes Sergius's being made a general because he "could throw away whole brigades instead of regiments" (Shaw, 1951, 150). Bluntschli reveals to Raina that Sergius's heroism was caused by his horse bolting into the enemy lines, an act that she steadfastly denies.

In opposition, the operetta represents Alexius (Sergius) as the glory side of romantic militarism, outfitted in a shiny uniform and unaware of his pomposity. In his song, Alexius describes himself as "Alexius the Heroic."

No enemy lives when Alexius is nigh,
In battle I'm always victorious,
No hero of old more courageous than I,
Not one ever lived half so glorious.
The deeds I have done I can scarcely believe.
My foes how they grieve, you cannot conceive.
I tell you the truth for I never deceive. (*Soldier*, 1925, 1–23)

The irony of these lines, of course, rests in the audience's awareness of how his horse's bolting at the wrong moment led him into his apparently brave charge against the Serbians (called Servians in several scripts).

Shaw drew on contemporary facts and reported anecdotes of English military life for his characters, primarily those of Generals Horace Porter and Gordon. One story has General Gordon of the Boer War affirming that "courage, like everything else, wears out" (Carr, 1976, 1992); Shaw transmutes this into Sergius's concession that war is the "dream of patriots and heroes! A fraud, Bluntschli. A hollow shaw, like love" (185). Although the two heroes would seem to be polar opposites, they both are spokesmen for Shaw's views: Thus, Bluntschli states that "nine soldiers out of ten are born fools" (132), while Sergius protests that soldiering is the "coward's art of attacking mercilessly when you are strong, and keeping out of harm's way when you are weak. . . . Get your enemy at a disadvantage; and never, on any account, fight him on equal terms" (152–53). The operetta's Alexius, however, maintains his cheery militaristic demeanor to the end, when he sings that now that the war is over, "these heroes are in clover/all the fighting finished, done/we're prepared for love and fun" (198–201).

However confident Alexius is about winning the war, his characteristic uncertainty in love carries over into the film version. There, Karl Lang (who plays the part of Alexius on stage) has "real life" doubts about his wife's fidelity before and during their marriage. She flirts with the officers in the theater boxes, apparently attracted by the shiny uniforms. To test her virtue, Karl disguises himself as a Russian singer to woo her with his pretty words. (The idea of a Russian lover rather than a guardsman may have been inspired by the unnamed Russian officer who inspects Nadina's bedroom in the operetta.) Although the plot makes it clear to the audience that Maria is and has been faithful, the hero Karl is left with some doubt, especially when, in the closing scene of the staged operetta, his wife again flirts with the officers during their curtain call. The doubtful ending comes from Molnar's play where Karl disguises himself as a "guardsman" to tempt his wife, but he, too, is left uncertain of her fidelity.

Parody sometimes lies in the unconscious of conscious imitation of an action or a familiar pattern; such a pattern is the configuration of a vulnerable male being hovered over by three women of diverse ages and stations—the three Graces, the three Fates, the three queens of Arthurian legend. These three women usually parallel the triune goddess configuration with the wise mother-goddess Juno or Hera, the love-goddess Venus or Aphrodite, and the virginal-warrior goddess Athena or Diana. In the play, the hero Bluntschli falls asleep on Raina's bed with her mother Catherine and her sly maid Louka looking down at him. In the operetta, the same three female figures appear in a slightly different form. After an extensive search to the energetic song "Seek the Spy," the hero Bumerli falls asleep: Nadina, his rescuer, and her mother Aurelia, and her cousin Mascha sing over his prone body. Stage directions of the 1925 edition indicate that the women "sing a song about three women who sat by the fire and a young shepherd came into their hut, spending the night" (*Soldier*, 1925, 1–23). The song from the 1909 operetta "Romance" has the women "sighing alone one night . . . when came a man to their delight, who banished all their sorrow. He was a soldier young and strong" (*Soldier*, 1909, 66–77). Each woman creeps away lest she disturb his sleep until Nadina bends over and kisses him, singing the last verse.

Because the film shows only part of the operetta being performed, the convention of the three women is not as obvious, for the heroine Maria (Raina/Nadina) has neither a mother nor a cousin. She does have Madame Helene, a motherly personal dresser, who is old enough and earthy enough to qualify as the dragon-dowager of Shaw's original play. But Maria also has a flighty maid Liesel who acts as the Louka/Mascha character of a soubrette, played by comedienne Zazu Pitts, a character so ready to abandon her station as a maidservant that she is constantly losing her cap. Even in the distorted version of the play that the film presents, the need to maintain a familiar pattern exists in showing the three women hovering over the sleeping male.

The real hero of the story is not the chocolate solder but chocolate itself. Chocolate makes the difference where life and death, survival and capture, are pitted against each other. Although the soldier who carries chocolate candies in place of cartridges may seem to be a flagrant negation of the role of a romantic hero, he survives. To the hero of all these genres, chocolate is the means to sustain himself in enemy territory. Bluntschli admits that his side had sent the wrong ammunition and that he "hadn't even a revolver cartridge: Only chocolate. We'd no bayonets, nothing" (Shaw, 1951, 137–38). Inadvertently, chocolate provides survival for him in two ways. He surmises that Sergius was able to rout the Serbian forces because he "most likely had gotten wind of the cartridge business somehow and knew it was a safe job" (Shaw, 1951, 138). Just as the chocolate he ate in the field gave him the energy to climb to her room for protection, the chocolate creams that Raina gives him sustain his life.

Shaw uses other familiar conventions to nudge the audience's memory. Quite possibly, the brandy in the center of the chocolate creams counters the caffeine and contributes to the soldier's deep sleep. Bluntschli (and his brothers in other genres) are near death from a lack of sleep, rest, and food. He has not "closed [his] eyes for forty-eight hours" when Raina taunts him as a "very poor soldier" for not climbing back down into the battle. Shaw blends Cortes's statement that chocolate will sustain a soldier better than other foods in Bluntschli's comment that "to my last hour, I shall remember those three chocolate creams. It was unsoldierly; but it was angelic" (139). The playwright continues the death image by having Bluntschli refer to Raina as an angel (1215), an oblique reference to the angel of death. Because she has provided refuge for him, he will not fall on the stones under her balcony because the "angel" Raina stops him before he descends. In the gospel story of Christ's temptations, Satan claims that if Christ is really God, angels will prevent Christ from dashing His foot on the stones of the terrace below. Bluntschli combines the two ideas, claiming that "I shall sleep as if the stones were a feather bed" (1216). So exhausted is Bluntschli that he equates sleep with death: "[C]apture only means death; and death is sleep: Oh, sleep, sleep, sleep, undisturbed sleep . . . death ten times over first" (139).

The songs in the operetta also encapsulate the antiwar and death themes. Nadina's early paeans of praise to the picture of her fiance, Alexius, evokes the song "Come, come, my hero" (*Soldier*, 1909, 16–31), which establishes her romantic nature. However, the early duet between Nadina and Bumerli, "Sympathy," counteracts any sweetness because it is framed as verbal warfare between lovers with terms too strong for the context: A fugitive soldier invading a maiden's bedroom, threatening her with a pistol, and eating her food smacks more of a violent rape scene than a musical comedy, and the lyrics of the song reflect that motif. Bumerli complains that "the burden of a maiden's hate . . . is hard to carry" and that she "turns me out so late." Whereas "all death is gruesome, dark and drear," the soldier finds that he loves "beyond all measure" and therefore "treasures" his life once more as the heroine extends her sympathy until "death has no fears" for him (41–48).

Just as a dramatic metaphor serves as the central object within the production, in *The Chololate Soldier* there is actually a chocolate soldier—that is, a piece of sculptured chocolate. In Shaw's play, Raina speaks of making:

a beautiful ornament this morning for the ice pudding; and how that stupid Nicola has put down a pile of plates on it and spoilt it. (*To Bluntschli winningly*) I hope you didn't think that you were the chocolate cream soldier, Captain Bluntchli.

Bluntschli (*laughing*) I assure you I did. (*Stealing a whimsical glance at her*). Your explanation was a relief. (*Shaw*, 1951, 165)

While her father comments that it is strange that his daughter has taken up cooking, her reference to the chocolate "ornament" indicates that it must have been ordinary; Raina refers to it later. Ironically, the image of the chocolate soldier that must be broken for the lovers to contract a solid marriage is shattered by the butler's placing a "pile of plates" on top of it. In wooing Raina later, Bluntschli lists the household inventory of his hotels, as if the weight of "nine thousand six hundred sheets and blankets . . . ten thousand knives and forks" (Shaw, 1951, 1251) will somehow mend the shattered image of the chocolate soldier in her mind.

In the operetta, Nadina and Bumerli sing the duet of "The Chocolate Soldier" (*Soldier*, 1909, 32–40) apparently to a real image of a soldier molded in chocolate.

Oh you little chocolate soldier man
You're far too sweet and pretty,
Oh, you funny chocolate solder man,
For you I feel great pity.
Oh you silly chocolate soldier man,
Just made to please young misses,
So sweet you'd melt, If e'er you felt
A full grown maiden's kisses.

It is not certain from the script (and the operetta is so seldom produced) if there is an actual chocolate soldier made of candy on stage. The words of the song seem to indicate that such is the case, especially when Bumerli protests that he is "not a soldier made" (i.e., manufactured). A candy soldier could be called "sweet" and "pretty" and would "melt" if it "felt a full grown maiden's kisses." The clever wording reinforces the sexual overtones to the song by referring to the well-known fact that the melting point of chocolate is lower than that of the human body. A "full grown maiden's kisses," the kisses of a mature woman, would indeed cause the chocolate soldier to "melt."

Shaw's play actually places the dramatic climax, the scene of highest interest, at the beginning—What greater tension is there than a male invading the bedroom of a female? The rest of the play is an intellectual discussion of the classes and a few fragile one-liners. The age of Raina provides the technical climax of the play, for the happy marriage of Raina and Bluntschli depends on his understanding that she is not a schoolgirl recently released from the nursery. He fears that "all that adventure which was life or death to me, was only a schoolgirl's game to her—chocolate creams and hide and seek" (Shaw, 1951, 1250). While he discovers that she is a "full grown" woman of 23, he reminds her that he first appealed to her as a "fugitive, a beggar, and a starving man" (1251). Like the prince awakening Sleeping Beauty with a kiss (chocolate again), he woos Raina with chocolate.

Once more chocolate keeps starvation at bay. Early in the operetta, the three women bemoan the absence of their men at war with the line that "if we live too long alone/we shall be but skin and bone" (*Soldier*, 1909, 16). When Raina, Nadina, and Maria are seduced from one love to another, it is accomplished by chocolate, and the reason may lie in a historical fact. Shaw based his chocolate theme on the stories of the English military surviving on rations rather than on bullets. The play in 1895, the operetta in 1909, and the movie in 1941 were successful because of the familiarity of chocolate as a weapon of war and of peace. World Wars I and II proved the importance of chocolate to the soldier's well-being. Raina and Nadina are children of war to be tempted by sweets after the rationing of butter and sugars; they are the quintessential mistresses to be wooed by sweet words of sympathetic lovers; they are romantics to be captured by the war of words launched by warrior lovers. Bumerli expresses it best when he protests that he is not a "hero of romance" such as a prettified uniformed soldier might be. He is, he protests,

A warrior by trade, and not a soldier made,
I've studied shooting, practiced riding,
I've studied fencing, fate deciding.
I am a warrior by chance, and not a hero of
romance. (*Soldier*, 1909, 32–40)

However, in the final segment of the song, he parries Nadina's words that he would melt if he met a full-grown maiden's kisses by suggesting that "I'd like to try your kisses" (107).

In all versions, the formula of reducing the soldier to the status of a child's play toy, a soldier cast in chocolate candy, is consistent. In the stage directions, Raina diminutizes Bluntschli when "[She stoops over him maternally]. Oh, you are a very poor soldier: A chocolate cream soldier" (*Soldier*, 1925, 1218). Later she calls him "the little beast. . . . Oh! if I had him here, I'd cram him with chocolate creams til he couldn't ever speak again!" (*Soldier*, 1909, 1229). In the operetta, Nadina defines a hero, "a true soldier," as one "who doesn't eat chocolate" (*Soldier*, 1925, 1-11); she is amazed that he eats chocolate: "You—a soldier—an officer?" (*Soldier*, 1925, 1-10). She reduces the fugitive in her bedroom to a play toy, something she can sing to in an innocent way without revealing her growing emotions, something she can call "sweet and pretty . . . funny . . . silly" (*Soldier*, 1925, 1-11). In "Sympathy" the pity she feels for Bumerli is switched to the imaginary candy ornament that is made to "please young misses," but Bumerli retorts that he would "like to try your kisses" (*Soldier*, 1925, 107).

The filmed version has no such handy dramatic metaphor. The hero Karl Lang is the operetta's chocolate soldier to his wife Nadina; he is sugar sweet on stage and baking chocolate bitter with jealousy off stage. Tormented by the thought of his wife's previous (and purely fictional) lovers, he is not happy until he is convinced of his wife's fidelity. The similarity, however, between Karl and Bumerli dwells in their wearing military uniforms because an officer's braid can easily catch a maiden's eye. The costume that is prescribed for the operetta is generically Graustarkian, derived from *The Prisoner of Zenda* and perhaps from *The Student Prince*. No matter what the genre, the hero's costume is always a trim, colorful uniform. In the operetta and within the movie, the costumes of the two leads are extravagant: Karl never appears in his tattered fugitive uniform but only in his grand uniform; even his pajamas imitate a Russian style with a high collar, smooth button placket, and sashed waist. When Maria plays Nadina, her frothy skirt and billowing sleeves are embroidered with Balkan symbols, her waist cinched with a dark peasant bodice, adding a typical beribboned Balkan headdress with a veil attached for the wedding scene. This "dressing-up" quality resembles the overly decorated prettiness of the chocolate boxes so popular in the last century. The operetta's candy-land scenes have toy soldiers parading around candy canes and lollipop trees while a candy-striped attired girl dances before them with a tray of chocolate candy.

Shaw and his followers play on obvious and sly conventions where the outward appearance of an object becomes important. Like a fondant or nut that is sweeter for bearing a coat of chocolate, all the adaptations of the chocolate soldier make use of disguise and deception to further complicate their plot lines. Raina gives her father's coat to Bluntschli to help him escape, and when the coat is returned by Bluntschli, its presence becomes an embarrassment because it indicates that Bluntschli has been in the household before. So also does a "coat" of chocolate preserve the soldier from harm. When Major Petkoff finds Raina's picture addressed to the chocolate cream soldier in the pocket of the coat, the ending of the play is precipitated.

In place of the revealing inscription on the picture, the operetta inserts the convention of a letter in the private duet between Nadina and Bumerli. At the same time she reviles him, Nadina also reveals her love with her inadvertent closing of the letter with the word "love." This "letter" song, which lets her reveal her emotions, is a form of the photograph that the play's heroine has tucked into the coat pocket for Bluntschli to find.

In the operetta, this disguise and deception convention is turned into a more serious charge that the women have somehow been unfaithful, a theme carried over in the filmed version. The crises are embedded in the sextet to Colonel Popoff's coat, "The Tale of the Coat" (*Soldier*, 1925, 113-36). The finale of act II, when Bumerli is revealed to be the man in Nadina's bedroom, Alexius considers himself a lover betrayed and Popoff a deceived father. The other two women, Aurelia (Catherine) and Mascha (Louka) are accused of infidelity also as the song weaves accusations and denials around the coat. The tension is broken by Bumerli's abject plea for forgiveness, also a song, which convinces everyone of his innocence and that of the women.

Another disguise or covering device in the play deepens the characterization. As the Bulgarian soldiers search Raina's room, Bluntschli throws her cloak to her so that she can cover her nightdress, even though it may mean his capture. Only after this noble gesture does the tie-in with chocolate and romance begin. When he admits that his gun is empty, Bluntschli establishes his preference for food over bullets: "What use are cartridges in battle. I always carry chocolate instead" (Shaw, 1951, 135). But Raina replies "[Outraged in her most cherished ideals of manhood] Chocolate! Do you stuff your pockets with sweets—like a schoolboy—even in the field?" (Shaw, 1951, 135). Yet she is willing to protect him and mother him as Bluntschli admits "as if I were a little boy and you my nurse" (Shaw, 1951, 1213). Her form of mothering is to provide the chocolate creams.

Having Bluntschli a Swiss national doubles Shaw's antiwar effect. Just as Swiss chocolate is renowned for its mildness, so also is Swiss neutrality admired. When Blunschli appears as a professional soldier who abjures ammunition, Shaw presents his practical side when he carefully lists his assets for Raina's parents. Sergius and Petkoff admit that they have been outmaneuvered financially by the Swiss captain who was a "commercial traveler in uniform" (Shaw, 1951, 1248). Raina admits that she gave her heart and her candies to "her chocolate cream soldier" (Shaw, 1951, 1251). Nadina's song declares her "happy, happy wedding day" in the operetta. In the film, Maria is wooed again by the sweet words of "Forgive" sung to her by Karl. The lovers unite, and the world is at peace once more.

Thus, in the peaceful Victorian era that preceded the dissolution of Europe in World War I, a British drama about a Balkan kingdom with a Swiss hero set to music by an Austrian composer in a Viennese operetta, rewritten by German librettists, and translated by an Englishman made a hit in America on Broadway for 26 nights and on the American movie screen for decades. Whether it was *Der Tapfere Kassian* or *El Soldadito de Chocolate* or *Le Soldat de Chocolat* or *The Chocolate Soldier*, the image of the chocolate soldier became, and remains, and international hit and continues to delight chocolate lovers everywhere.

NOTES

1. Shaw derived his title from the first line of Dryden's translation of Vergil's *Aeneid*. The character of Raina is somewhat like Dido of Carthage who dies when her romantic ideal of love is shattered by Aeneas's departure for war and conquest.

2. Theatrical legend has it that Rex Harrison, the original Henry Higgins in *My Fair Lady*, carried a copy of *Pygmalion* on the set and insisted that the Shaw dialogue remain untouched.

3. *The Student Prince* may have contributed two names to the film version. The student prince is Karl Franz, and Franz is the name of the friend Karl uses as an excuse to leave the dinner table when he disguises himself as the Russian. See *The Chocolate Soldier. Der Tapfere Soldat*. Operetta in three acts. Music by Oscar-Straus. Lyrics by Rudolph Bernauer and Leopold Jacobson. English version by Grace I. Colbron.

REFERENCES

Carr, Pat M. *Bernard Shaw*. World Dramatists. New York: Frederick Ungar Publishing Co., 1976.

The Chocolate Soldier. Based on Ferenc Molnar's *The Guardsman*, 1941, with music and lyrics from *The Chocolate Soldier*, music by Oscar Straus, English lyrics by Stanislaus Stange, and original lyrics by Rudolf Bernauer and Leopold Jacobson. Screenwriters Leonard Lee and Keith Winter.

The Chocolate Soldier. Der Tapfere Soldat. Operetta in three acts. Music by Oscar Straus. Lyrics by Rudolf Bernauer and Leopold Jacobson. English version by Grace I. Colbron.

The Chocolate Soldier. An opéra bouffe in three acts. Music by Oscar Straus. Lyrics by Rudolf Bernauer and Leopold Jacobson. English version by Stanislaus Stange. Directed by F. C. Whitney.

Duchartre, Pierre Louis. *The Italian Comedy*. Trans. Randolph Weaver. New York, Dover, 1966.

Morton, Marcia, and Frederic Morton. *Chocolate: An Illustrated History*. New York: Crown, 1986.

Shaw, George Bernard. *Arms and the Man. Literature*. Ed. Robert DiYanni. New York: McGraw-Hill, 1990.

Shaw, George Bernard. *Arms and the Man. Seven Plays*. New York: Dodd, Mead, 1951.

Whitman, Robert F. *Shaw and the Play of Ideas*. Ithaca, N.Y.: Cornell University Press, 1977.

CHAPTER 6

Candy, Cheka, and Controversy: The Propaganda Failure of Alexander Tarasov-Rodionov's 1922 Novel *Chocolate*

Robert Fyne

More than 76 years have passed since Alexander Ignatyevich Tarasov-Rodionov—a staunch Bolshevik who participated in the early 1905 Revolution, was a leading activist during the October Revolution and a former Red Brigade battle commander, fought during the 1919–1920 Civil War, and was a onetime examining magistrate for the new Communist government—launched his literary career with the publication of his first propaganda novel in 1922. *Chocolate* rocked the existing *status quo* and subsequently set into motion a series of almost predictable, but fatal, events that culminated some 15 or 16 years later (either in 1937 or 1938) with his sudden and unreportable death, another unknown cipher, fallen victim to the Stalin purges of the late 1930s.

But none of these portentous events were looming in 1922 when the 34-year-old Tarasov-Rodionov emerged as an instant literary celebrity on writing *Chocolate*, the story of an innocent Cheka leader whose execution is necessary to appease the masses, first appeared on the Moscow newsstands in the Soviet magazine *Young Guard*. Almost immediately, *Chocolate*, a novel that questioned the methods the Cheka employed to maintain their power, was transformed into a *cause* célèbre as supporters defended its propaganda value while opponents virulently denounced the so-called anti-Communist theme. Overnight, a virtually unknown writer had started to erode a political ideology, and within 2 years, in 1924, *Chocolate*, because of its popularity, was reprinted in book form. And for the next 10 years, while Tarasov-Rodionov wrote other novels and essays, this first publication would always remain the political albatross dangling from his neck, the subject of an irreducible and unresolved controversy within the ranks of the Communist Party.

However, no such controversy existed when *Chocolate* was translated into English some eight years later (in 1932) by Charles Malamuth. Apparently, unaware of the events of the previous decade, the novel did little to stir up any interest. An unnamed *New York Times Book Review* critic acknowledged the "austere power of the story" but quickly labeled *Chocolate* as mere "Bolshevik propaganda" ("A Communist Martyr," 1932, 15). Equally anonymous, the *Saturday Review* pronounced that the "novel was already dated ("Years of Horror," 1932, 13); but Edwin Seaver, writing in the *New Republic*, argued that *Chocolate* would "endure as a revolutionary classic" (1932).

Literary criticism soon followed. Robert A. Maguire (1968) branded Tarasov-Rodionov (along with Bednyis and Lebedinskiis) "a second-rater." Vyacheslav Zavalishin (1958) called *Chocolate* "a thesis novel which had the effect of a severe electric shock." In 1935, Gleb Struve said that "*Chocolate* was an interesting and piquant work," but in 1971 he apparently changed his tune when he wrote that "*Chocolate* is poor literature. . . . [T]he characters are unreal, the story smacks of cheap melodrama; the style is poor." But Edward Brown (1973) praised the novel and stated that "*Chocolate* has a feature that most Soviet novels lack: An interesting and suspenseful intrigue" (1923, 215).

As a standard work of fiction, *Chocolate* must be read on three levels of awareness: (1) the spoken language of the protagonist, Comrade Zudin, who is the head of the local Cheka, a strong-willed man who slowly transmogrifies into a mere concession after he realizes that he is "guilty of everything"; (2) the unspoken thoughts of Zudin, whose ideas permeate much of the novel but are never manifested, and (3) a small but significant form of the Joycean stream-of-consciousness technique, those images and dreams that in their own phantasmagorical way reveal to Zudin the hopelessness of the situation he has created for himself. These three qualities allow the novel a certain amount of lyricism, a trait that may obliterate the label of "propaganda" and then allow *Chocolate* a position—no matter how minor—in *belles lettres*. Parenthetically, there are many novels—of the same intrinsic worth—that have never received the recognition they deserve. (William March's excellent World War I novel *Company K*, published in 1933, is a perfect example.)

It is somewhere in a large Russian city—located on the banks of a frozen river—during the Russian Civil War (the place location is never mentioned and all allusions are usually ambiguous or delicately obfuscated; the date, however, must be 1918 or 1919) when *Chocolate* begins. Panic and confusion, disorder and mistrust, are everywhere within the ranks of the ill-disciplined and ill-recruited Red Army; foreign spies, *agents provocateurs*, and enemy agents—both real and imaginary—seem ubiquitous. Food and clothing are scarce; morale is low, and the ragged citizenry, looking pale and haggard, linger in the throes of penury. Suspicion and mistrust permeate each page as cynical Russian peasants eye their neighbors, staring at their closed curtains and locked doors. Everyone and everything are suspect. Pessimism is rampant as the confused population sits on the edge of their own darkness—the enemy is just 25 versts away—fearful that their new-found Revolution, like so many others before it, is doomed to a horrible collapse. Gossip and slander, "like fat snakes in a black hole," form public opinion.

As usual, the Cheka struggle to bring a modicum of order to this chaotic situation. Arrests and executions become routine as stern-faced Leather Jackets round up anyone on the slightest pretense of antirevolutionary activities. Controlling this dreaded group is the local Cheka chief Comrade Alexey Ivanovich Zudin (Alyosha, the protagonist), an old and loyal member of the Communist Party (since 1903, he reminds his underlings) who once suffered imprisonment and exile to Siberia for the Cause. He is determined to rid the new Soviet government of her current enemies: The Whiteguards, manufacturers, landlords, Finns, and Poles—those enemies who are financed and motivated by specific capitalist countries: France, Germany, England, America, and China.

As a family man, Zudin is not oblivious to domestic problems. His two children have no stockings to wear; there is no soap in the house; milk and butter have been absent from the family table for months, and the only staple is horse meat, meat that is often rancid. When berated by his wife for not using his influence as Cheka chief to obtain better food, he reminds her that such favoritism would only violate the spirit of the Revolution and cautions her able loyalty, asserting that the real enemies of communism are those from within, those opportunists interested in their personal pleasure and comfort.

It is this introductory material that sets the tone of *Chocolate*. As the leader of the local secret police, Zudin stands firmly behind the principles of the Bolshevik Revolution, even though some of the tenets seem obscure. A strong, proud, able man, Zudin is an idealist, and his bold, haughty, imperious attitude about objectivity often distorts his judgment and reasoning. His perception about human nature seems naive and untested, and there is a noticeable soupçon of altruism in many of his activities, a trait that structurally must stand as the harbinger of those foreboding events soon to come. Only through a formal sense of order, with the Cheka in control, he contends, will the Revolution succeed.

From this point, the plot moves quickly. Some counterrevolutionaries have been arrested, and included in this hapless group is a local prostitute, Yelena Valentinovina Valts, a sensuous woman, who epitomizes feminine opportunism and bourgeois decadence. Her initial claim to be a more innocent bystander is suspect, and she is herded to the Cheka chief for interrogation. At first, Zudin is amused by her tale—a lost ballet dancer searching for her troupe—then he warns her of the dire consequences for consorting with the enemy. Soon she confesses to being merely a "bedroom convenience" and begs forgiveness. Hearing her imputations, Zudin loses his iron grip, and his objectivity disintegrates. In a moment of sincerity—coupled with his own idea of altruism—Zudin admonishes her poor judgment and suspends punishment. Her own neck now saved, Yelena Valentinovina promises reform and adjuration. Impressed by her entreaties, Zudin takes one step further by furnishing her a position—a job—in Cheka Headquarters as one of the record keepers. As a supernumerary, her assignment will be to alphabetize the current cases under investigation.

At this point, another characterization has developed. Oblivious to the dogma of the Revolution, Valts's opportunism oozes out in every situation, and she is—as Xenia Gasiorowska (1968) has pointed out—imbued with "a vulgar sexiness and insidious sex-appeal," two traits that the hardened, but naive, Cheka leader cannot discern. As a *femme fatale*, Valts knows every level of the former bourgeois society, and many men still lavish her with gifts and luxury. Now employed by the Cheka, her situation, which structurally is implausible, is necessary to further plot development (coincidences are found on every level in *belles lettres*). Valts soon realizes the fortuitousness of such a position, a situation she foresees will only enhance her welfare.

Two important events unfold: First the attractive Valts attempts to seduce Zudin, but the Cheka chief, while capitulating to her voluptuous advances, is frustrated by her moronic anti-Bolshevik remarks and, seated in the privacy of his office, literally throws her off his lap late one evening—a scene, by the way, witnessed peripherally by the cleaning woman. Second, another coincidence occurs when Valts undaunted by her seduction failure discovers an old folder, which has been misfiled, describing a bureaucratic mistake responsible for the incarceration of an innocent man. Now she decides to act. She will bring this mistake to Zudin and point out the circumstances for the false imprisonment and—understanding the chief's sense of justice—will be instrumental in having the innocent man freed, an event she plans to capitalize on.

Complications and intrigues follow. Valts must now ingratiate herself once more with Comrade Zudin, and a third important coincidence happens. An old lover—an English spy running from the Cheka—pops up unexpectedly and, after an evening of dalliance and intimacy, gives Valts an unusual present: 20 pounds of Cailler's chocolate, a premium brand and unseen for months in wartorn Russia. Soon she is standing in Zudin's living room, but this time she is visiting the Cheka chief's family. After a few moments of pleasant amenities, Valts tells the confused wife that she has brought a few presents for the children—2 pounds of chocolate and a few pairs of lisle stockings. Stunned by the extravagance of the gifts, the wife graciously accepts the secretary's offer.

Returning home that evening, Zudin is first nonplussed by this show of magnanimity by his clerk—a mere underling—but then berates his wife for accepting such generosity, arguing that the gifts resemble a bribe. A heated discussion follows, but against his better judgment, the Cheka chief—watching his young son devour half the chocolate—permits the presents to remain, justifying his decision to appease his wife's vanity. Later on, Zudin criticizes Valts for being in his home—it is a breach of social stratification—but once more, the sensual clerk is able to smooth-talk her way out of this predicament when she realizes Zudin's vulnerability to her charms.

Soon Valts initiates her extortion scheme. Obtaining Zudin's formal signature on a prisoner release form, she proceeds to demand payment from the victim's terrified family the sum of 20 pounds of gold. Frightened by the woman's credibility—she represents the Cheka—the family acquiesces to her threats and delivers the gold coins. Subsequently, the prisoner is released when Valts produces Zudin's certificate of authority.

Unaware of these events, Zudin is faced with a serious problem. A loyal Cheka officer is murdered by the Whiteguards, and Zudin, livid with rage, orders the execution of 100 prisoners as retribution. The entire scene is ruthless; in a fit of rage, Zudin demands terror and warns of more mass executions, more reprisals, more deaths. "To avenge one individual we shall strike at their whole class," he raves (1922, 69).

This episode reveals the dichotomy in Zudin's personality. On one side, he is a kind family man, an individual of warmth and compassion, a person of honor and integrity, willing to make sacrifices and endure hardships for the "better world" promised under the new Communist Revolution. But when angered, he becomes uncontrollable, incoherent, and brutal, demanding death to all enemies of the Cheka. His primitive philosophy—that the end justifies the means—is a pseudopragmatic concept, that he and his followers blindly obey, unaware, at this time, that he, too, will soon fall victim to such a primitive mentality.

While Zudin is implementing his campaign of terror, Valts's extortion attempt backfires, and she is quickly arrested. Frightened, realizing her crime is punishable by summary execution, she panics and pleads for her life, arguing that the Cheka chief, himself, sanctioned and encouraged her acts. Soon Zudin is arrested and charged with taking bribes, allowing extortion, and participating in counterrevolutionary activities.

At this point it is easy to discern that the content of this plot development in *Chocolate* is only the exposition of the novel. The information is basic and simple: A loyal Communist member—the chairman of the local Cheka—is arrested and charged with a capital crime. On the surface, the man is innocent (so was Billy Budd), but we are dealing with a Soviet novel, and what follows soon becomes a moot point, a matter of debate and rationalization, a matter that places expediency over justice, of control over chaos, of strength over weakness.

The interrogation of Zudin, held *in camera*, is, as Zavalishin (1958) has stated, similar in content (lacking the brutality) to Rubashov's predicament in Koestler's *Darkness at Noon*. And so it is here in these last 100 pages that one can comprehend that Tarasov-Rodionov, unknowingly, was ringing his knell by caricaturing the Cheka officials as both odious and simple. Zudin listens to each word as his cohorts denounce him for taking bribes, for accepting the two pounds of chocolate, for reveling in luxury while the citizenry lacks basic necessities. Over and over again, Zudin is denigrated as an enemy of the state, a bribe-taker, an official who has violated these sacrosanct principles of the October Revolution. One of the ironies of this kangaroo court—as Brown (1973) has aptly indicated—is that no mention is made of Zudin's irrational (and somewhat paranoid) behavior for the reprisal killing of 100 innocent prisoners. But, rather, in their own interpretation of revolutionary justice, the accusers reiterate their charges that Zudin is "guilty of everything."

At this time, there is a certain stoic quality about Zudin's behavior when he hears the words "guilty of everything." His predicament, while basically innocuous, has proscribed him to certain doom through the process of revolutionary logic. The opinion of the masses, the investigators claim, must be satisfied; already the gossip of the cleaning woman, the quidnunc present during the attempted seduction scene, has linked the Cheka director to both sex and bribes. And finally, the tribunal pronounces that the exoneration of Zudin would destroy the control of terror, a manipulative lever that Zudin had originated, so necessary for the work of the Cheka.

The council announces its edict: The death—or in Zudin's case, the sacrifice—of any individual is justified if it will benefit unforeseeable thousands, if it will free the masses from exploitation, starvation, misery, and suffering. Moral or ethical considerations are inconsequential. By implication, by nuance, by association, Zudin is "guilty of everything," and without his execution, the power of the Revolution will erode as the masses falter in their loyalty and trust to Bolshevism. Even Zudin understands the council's reasoning when an old comrade laments, "[Y]ou are guilty, you were guilty, you have roused the suspicions of the masses so that our entire cause may be lost. . . . [A]ren't you an old revolutionist? . . . We must punish you to make an example of others. . . . [T]hink only of the future" (1922, 69).

Zudin's death is glorified in the final pages in a scene that would make the brightest purple prose blush. Walking toward his executioners, the former Cheka chief gloats in self-aggrandizement, happy in the knowledge that his death is perpetuating world communism. The feeling is complemented by the resounding music of the peasants, marching off to fight the distant enemies, singing their "*Internationale.*" This entire scene, parenthetically, resembles a short episode found in Lewis Milestone's 1943 Hollywood propaganda film *The North Star*.

Overlooking many of the defects in style—the frequent use of coincidence and the highfalutin idealism (especially in the dream sequences)—*Chocolate* is a valuable work of Soviet fiction because of its treatment of the private workings of the Cheka, especially in describing the means of terror for control of the population. One could only speculate why Tarasov-Rodionov would take such a controversial subject as the theme for a beginning novel, a book that subsequently provoked such public opposition because in questioning the innards of the Cheka, the author was, in reality, challenging the secret police's very existence. Maybe, as Brown (1973) has stated, Tarasov-Rodionov did not understand the deadly nature of the questions and theme he was raising. Perhaps, in his own naive way, the author was asserting that literature—as an art form—transcended both politics and governments. (But did it transcend a revolution?) Surely Tarasov-Rodionov must have drawn on his own participation in the Bolshevik movement as a course (or inspiration) for *Chocolate*. It still isn't clear, in many minds, whether or not the book contains propaganda value. On the one hand, the novel insists on scrupulous adherence to dogma, because in the end, such behavior, no matter how vile, will ensure world communism; on the other hand, *Chocolate* may be read as an indictment of Red terror, because the subject of innocence or guilt is never an issue—only those means required for expediency.

Regardless of any speculation, Tarasov-Rodionov did not enjoy any of the benefits of literary fame. In 1928, he published *February*, an eyewitness (and highly complimentary) account of the Early Revolution, a novel written in diary form, devoid of any of the polemics or ambiguities that are found in *Chocolate*. Two years later, a third volume, *July*, appeared. A fourth book, never released, was titled *October*.

A few years later, in 1937 or 1938, Tarasov-Rodionov, like his ill-fated Cheka hero, was also found guilty of everything. Accused of Trotskyism, he was arrested and never heard from again. And like so many others, some three decades later, as George Gibian has acknowledged, Tarasov-Rodionov was rehabilitated and returned to the roster of Soviet authors, his novel *Chocolate* now wearing the imprimatur "ideological error."

REFERENCES

Alexandrova, Vera. *A History of Soviet Literature*. Garden City, N.Y.: Doubleday, 1963. 38. A one-paragraph reference to Tarasov-Rodionov's writings emphasizing his disgrace, arrest, and obvious death caused by the Stalin purges.

Borland, Harriet. *Soviet Literary Theory and Practice during the First Five-Year Plan 1928–1932*. New York: Greenwood Press, 1950. 150. A short reference describing a statement—made by Tarasov-Rodionov—about Soviet writer Leopold Averbakh.

Brown, Edward. *Russian Literature since the Revolution*. New York: Macmillan Company, 1973. 147–50, 215. Excellent discussion of *Chocolate* with strong references to the influence of Andrey Bely.

"A Communist Martyr." Review of Tarasov-Rodionov's *Chocolate*. *New York Times Book Review*, April 24, 1932. 15. Generally favorable review discussing the novel's propaganda value.

Eastman, Max. *Artists in Uniform*. New York: Alfred A. Knopf, 1934. 14.

Gasiorowska, Xenia. *Women in Soviet Fiction 1917–1964*. Madison: University of Wisconsin Press, 1968. 144, 165. Short references to the characterization of Yelena, the *femme fatale*, in *Chocolate*.

Hingley, Ronald. *Russian Writers and Soviet Society 1917–1978*. New York: Random House, 1979. 139. Brief reference to the Cheka theme in *Chocolate*.

Maguire, Robert A. *Red Virgin Soil*. Princeton: Princeton University Press, 1968. 77, 162, 232, 297, 367. Numerous references to Tarasov-Rodionov's career as a Soviet writer; no references to *Chocolate*.

Ruhle, Jurgen. *Literature and Revolution*. New York: Praeger Publishers, 1965. 473. Statistical reference to Tarasov-Rodionov's death.

Struve, Gleb. *Russian Literature under Lenin and Stalin 1917–1953*. Norman: University of Oklahoma Press, 1971. 92–93, 138–39, 170, 280, 282. Detailed accounts of Tarasov-Rodioinov's writing career. Good reference material.

Struve, Gleb. *Soviet Russian Literature*. London: George Routledge and Sons, Ltd., 1935. 100, 101, 156, 261.

Van Der Eng-Liedmeier, A. M. *Soviet Literary Characters*. Amsterdam: Mouton and
    Company, 1959. 13. Interesting footnote discussing the dénouement of *Chocolate*.
"Years of Horror." Review of *Chocolate* in *Saturday Review*, May 7, 1932. 713.
    Generally favorable review citing the historical accuracy of the novel.
Zavalishin, Vyacheslav. *Early Soviet Writers*. New York: Praeger Publishers, 1958.
    215–17, 241, 282. Good background material comparing *Chocolate* to Arthur
    Koestler's *Darkness at Noon*.

CHAPTER 7

Chocolate for Rrose: Marcel Duchamp's *Chocolate Grinder* and *The Large Glass*

Erdmute Wenzel White

There is no more metaphysics in the world than chocolate.
—Fernando Pessoa, *Tobacco Shop*

Chocolate, in its original meaning *xocoatl*, a nourishment of the gods, right-fully belongs to the artist and poet. Marcel Duchamp, master of the avant-garde, transcendent satrap of the Collège de Pataphysique, and Dadaist by choice, was fascinated by passions of chocolate so esoteric as to defy the imagination. His chocolate reflections on paper, on canvas (see Figure 7.1), or in glass are forever dissimilar and as cryptic as hermeticists' texts. Chocolate, in this instance, goes well beyond energies occasioned by known forces and substances. For Marcel Duchamp, chocolate ultimately stands for the place of mind itself, thus taking the idea of "chocolateness" into its fullest mystery.

Characteristic of the relationship between chocolate and the arts is the wide range of dialogue, combining "life-size" economics with the essence of contemplative flight. The Dada-Gallery, Zürich, 1917, was sponsored by the Swiss chocolate manufacturer Sprüngli. The Peter Ludwig Collection, now the Ludwig Museum, Cologne, specializing in Art of the Sixties, is equally endowed by wealth obtained in chocolate fabrication. The Sprengel Museum, Hannover, is yet another exaltation of chocolate fortunes. The latter houses, moreover, some of the great works by Kurt Schwitters, the artist famous for gathering discarded wrappers from sidewalks and gutters and lifting them onto his canvases.

Unlikely and unsuspecting persons, lovers of chocolate bars, have contributed to the flowering of modern art and the conservation of Merz cathedrals. Artists such as Dieter Roth and Joseph Beuys have, on occasion, worked directly in chocolate, as did Marcel Duchamp. *Puddingbücher* and *Schokoladenbilder* by Roth celebrate the chocolate point of view, as does Beuys's elevation of the ordinary chocolate Easter bunny to a complex iconic marker. Beuys's chocolate connection resonates far and unexpectedly as in his *How to Explain Pictures to a Dead Hare* (1965, action). Whether such imagery is semantic, procedural, or tactile, the chocolate substance seemingly embraces all categories. While inviting more than meets the eye, its essence remains nameless, an entity that is, which in Duchampian logic holds and generates the very secret of desire.[1] Chocolate as perfect aphrodisiac, while obvious, creates its own reverberations without the slightest claim to originality. What is singular about Duchamp, however, is his system of perplexities (*cervellités*), which allows the notion of the raising of desire to be comparable to the "raising of dust," literally.

Duchamp's object dedicated to "dust breeding," *The Large Glass*, took 13 years and was officially "unfinished" in 1923, with the accidental breaking of the glass panels on their return from exhibition. When the calamity was discovered a few years later, Duchamp set out patiently to repair thousands of fragments. The accident must have pleased him, since the shattered surfaces add yet another visual demonstration to the punning dimensions of the dangers of transport.

Our visual sense is an uninteresting one, according to Marcel Duchamp. Painters paint the same picture over and over, preoccupied with visual appearances. Duchamp, on the contrary, puts painting at the service of the mind. Painting, he insists, must be "antiretinal," that is, free from the dictates of canvas-born sensation. The art of Marcel Duchamp painstakingly suspends the protocol of visual intelligibility. His optics and physical implementations are "subsidized" by language, itself determined by delirious semantic trickery. Duchamp's work elicits visceral and eccentric reaction. He resists theorizing by deliberately subverting his own taste and by systematic proliferation of intent. Duchamp's answer to the art of impressions, *The Large Glass*, is a spectral text, neither a visual event nor a purely conceptual one. (For a twelfth-century version, see Figure 7.2.) Although color, line, and taste act as irritants, they remain aloof from physical figuration (Figure 7.3). What is unique about Duchamp, is not the mingling of the senses but the creation of an antiworld, a neutrum between emptiness and form. The utopian process concerns cessation of color and its rebirth as a pure and flawless "physical idea."

My own approach to the artist's work rests on indecisive reunion of words and senses slightly bent. The intent is to cultivate a speculative realm where sensory values change essences, confirming reversibility of phenomena and ideas. Placed both at the beginning and end of resemblance, *The Glass* emerges intact from the present procedure. The interpretation set forth here is conspirtorial. Propelled by Duchampian interventions, it draws on chance and necessity to project the motions of meaning.

In 1911, Marcel Duchamp's brother, Duchamp-Villon, asked each of a number of artists to contribute a work for his kitchen. Duchamp's contribution was *Coffee Mill* (*Moulin à Café*), oil on cardboard (Figure 7.4). The mill relates to events that master and abolish time, showing its handle simultaneously as it revolves. Harriet and Sidney Janis observe that this wedding gift, made casually, constitutes a key work in Duchamp's subsequent development: "This

Figure 7.1
Chocolate Grinder

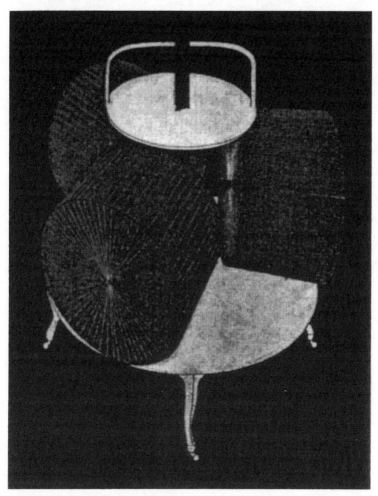

Broyeuse de Chocolat (Chocolate Grinder [No. 2]), February 1914 (Paris). Oil and thread on canvas, 65 × 54 cm. Philadelphia Museum of Art, The Louise and Walter Arensberg Collection.

Figure 7.2
Marcel Duchamp's *The Large Glass*

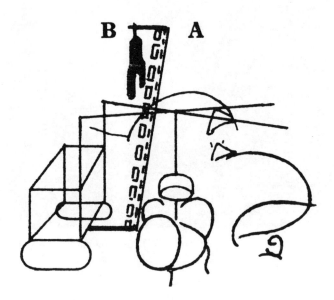

The twelfth-century Nuttall Codex includes a work of art in which a royal Mesoamerican couple shares a cup of chocolate to seal their marriage contract. Its twentieth-century version is an extraordinary object, Marcel Duchamp's *The Large Glass*.

ERRATA

Chocolate: Food of the Gods

Please note that the artwork on page 71 was inadvertently printed upside down.

Figure 7.3
The Large Glass or *The Bride*

La Mariée Mise a Nu Par Ses Célibataires, Même (Le Grand Verre) (The Bride Stripped Bare by Her Bachelors, Even [The Large Glass]), 1915–23. Oil, varnish, lead foil, lead wire, and dust on two glass panels (cracked), each mounted between two glass panels, with five glass strips, aluminum foil, and a wood and steel frame, 227.5 × 175.8 cm. Philadelphia Museum of Art. Bequest of Katherine S. Dreier, 1953.

Figure 7.4
Coffee Mill

Moulin à Café (Coffee Mill), 1911. Oil on cardboard, 33 x 12.5 cm. Arturo Schwarz, Centro Studi SADE (Surrealism and Dada, Even), Milan, Italy.

incident served to release the inventive and fecund personality of Duchamp as it exists today, as if inadvertently he had exposed to light and air, to the necessary elements, a nucleus from which his own psyche could develop and grow. Duchamp regards the Coffee-grinder as the key picture to his complete work."[2] *The Large Glass* (1915–23) also comprises *Chocolate Grinder (Broyeuse de Chocolat)* and *Watermill (Glissière contenant un Moulin à Eau)*, (1913–14). The nucleus of *The Large Glass* thus existed before Duchamp's trip to Munich, where he visited from July to August 1912.

In Munich, Vassily Kandinsky and Franz Marc had just published the *Blaue Reiter Almanach*, which appeared in May 1912 at Piper Verlag. It closely followed Kandinsky's *Über das Geistige in der Kunst*, a treatise Duchamp may have translated for his own use.[3] The almanac, according to an October 1911 press release by Kandinsky, was devoted to the complete renewal of art, called "die grosse Umwälzung" (the great rotation of values). The volume included an article by Roger Allard, which examines the achievement of French artists in search of new form. The critic refers to Marcel Duchamp as one of the seminal artists of the time, his notoriety due, in part, to *Nude Descending a Staircase*, completed in January 1912. To illustrate the revitalization of the age, Allard's essay includes works by Cézanne, Le Fauconnier, and a stunning, full-page reproduction of Henri Matisse's *La Danse* (1909–10) from the Shchukin collection, a work emanating energy and glorification of instinct and desire.[4]

Enjoying prominence in Munich art circles, Marcel Duchamp traveled to Germany to see for himself and to participate in the creation of a new canon. *The Large Glass*, developed after his stay in Munich, no longer fits any known category of art but sets in motion the inexhaustible range of optical and mental effects that would characterize his subsequent work. In keeping with his penchant for punning and tongue-in-cheek delectation, Duchamp's *Chocolate Grinder*, featured in *The Large Glass*, offers "optical evidence" of "die grosse Umwälzung" announced by his friends of the *Blaue Reiter* group.

Following Marcel Duchamp's statement that he regards his coffee mill as the key to his complete works, the present chapter will focus on the chocolate mill centrally located in the lower part of *The Glass*. The change from coffee to chocolate was occasioned, presumably, by superior formal beauty and by semantic locomotion. The chocolate mill creates the network of laws of attraction and gravitation that provides the indispensable support of *The Bride* portrayed in the upper half of *The Glass*. As spatial form and chocolate fiction, the chocolate machine, like the 1911 coffee mill, refers to motion arrested, now interiorized, "sewn into perspective." Recast, detached, and positioned to oscillate, it is set to demonstrate the divisions of space and meaning.

Standing nine feet high (108 × 67 inches), *The Large Glass* is a climactic work, a search or statement of self-identity constantly fluctuating between determinism and wildest chance. Its full title is the oddly phrased "La Mariée Mise À Nu Par / Ses Célibataires, Même" (The Bride Stripped Bare By Her Bachelors, Even), which the artist insists is nondescriptive but should be treated "like an invisible color." Despite the reminder, a host of subtitles such as "agricultural machine," "this business/has much to offer . . .)," "apparatus— instrument for farming," or "delay in glass" comment and express intention, adding highly charged emphasis while denying its consideration. *The Large Glass* is the Dada work *par excellence*, an elegant, haunting game of indefinite incompletion and implausible mental leaps, at once threshold of the history of modern art and personal rite of passage.

The Glass is new and powerful for the sheer variety of perceptions granted. Architecture of incorporeal phenomena, it embraces the viewer's mirror image, the volume behind the glass—a gallery site or Katherine Dreier's backyard—and the shadows cast by the component parts of the work. Imbued with light and air, the work specifically refers to watercolor, the most revealingly fluid means of painting. Its double panes are delicately tinged *eau de Nil*. However, in characteristic *volte-face*, Duchamp bypasses the material aspect of the medium, except in real paint applied to the sensuous "cinematic blossoming" of *The Bride*. Like watercolor, *The Glass* openly displays its substance and structure, yet it does so only to deflect from its anomalously complex procedural qualities. Made of seamless force fields of visual and semantic information, effects are created before our eyes, offering glimpses of mental fabrication. Energized by semiopaque textures of verbal punning, the trickery of words mirrors the *trompe l'oeil* effect of a glider/chariot/sleigh "moving" in *inframince*, the severely compressed space between two panes of glass.

When Duchamp returned from Munich after his two-month stay, "the scene of my complete liberation,"[5] he announced that as far as he was concerned, painting was finished, and with few exceptions, he abandoned conventional forms of painting and drawing. His drawings, henceforth, tend to be scientific illustrations or technical sketches, although painting and drawing were not altogether excluded, as exemplified by his 1953 work entitled *Moonlight on the Bay of Basswood*, a drawing on blue blotting paper of the shoreline of a Minnesota lake. The composition is done in ink, pencil, and crayon but also in talcum powder and in real chocolate. Having come full circle in chocolate magic, next to the glittering absorbency of talc, the very idea of chocolate closes the eyelid.

At about his return from Germany, Duchamp began to jot down working notes on single pieces and scraps of paper, published as loose fragments in 1934, his *Green Box*. In 94 thoughts, meticulously printed, the artist engages in space-time calculations and idiosyncratic systems of measurements that, in his own words, stretch the laws of physics just a little. The personal liberation Duchamp refers to is demonstrated by visual and semantic transformation of *The Bride* image. In January 1, 1910, the artist provided a cartoon for *Le Courrier Français*, which depicts a walking doll with a legend taken from an advertise-ment: "Bébé marcheur, dormeur à cils, envoyant des baisers des deux mains, complètement articulé, béguin, costume soie, chemise garnie de dentelles. Se déshabillant." These "real" attributes of the doll and the word plays such as the meaning of "béguin" as "passion amoureuse passagère" and the bonnet of a sort of nun, "une religieuse qui, sans prononcer des voeux, vit dans une sorte de couvent," are also present in the final *Bride*, where despite her "blossoming," she is forever separated from the bachelors by a "cooler." The porcelain bride can be undressed ("se déshabillant"), which might also mean "in the act of undressing." Similarly, *The Bride's* clothes are *listed* as absent in *The Large Glass*. As in the case of the "free nun," a viewer is left with inexplicable clues and complex interrelated functions that are neither true nor false, continually feeding on reversals and paradoxical linkings, keeping the mind in suspension. "There is no solution, because there are no problems," Duchamp answered Richard Hamilton when the latter submitted his speculations upon the meaning of *The Bride*.

Duchamp's first Munich sketch for the Bride approximates the final title, *The Bride Stripped Bare By The Bachelors" (La Mariée Mise À Nu Par Les célibataires)*, July-August 1912. A pencil and wash on paper, it depicts a woman surrounded by two males. It seems that at this moment Marcel Duchamp hit on the "theme" of his *The Large Glass*, namely, how alien concepts, related by linguistic inversion, fit an underlying subversion of logic. Inscribed in the lower center of the work are the words: "Méchanisme de la pudeur/ Pudeur mécanique" (Mechanism of chastity/Mechanical chastity). In this sense, *The Large Glass* might conceivably be said to describe the plumbings of eroticism.

The "chastity" drawing was followed by two Munich "virgins," both dating July 1912, by *The Passage from Virgin to Bride (Le Passage de la Vierge à la Mariée)*, oil on canvas, and finally, by *Bride (Mariée)*, dating August 1912. This succession of brides and her post-Munich appearance in *The Large Glass*, from porcelain doll to bridal transformations into idea and transparency, is accompanied by a formal switch from canvas to glass. A window suspended in space, it challenges the gaze to travel through its actual locale, beckoning beyond to ideal images of mind. Vision and capacity of realization are startlingly, more fully apprehended. "Meaning" flows beyond site boundaries, shuttling freely between immaterial light and light traveling through glass. While there is speculation concerning the artist's use of glass, Duchamp was familiar with Bavarian *Hinterglasmalerei*, votive, folkloric paintings done on glass, which were popular at the time with the *Blue Rider*. Kandinsky, Marc, and Münter adopted glass painting for their own use. Their frequent subject, the pouring of the Spirit, is deeply implied in *The Large Glass*, as well as the related notion of the *Geistesblitz*, the sudden flash of inspiration.

The history of *The Large Glass* is complex and embraces such striking aesthetic procedures as the already mentioned dust breeding (*élevage de poussière*), recorded in 1920 by Man Ray's photographs, which register the monthly accumulation of dust as the work lay on its face in the studio, the final fixation of selected dust areas by means of drops of varnish, and the unforeseen breaking of the glass in 1923. Although it was made of plate glass, Duchamp specifically speaks of his object as a "painting": "When I came to New York in 1915, I started this painting, repeating and grouping together in their final position the different details" (*MD* 296). Indeed, Duchamp considered his application of varnish as "a kind of color," and the tinge of the plate glass is yet another subtle form of color. The central element of *The Large Glass*, the imposing *Chocolate Grinder (Broyeuse De Chocolat)* itself, must be related to the painterly act of grinding color, while the dusted surfaces, in turn, evoke delicate dustings of chocolate powder.

The Bride Stripped Bare By Her Bachelors, Even lists the following ingredients: Oil, varnish, lead foil, lead wire, and dust on the two panels (cracked), each mounted between two glass panels, with five glass strips, aluminum foil, and a wood and steel frame. Distilled from a heightened, private language of forms and symbols, the Chocolate Grinder is located in the center of the so-called Bachelor Apparatus that occupies the lower panel. It was suggested by an actual chocolate grinding machine Duchamp saw in the window of a confectionery shop in Rouen. This contraption of chocolate machinery, considered to belong to the male part of the work, will lead us far afield into disconcerting yet reassuring madness, embracing at once the minute shifts of the darkness of passion and impersonal, metaphysical hilariousness. The Grinder is, above all, a most dramatic and deliberately paradoxical portrayal of the chemistry of chocolate as essence of creative mystery. Thus, the triumph of chocolate may lead, by chance, to a science of one's fantasy.

The second motif of the Bachelor Apparatus, linked to the Grinder by means of scissors and diverse capillary tubes, is a sleigh or chariot, an elegant Glider (1913–15): "[T]his Glider is also a machine sliding on its two runners . . . designed to slide back and forth at a jerky pace, activated by the erratic fall of a bottle of Benedictine" (*MD* 276). Lengthy litanies are recited on its journey, tentatively listed as follows:

The Litanies of the Chariot:

> Slow life.
> Vicious circle.
> Onanism.
> Horizontal.
> Round trip
> for the buffer.
> Junk of life.
> Cheap construction.
> Tin, cords, iron wire.
> Eccentric wooden pulleys.
> Monotonous fly wheel.
> Beer professor.
> (to be entirely redone).[6]

Attached to the Glider are the nine malic molds, also called "Cemetery of Uniforms and Liveries," which depict a priest, delivery boy, gendarme, cuirassier, policeman, undertaker, liveried servant, busboy, and stationmaster. Significantly, we don't see them, since each precise uniform is *inside* its external mold, is a hollow livery, and is thus obliterated to the eye. Other elements of the lower Bachelor Machine are sieves or a parasol, regions of the waterfall, the three splashes, the sculpture of drops and the "Wilson-Lincoln" effect, as well as the Butterfly pump. There are further objects or events designated as corkscrew, weight with nine holes, Mandala, which is a magnifying glass to focus the splashes, Marbles, and a proposed Boxing Match. While the bachelors are grinding their chocolate, the Bride, referred to as "Pendu femelle," hangs above them in the window's upper section. The Bride's Domain lists 10 further items, among them the Inscription of Milky Way (the cinematic blossoming), the draft pistons or Nets, Nine Shots, Bride's garment, grilled cooler (isolating plates), the region of the picture of cast shadows, the mirror image of the sculpture of drops, horizon and a Juggler of Gravity (also called the Trainer, Handler, or Tender of Gravity). Such names as "region of the picture of cast shadows" suggest Platonic states instead of geographic location. The "cinematic blossoming," referred to as the halo of the Bride, according to Duchamp, is the "emanation of the sum total of her splendid vibrations" (Hamilton, n.p.). There is, finally, one other thrice-reflected presence in *The Large Glass*. Below the Mandala, Duchamp later added the *Témoins Oculistes*, Oculist Witnesses (French: Eyewitnesses), made of actual oculist charts. Taken from carbon paper, they were made of silvered sections laboriously scraped away from the glass.

The *Témoin* appears in the 1918 Buenos Aires Glass with the following instructions: "A regarder (L'Autre Côté du Verre), d'un oeil, de près, pendant presque une heure" (To be looked at [From the other side of the Glass] with one eye, close up, for almost an hour). While charts and Mandala reinforce the role of the observer, the voyeuristic tingle, they mark an independent agency of triple integrity and silvering, mirroring reflection. The pleasure of the chocolate event is *ours* to experience, its aesthetic progress minutely charted and recorded in the glass. Chocolate speculations are traced by an eye of paradoxical vision, sculpting either lyric halos or that which clouds the mind. This, perhaps, Tristan Tzara meant when he spoke of "chocolate in the veins of men" (chocolat dans les veines de tous les hommes).[7] "Veine" is both chance and artery or vein. Taken to its logical conclusion, chocolate, according to Tzara's curious linguistic convergence, is captivated/captivating or canned chance. Duchamp simply added the precision of transparent luck, or luck in glass, a game of now you see it, now you don't.

Oblique reference to the artist himself is woven into the very texture of the main title, a hidden, ambiguous presence, both male and female, as expressed by the complementary architecture of the sentence: "La *Mariée* Mise À Nu Par Ses *Céli*bataires, Même." Verbal ensnare and discovery signal a private obsession suggested by Duchamp's *Adam and Eve* (after Cranach), for which he posed nude in Francis Picabia's *Ciné Sketch*, 1924, and his own impersonation as the transvestite Rrose Sélavy (Figure 7.5), for whom Duchamp had printed baggage tags. We recognize a purposeful progression from complementary opposites as in *Adam and Eve* to androgynous Rrose to still another transmutation into purely imaginary realms in glass; from immediate presence, albeit on film, to the male Rrose, a figure of mental displacement who carries the accoutrements of "real" life, to ultimate unity in *double* glass. A reading of the twice-repeated initial consonant of Rrose Sélavy, allows the following phrase: "Eros is Life" or "That's Life!" Duchamp's perception of life as an aggregate of pleasure-directed principles typically contains a new convergence of inner and outer, since Eros itself is twofold, being at once that which keeps intact energy of awareness and its arresting quality, the beauty of a rose, for example. It is here, at the crossroads of meaning, that we should return to the Chocolate Grinder, since in Marcel Duchamp's own words, it is poised "at the place (still ascending) where eroticism is revealed (which should be one of the principle cogs in the Bachelor Machine" (Hamilton, n.p.).

A celebration of eroticism, the implausible Grinder is spinning in posed fervor. At once impotent and powerful, it operates under its own power. We are alerted to this fact by a pen and pencil on paper of 1959, entitled *Cols Alités (Bedridden Mountains)*, which has the chocolate engine hooked up to an electric pole. The grinding machine is a locus of trinity, which consists of three rollers, their glittering necktie, and a circular platform, namely, a three-legged, seductive Louis XV chassis. The *Green Box* notes concerning the Chocolate Grinder are numerous and detailed. Some are done on *brasserie* slips (Brasserie de l'*Opéra*, restaurant, Rouen). Figures 7.6 and 7.7 describe the apparatus (so it *is* an "agricultural machine" and defines its enabling function as a "Principle of [Spontaneity]").

Several preparatory studies led up to the Grinder's final placement in glass. The first work, oil on canvas, dating from 1913, was followed by complicated plans and elevation studies of the entire Bachelor Apparatus. About his magnificent 1914 *Chocolate Grinder*, oil and thread on canvas, Duchamp writes: "From 1913 on, I concentrated all my activities on the planning of *The Large Glass* and did a study of every detail" (*MD* 272). The Grinder, above all, meant complete artistic freedom: "Through the introduction of straight perspective and a very geometrical design of a definite grinding machine like this one, I felt definitely out of the cubist straightjacket" (*MD* 272). The lines of the three rollers are made of threads directly sewn into the canvas, providing an effect that, according to Duchamp, "is like an architectural, dry rendering of the chocolate grinding machine purified of all past influences" (*MD* 272). The title of the canvas is carefully printed in gold letters on a leather label. Thick, resistant leather becomes the tactile equivalent to chocolate, with golden lettering evoking its luxury and richness. The threaded Chocolate Grinder is the first complete version. Another contemporaneous study shows the bayonet, the stem that generates all other things, but still without the Louis XV support. Now sewn

Figure 7.5
Rrose Sélavy

Rrose Sélavy by Man Ray (1920–21). Gelatin silver print of Marcel Duchamp. Collection of the J. Paul Getty Museum, Malibu, California. Copyright © 1922, Mann Ray Trust/ ADAGP-Paris/ARS-USA.

Figure 7.6
Description of the Chocolate Grinder

<u>the Chocolate Grinder</u>

is essentially composed . . .

The <u>chocolate</u> of the rollers, coming from one knows not where,
would deposit itself after grinding, as milk chocolate . . . . .

(insert a letter referring to a diagram) with brilliant shimmering
The <u>necktie</u> would have been of aluminum foil stretched and

stuck down, but the[3] <u>rollers always turn beneath.</u>

the Bayonet ^(X) Helps to hold up the compression bar
and the large scissors and the isolating plates.

First-class article.

The grinder is mounted on a Louis XV nickeled
<u>chassis.</u>

reconsider it
Adage
Principle of [Spontaneity] (which explains the gyratory mt of the grinder without other help)
<u>The bachelor grinds his chocolate himself—</u>

<u>commercial formula, trade mark, commercial slogan</u>

<u>inscribed like an advertisement on a bit of glossy and</u>

<u>colored paper (have it made by a printer)—this paper stuck</u>

<u>on the article "Chocolate Grinder"</u>

Source: Marcel Duchamp, George Heard Hamilton, and Richard Hamilton, trans., *The Bride Stripped Bare* (Stuttgart: Hansjörg Mayer, 1976), n.p.

Figure 7.7
"Given an *Object in Chocolate*"

Given an <u>object in chocolate.</u>

                                              other

1st its appearance = retinal impression (and sensory

                                              consequences)

2nd its apparition

                                              in negative

The <u>mould</u> of a chocolate object is the (negative) apparition
of the <u>surface</u>   one or
of the <u>plane</u> (with several curvatures) generating 1st (by

elementary prilllism) the (colored) form of the object

                         native colors

2nd. the (mass of <u>elements of light</u>) (<u>chocolate type</u>

⁺
in the conditional
tense. if one ...   elements): ⁺ in the passage from the <u>apparition</u> (mould) to the <u>appear-</u>

<u>ance</u>, the plane, composed of elements of <u>chocolate type</u> light

determines the apparent chocolate mass

by <u>physical dyeing</u>

a)   <u>in negative</u>   <u>for the colored form</u>
  the (negative) apparition (determined <u>conventionally</u> by the

linear perspective, but always in an environment
                     (for example)
of n—1 dimensions. for an object of n dimensions.); In the
             in negative
same way this (negative) apparition, for

the phenomenon of <u>Physical Dyeing,</u> is determined by

the source of light becoming in the <u>apparent</u> object

lighted mass (<u>native colors.</u> = apparition in negative of the

<u>apparent</u> colors of the substance of the objects.)

Note: This chocolate inscription generates a relationship between the apparent chocolate mass and "physical dyeing."
Source: Marcel Duchamp, George Heard Hamilton, and Richard Hamilton, trans. *The Bride Stripped Bare* (Stuttgart: Hansjörg Mayer, 1976), n.p.

into perspective, complete, the 1914 Grinder is not only a reclaimed object but also the "soul" of a machine, rendered virgin, pure, "purified of all past influences," is devoid of past, self-contained, *free* ("Munich was the scene of my complete liberation").

In 1917 the motif appeared on the cover of the Dada magazine *Blind Man, revue*, revisited and looked at again. The next time we see the Grinder, it is covered with dust, as in the 1920 Ray photograph. Cleared of the past, resuscitated in *The Large Glass*, it has acquired the spare, powerful lightness of a ballerina. Finally, in 1968, the Grinder rises skyward in Jasper Jones's transparent balloons for Merce Cunningham's ballet *Walk-around Time*. As dancers walk among the elements of *The Large Glass*, the Chocolate Grinder, concerned with real and intellectual motion, fittingly, turns figure of dance. If we read the title of the Grinder's last, "landscaped," hooked-on appearance, it spells not only "Bedridden Mountains" and "Mountains in Bed" but also "Causa- lité" (Causality). While such linguistic coincidences question the validity of language, it is precisely the causality of occult coincidences that governs *The Large Glass*, including the following Duchampian semantics for the inner land- scape of chocolate, suited only to perfect surprise of chance, exquisitely fusing transparencies of language with the sibylline exactness of his own visual text.

"Choc-au-las" is pure essence of illuminating, internal semantic energy, spelling out what may be translated as "choc or impetus to weariness, to what is worn out/tired (las)" or "*élan vital* as opposed to the forces of death." "Chocolat," in its verbal dream, rent apart and purified of its usual meaning, justifies and proves Duchamp's visual and conceptual *Chocolate Grinder*. Seeing, in this instance, captures the beginning in a word.

At the virgin point of spin, the Chocolate Grinder's ultimate heuristic thrust is crushing but unifying, pulverizes while elevating to new coherence. Its acropetal Muse, proceeding from base to apex, is a unique beauty of fluttering giddiness, abundance of free spirit. Encased in unreachable space, a "delay in glass" or act of intercession, the hovering Bride is Duchamp's meditative summons and invocation to the Muse (porter aux nues = to exalt), right down to the litany and sacred chant. His Muse, fading in and out of sight, as in "Muse à nue[s], in the high clouds," it seems, also fell for him, Marcel Duchamp. "Même" or "m'aime" (she loves me) he later added to the previously symmetri- cal title of *The Large Glass*. That the artist's offering came in the form of chocolate was clearly meant to provide a familiar ground of reference.

NOTES

1. In Casablanca, on the Boulevard el Hansali, hashish sellers offer their dreams murmuring, "Chocolat! Chocolat!" Chocolate illusions project not only high spirits and imaginary pleasures but the motions of ascendant lunacy, staged, for example, by Vivienne Haigh-Wood, T. S. Eliot's wife, who dribbled chocolate through the mail slot of her husband's office at Faber & Faber. Duchamp may have been inspired by

"Chocolat," who was one of two famous clowns portrayed by Toulouse Lautrec in *La Revue Blanche*. Recently, the Swiss Institute, New York, devoted an exhibit to chocolate as an art form, April 6–May 20, 1995. Artists included Marcel Duchamp as well as many contemporary artists.

2. Harriet Janis and Sidney Janis, "Marcel Duchamp, Anti-Artist," *View* 5, no. 1 (March 1945); this work also appeared in *The Dada Painters and Poets*, ed. Robert Motherwell (New York: Wittenborn, 1951), 306–15.

3. The annotated copy of Vassily Kandinsky's *Über das Geistige in der Kunst* was found in Jacques Villon's library. According to Alexina Duchamp, Villiers-sous-Grez, the handwriting is that of Raymond. For a note on the subject, see Thierry de Duve, *Pictorial Nominalism. On Marcel Duchamp's Passage from Painting to the Ready made* (Minneapolis: University of Minnesota Press, 1991), 204, no. 1. Passages of *Über das Geistige in der Kunst* were translated by Alfred Stieglitz in *Camera Work* in 1912. Stieglitz also provided the photo of Duchamp's famous urinal, *Fountain by R. Mutt*, which was refused at the first exhibition of the New York Society of Independent Artists. The photo, subsequently published on an interior page of *Blind Man*, May 2, 1917, was taken in front of Marsden Hartley's *The Warriors* (1913). The same number of *Blind Man*, prepared by Henri-Pierre Roché, Beatrice Wood, and Marcel Duchamp, boasted the *Chocolate Grinder* on its cover. *Fountain* was redubbed *Buddha or Madonna of the Bathroom*.

4. Matisse's work, chosen by Kandinsky for the Allard article, underscores space/time preoccupations which would fascinate Duchamp for years to come. *La Musique* by Matisse, the second panel for the Shchukin house, is included in Kandinsky's essay "On the Question of Form." For an analysis of these works, see Pierre Schneider, *Matisse* (New York: Rizzoli, 1984), 285.

5. *Marcel Duchamp*, catalog (New York: Museum of Modern Art, 1972), 263. (Hereafter referred to as *MD*.) While my perspective is different, I would like to draw on evidence presented by David Antin, who first discussed Marcel Duchamp's loving muse (*même/m'aime*) in "Duchamp and Language," and on Laurence Steefel's reflections devoted to "Marcel Duchamp and the Machine." Both articles are published in *MD*. For a discussion on artistic practice that Marcel Duchamp may have experienced in Munich, see Peg Weiss, *Kandinsky in Munich. 1896–1914* (New York: Salomon R. Guggenheim Museum, 1982). The article by Thierry de Duve, "Resonances of Duchamp's Visit to Munich," published in *Dada/Surrealism* 16 (1987): 41–63, discusses Duchamp's stay in the Bavarian capital. This article and subsequent work, however, fail to mention that Marcel Duchamp is actually cited in the *Blaue Reiter Almanach*, establishing an important and direct link of the French artist to Munich expressionists. De Duve's work is reprinted in *Marcel Duchamp, Artist of the Century*, ed. Rudolph Kuenzli and Francis Naumann (Cambridge: MIT Press, 1989); in *Nominalisme pictural: Marcel Duchamp, la Peinture et la Modernité* (Paris: Les Editions de Minuit, 1984); and in *On Marcel Duchamp's Passage*. Certain passages from *Über das Geistige in der Kunst*, anticipate Duchamp's strategy of nonretinal and hypothetical spaces. The true father of concept art was perhaps not Duchamp but Kandinsky. The Russian artist was prominent also with the Zurich Dada group. His poems were performed during their soirées and were published in magazines. In 1917, Hugo Ball gave a public lecture on Kandinsky, and a special room at the Gallery was named in honor of the painter. In 1914, Ball, Kandinsky, and other *Blaue Reiter* artists collaborated in an attempt to revitalize Munich theater.

6. The Bride Stripped Bare (Stuttgart: Hansjörg Mayer, 1976), n.p. Translated by

Marcel Duchamp, George Heard Hamilton, and Richard Hamilton; (henceforth cited as Hamilton).

7. Tristan Tzara, *Oeuvres Complètes* (Paris: Flammarion, 1975–77), 1: 366. "Chanson Dada" celebrates the hygienic qualities of chocolate, a concept dear to Marcel Duchamp. "Mangez du chocolat / lavez votre cerveau / dada / dada / buvez de l'eau." Just as chocolate seems to evoke opposite realms of the spirit, it connects the rhythms of the body. Rosalind Kraus quotes a French nursery rhyme that Duchamp would certainly have known: "Fais dodo / 'Colas mon petit frère; / Fais dodo / T'auras du lolo; / Maman est en haut, / Qui fait du gâteau; / Papa est en bas, / Qui fait du chocolat." The lullaby depicts the Bride baking a cake and providing milk and the bachelor making chocolate. Kraus reminds us that French parents may actually sing "Papa est en bas, / qui fait du caca," a version that does not disturb the five-syllable rhythm of the lullaby. See Rosalind Kraus, "Where's Poppa?" in *The Definitively Unfinished Marcel Duchamp*, ed. Thierry de Duve (Cambridge: MIT Press, 1991), 433.

CHAPTER 8

Has Modernism Failed the Chocolate Box?

Diane Barthel-Bouchier

To the modernist movement, the chocolate box was a symbol of outmoded, mawkish, Victorian design: Of everything it was revolting *against*. In 1937, esteemed art and architectural critic Nikolaus Pevsner, attempting to translate the German term *kitsch*, defined it as "any over-sentimental, over-sweet, luscious, in short, chocolate-boxy production in art, music, and literature."[1] Indeed, the chocolate boxes of the 1920s and 1930s were largely sentimental holdovers of Victorian romanticism. Modernism was meant to replace this old-fashioned mode with bold new designs. As glass skyscrapers replaced beaux arts wedding cake structures, the Bauhaus sought to revolutionize design in everyday life. Lamps, rugs, and teapots became rationalized and stylized. So, too, that totem of taste, the chocolate box, would become modern in design, thereby contributing its small share toward improving the daily life of working men and women.

Today it is over 60 years since Pevsner identified the chocolate box as an emblem of bad taste. It is now an empirical question as to whether the chocolate box has adopted modern design or whether earlier motifs predominate. Analysis of a sample of chocolate boxes revealed a mixed finding, which, however, was very suggestive as to the social context of chocolate boxes, which can be expected to influence their design.

METHOD

A sample of 20 chocolate boxes was gathered. Reflecting the fact that modernism aspired to and indeed became an international style, efforts were made to maximize the number of nations from which boxes were sampled. Italy, Germany, Switzerland, England, and the United States were thus represented. Where there was a range of weights, only 1 box, in the popular 6 to 10 ounce gift size, was selected. Further, since, as Nikolaus Pevsner rightly warns, bias may be introduced through the particular retailer's taste, a number and range of outlets were used as sources. These included a drugstore, a card shop, a gift shop, two chocolate specialty stores, and one international food market. This range of stores also helped reduce any class bias in the sample. Prices of the boxes ranged from $4.99 to $13.99.

It is difficult to isolate the changing tenets of taste. Modernism emphasized clear, strong patterns and nonfigurative over figurative designs. It was responsible for new typefaces and a distinctive Bauhaus style, among others. It also embraced rationalism and honest products. Thus, as a first step in the analysis, each chocolate box in the sample was categorized as to whether or not it had a figurative design or whether, as a separate category, the actual product was in some way depicted (design, photograph, see-through plastic, suggestive of "honesty in advertising"). The sample divided as follows:

Figurative	Nonfigurative	Chocolates Depicted
6	9	5

Boxes with only minor figuration, such as a stylized bow or brand insignia, were included as nonfigurative. Among those with chocolates depicted, the majority showed the chocolates through clear plastic (4), with one showing a soft photograph of the chocolates against a bouquet backdrop.

This simple categorization reveals the prevalence of nonfigurative over figurative, with a substantial proportion showing the product itself. To this extent, therefore, the data suggest that modernism has not failed the chocolate box: That a modernist tendency toward abstraction and clarification of design has had an impact on chocolate boxes. Both change in design and cause for it are difficult to prove without examples from earlier decades and archival and interview research with those responsible for product design.

QUALITATIVE ANALYSIS

While we do not have access to design decisions, we do have Pevsner's 1937 critique of chocolate boxes then-extant. In *An Enquiry into Industrial Art in England*, Pevsner devotes substantial space to packaging in general and Cadbury's chocolate boxes in particular. He chose Cadbury's both because it is one of the leading British manufacturers of chocolate and because its then-new factory on the outskirts of London was a highly regarded modernist plant. Pevsner then, reasonably enough, considered whether or not the boxes produced in this plant would also reflect what was in his mind good design. The Cadbury management, he writes, "would certainly like their packings to be in harmony with their clean, simple and bright factory buildings, and with their epoch-making garden city, but they know that they must act slowly and step by step."[2]

Cadbury's experience regarding the popular appeal of quality designs was, as Pevsner reported, "wide and depressing." Designs for Christmas boxes in particular were "deplorable." An experiment in commissioning leading artists led to disappointing results, though this may, as Pevsner suggests, be related to the themes they chose to depict: "Neither a circus scene nor a still life of fruit has a natural and easily understandable relation to chocolate."[3]

Sixty years is surely time enough for the public to respond to new tendencies. Thus, to move beyond the simple categorization above, we will use a more qualitative approach to better appreciate the contemporary designs. Starting with Pevsner's distinction between designs that are "over-sentimental, over-sweet, luscious" ("chocolate-boxy") and those that are "clean, harmonious, simple," the following points can be made regarding the sample of chocolate boxes gathered.

First, the most chocolate-boxy chocolate boxes were the two British boxes included in the sample. Mackintosh's Quality Street chocolates and toffees featured a brightly colored tin with Regency figures (a woman in pink, green, and white ruffles; a man in a red, gold, and black uniform). They stood against a background of pink, yellow, and tan townhouses and a foreground with the product label. This frankly fussy design was then further surrounded with another magenta and gold box (cut out to show the tin's design) illustrated with images of the chocolates in fancy wrappers. The design was thus both "sentimental and sweet." Cadbury's Milk Tray, the second British entrant, better fits Pevsner's adjective "luscious." A single white and gold orchid was displayed against a deep purple background of softly variegated shading. "Cadbury's Milk Tray" was written in elegant gold and white script across the left-hand corner, balancing the orchid on the right. Both chocolate boxes were the sort one might bring mother or a sentimental aunt. The Mackintosh box looks like an illustration to a romance novel, while the Cadbury's orchid hints at discreet sensuality.

Two classic mainstays of the lower-priced American market, namely, Whitman's Sampler and Fanny Farmer, also have sentimental and sweet imagery— but of a more restrained variety than that found in the British boxes. Whitman's Sampler plays on the association of a sample of chocolates with a cross-stitch sampler, in its old-fashioned yellow check boxes with small bird, flower, and house motifs. On one side is written: "Started in 1842." Fanny Farmer also draws on old images of the female world by depicting a high-collared female silhouette, presumably Mrs. Farmer, and above that the label "An American Collection." If Jessie Bernard is right that the female world is defined by love and duty, then loving, dutiful women will be rewarded with such traditional and restrained chocolate boxes.

With these two boxes representing American traditional, another brand is American postmodern. The Beverly Hills chocolate box is bright hot pink, with a white architectural motif complete with green palm trees suggesting this Californian luxury outpost and the promise that the contents represent "the richest chocolate in the world."

As opposed to these uses of figurative design connoting images of femininity and luxury, another American brand, Russell Stover, uses the dominant symbol of gift giving: The bow. So, too, does Tobler's "Tradition." Both boxes are clean designs comprised only of attractive lettering (more modern in the second instance) and the stylized ribbon against a shiny white background. Both rely on the tradition of giving chocolates—and their own tradition of making chocolates (Stover's are "home-fashioned").

The Italian brand Perugina, found in several outlets, offers a choice between figurative and nonfigurative designs in its gift collections. The figurative designs included a dark blue box with a color photograph of the Trinità dei Monti fountain in Rome pictured against a bright blue sky. It is a moot question as to whether Pevsner would have approved, insofar as this design has nothing to do with chocolates in general, but has some connection with Italian chocolates in particular. His major complaint was against "sham materials and sham technique," and he does, in fact, ask himself, "Is there really so much harm in the blatant blue sky of Naples?"[4] Other Perugina designs were variations of the floral, perhaps in part because of the season when sampling occurred (early spring). While some were more contemporary treatments than others, all tended more toward the "clean, simple, and harmonious" than toward the "sweet, sentimental, and luscious."

Considered within the context of modernism, the Perugina nonfigurative boxes hold especial interest. They are as glossy, clean, and well crafted as a modern skyscraper. While the overall design is modern, effective use is made of symbols of tradition and luxury. One box is labeled "Maitre Confiseur"; another, filled with silver-and-gold-wrapped chocolate, is "Jewels." A stylized horse insignia furthers the impression of aristocratic pleasure. The Baci chocolates likewise depend on strong glossy colors (dark blue offset by white print) and a mix of modern and traditional lettering to convey this impression of aristocracy.

Indeed, symbols of luxury and extravagance are found in all three of the above major categories. Gold, silver, and white are favorite colors, while choices of lettering and insignias suggest refinement. Besides Tobler's white and gold "Tradition," the sample included Lindt's "Connoisseur" and that type of very rich chocolate known as "truffles." At the top of the market, Gucci sells its designer chocolates in glittering gold boxes.

DISCUSSION

At its more idealistic, modern design was meant to place the masses in a position of equality vis-à-vis their right to live surrounded by beautiful, functional objects and, further, to work in tandem with other social improvements toward a more egalitarian society. On this point, Pevsner himself is very clear: "The battle has to be fought on all fronts. Not one of the subjects is less essential, not one can be neglected, neither slum-clearance nor the renovation of school buildings, neither the levelling up of class contrasts nor the raising of standards of design."[5]

If the average worker has been given more modern chocolate boxes over the past 60 years, as this international sample suggests, he or she has also been given boxes that celebrate luxury and wealth. To some extent, then, the course of chocolate box design has paralleled the course of modern design. A movement that, in its Bauhaus phase, dreamed of serving socialist purposes has effectively furthered capitalist consumer society, as modern design itself has become accepted as another capitalist good, another "style."

A second point must be made regarding the social significance of chocolate. The chocolate boxes described above are not meant to be purchased and consumed by one and the same person. This act of self-pleasuring resembles others and carries with it associated feelings of weakness, guilt, and overindulgence. Chocolates in attractive boxes are designed to be given as gifts. The likely recipient is female, although children of both sexes (like the female, socially immature and prone to weakness) may be so gifted.

Chocolates were once an accepted gesture within the courtship ritual—and in some outlying areas, still are. Women were supposed to give in to the men as they gave in to the sweets. Chocolates symbolized the impending breaking down of sexual resistance. To give a whole box of chocolates to a man was a sexual *non sequitur*, although a woman could reenact Eve's role by tempting him with just one or two out of her own box or, as today's commercials suggest, by offering a discreet after-dinner mint that does not threaten his masculinity with any suggestion of need, want, or unseemly desire.

As the designs suggest, chocolates are associated with flowers, the other half of the sexual bribe. Flowers also symbolize the female: As George Bataille pointed out, both put on a colorful show to attract fertilization.

Today, some men and women find such courtship gestures reprehensible, oppressive, and/or simply old-fashioned. Some deliberately casual designs appeal to customers who would object to traditional designs. While many traditional red, pink, and yellow plush Valentine's hearts are still sold, one now finds jokey packaging, as if romance were an embarrassment.

The answer as to whether modernism has failed the chocolate box, then, must therefore be twofold. On one level, modernism as a set of design principles stressing the clean, the simple, and the harmonious has been accepted by many chocolate box designers and, presumably, customers. Pevsner as a modernist who insisted above all on "honest" design would have approved of boxes that openly display or, in a nonmisleading fashion, portray the product sold. He would also have approved of the attractive and bold designs of many of the nonfigurative boxes and the contemporary handling of much figurative design. On the other hand, he would have reason to continue his "enquiry into industrial art in England" in order to understand why English chocolate boxes remain relatively traditional when compared to other chocolate boxes: Why they remain, in short, so chocolate-boxy. More research must be done on this important point.[6]

More research must also be done on seasonal themes and variations. I have already suggested that Valentine's boxes are more traditional than those that follow in the early spring. It is quite possible that other holidays, such as Mother's Day and Christmas, as traditional, nostalgia-riddled occasions would also encourage more traditional designs. Some chocolate manufacturers, for example, provide some form of seasonal slips, clear wrappers with seasonal designs (Easter eggs and bunnies) or boxes with similar motifs (for Mother's Day, a pink box with long-stemmed roses) that simply are placed over the usual box and can be taken off once the holiday is passed, should the chocolate remain on the store shelves.

Returning to the analysis, on a second level, the chocolate box has used modernism to suit its own purposes. Much of the initial underlying political program of modernism had to do with changing the relations of production and improving the lot of the worker. But chocolate denies having anything to do with this; it denies its own status as a factory product produced by unglamorous workers. What it represents instead is the whole other side of life comparatively neglected by social and political theorists with their emphasis on work, production, saving, and investment. Chocolate, by contrast, is part of what Georges Bataille recognized as that part of life that is *excessive*: extra, surplus, having more to do with losing control than with gaining it, with spending rather than saving, with sex rather than salvation. As a luxury object, and an object rich with symbolic meaning, it does not fit easily into the modernist political program.

What chocolate boxes do is to take modern design and translate it into luxury design, clearly communicating that chocolate is an "honorific food," not in any way necessary to life but useful as a symbol of status and wealth in social relations. What is especially significant is how modernism has accompanied the chocolate box on the road from socialist honesty to capitalist luxury. Mies van der Rohe, once a Bauhaus designer, excelled at creating capitalist monuments, the Seagram building chief among them. Such findings suggest, then, that a taste for modern design and a taste for luxury may not be contradictory but may be found close at hand in the not-so-humble chocolate box.

CODA

Some scholars have queried whether the chocolate box is suitable as a subject of serious inquiry. Without too much deliberation as to the state of their intellectual tastebuds, one might suggest to them that this inquiry has contributed to the broader question, Has Modernism Failed? This chapter suggests that this question only makes sense when it is brought down to earth: Has modernism failed whom—or what, for what reasons, and with what consequences?

NOTES

1.   Nikolaus Pevsner, *An Enquiry into Industrial Art in England* (New York: Macmillan, 1937), 12.

2.   Ibid., 123.

3.   Ibid., 125.

4.   Ibid., 12.

5.   Ibid., 215.

6.   Funding sources are being investigated.

CHAPTER 9

Chocolate Imagery in Avant-Garde Art

David W. Seaman

When avant-garde artists attacked conventional society at the beginning of the twentieth century, releasing a whole range of repressed imagery, it is not surprising that chocolate was among those images. Yet it is remarkable that chocolate imagery appeared in the work of some of the most significant writers and painters and enables us to understand something of their artistic goals. In this chapter, we will examine the use of chocolate imagery in the work of Dada leader Tristan Tzara and Surrealist Marcel Duchamp before exploring the lurking fondant presence in the art of Salvador Dali.

One could almost claim that Zurich Dada flourished under the sign of chocolate since the "Sprungli-Haus" on Bahnhofstrasse, where the Galerie Dada was located, had a big sign across the front saying: *Chocolat Lindt & Sprungli*, as evidenced by a 1920 photograph in Hans Bollnger's *Dada in Zurich*.[1] This fortuitous sign probably had nothing to do with the chocolate images to follow, but it is a suitable reminder of the place of chocolate in Swiss society, the society that was the background for the Dada critique.

The first significant reference to chocolate in the work of Tristan Tzara, the Dada leader, is in his *Dada Manifesto 1918*, where he declares, "Morality is the infusion of chocolate in the veins of all men."[2] To understand this statement, we must realize that Tzara is in the process of excoriating all the received values society is most fond of. The context is instructive:

Morality was determined by charity and pity, two suet balls grown like elephants, like planets, that people call good. They have nothing good about them. Goodness is lucid, bright and determined, pitiless towards compromise and politics. Morality is the infusion of chocolate in the veins of all men. No supernatural force ordains such comportment, rather the monopoly of the idea sellers and the university profiteers.[3]

Chocolate is thus not only used here to represent the sluggish, warm, sweet, and sickening ("suet balls") beverage drunk by moral society; it is also the corrupt product of "idea sellers and university profiteers." The opaque chocolate of morality contrasts with goodness—morality is not good in the Dada canon—which is "lucid" and "bright."

Chocolate has the same stolid value in the 1917 poem "Circus," where the circus master enters in the first section, and immediately chocolate enters in the second:

> people wait
> cords hang down above
> music
> it's the circus master
> the circus master doesn't want to show he's happy
> he is proper
>
> II
>
> entrance
> of chocolate truth hazelnuts newspaper
> one assumes about corridors and trunks from
> door signs
> you are anxious but I am confident
> many soldiers with new gazes
> the narrow layers of air stretched out the strong
> light falls
> from the stairs
> filtration through the grillwork of relationships
> the elephants go to bed black satellites
> is this a prospectus of appearances? lead us under
>   the curtain
> and in the familiar dressing-rooms
> an unexpected finger suddenly touches us.[4]

Chocolate is here again associated with conventional values—"truth" lines up with morality, charity, and pity—and with elephants, underscoring the heaviness of the brown medium. It is also located in the circus spectacle, which recalls the Dada fondness for cabaret shows—Dada artists are the circus masters, Tzara states in *Mr. Antipyrine's Manifesto*[5]—and alludes to the spectacle of life.

Tzara's distaste of chocolate here coincides with his preference for the grotesque. Earlier in the 1918 manifesto, he discussed art and said, "[L]et it be a monster frightening to servile minds, and not sickly-sweet in order to decorate the refectories of animals dressed like men."[6]

There is a way, however, in which chocolate can be redeemed in Tzara's vision, and that is through its transformation in the human body. Already we have looked at the image of chocolate pumped into veins; we must also consider the digestion of chocolate and its excremental appearance. In the violent poem "For Marcel Janko," Tzara speaks of a young man who has diarrhea and then "farts luminously," which is a positive metaphor for the creative process.[7] In *Mr. Antipyrine's Manifesto*, Tzara indicates that Dada is "still a bunch of excrement, but we want to shit in different colors to ornament the zoo of art of all the consulate flags."[8] Chocolate as a body process can be creative.

For Marcel Duchamp, as well, chocolate becomes part of the body processes. His limited canon centers on *The Large Glass*, otherwise known as *The Bride Stripped Bare by Her Bachelors, Even*. This work incorporates the third version of the *Chocolate Grinder*, an image that Duchamp referred to as "a very important moment in my life."[9] The importance came from discovering the formula for the *Chocolate Grinder*: "I used to walk around the streets of old Rouen. One day I saw an actual chocolate grinder working in a shop window, and it fascinated me so much that I took it as a point of departure."[10]

Duchamp was initially fascinated by the mechanical aspect of the chocolate grinder, since he was looking for a dryer approach to art than the "splashing of paint."[11] But soon the many ramifications of the chocolate grinding process and the potential imagery blossomed in his conception. Duchamp's many notes on the subject, published in *The Green Bag*[12] in 1934 and also in *Salt Seller*, demonstrate the richness of the chocolate imagery. Once the chocolate grinder became part of *The Large Glass*, it could carry some of the qualities of the bachelor that it represents.

There is a fundamental sexual imagery in this piece, as the alternative title suggests. The chocolate grinder's function is indicated by the statement, "The bachelor grinds his chocolate himself" and reinforced by the assertion, "The chocolate of the rollers, *coming* from one knows not where, would deposit itself after grinding, as milk chocolate."[13] Can there be any doubt that chocolate is seminal fluid, essential to the creative process?

Duchamp fills many pages with notes about the mixing of colors for the different shades of chocolate. He distinguishes between the chocolate of the rollers, which contains Veridian green and a lot of ochre; the light chocolate, with ochre, sienna, and white in it; and the milk chocolate, which has a tasty mixture of Veridian green, Naples yellow, and yellow ochre or alternatively, white, black, vermillion, gold ochre, and Naples yellow.[14]

Chocolate is one of only a handful of major images in Duchamp's work, and he labored over it for years. Drawings of the *Chocolate Grinder* began in 1913, and the image was worked on until *The Large Glass* was considered "finished" in 1923. Meanwhile, Duchamp used chocolate as an example to illustrate his idea about molds and the way a mold transmits its shape and color to an object. For Duchamp, there is a difference between the appearance—"the sum of the usual sensory evidence"—and the apparition, which is the mold of it, divided between the "surface apparition" or spatial model, and the "native colors," which are not colors in the ordinary sense but "luminous sources producing active colors." Thus, in the case of chocolate, "a surface of native-chocolate color will be composed of a sort of chocolate phosphorescence completing the molded apparition of the chocolate object."[15]

Perhaps it is in the nature of chocolate to be a molded object; certainly the different forms of chocolate candies can attest to this, but for an artist, there are many other materials that might come to mind—wax and bronze, for instance. So we return to Duchamp's fixation on chocolate and his elevation of it to an aesthetic status, making it a viable image of creation:

The object is illuminant. Luminous source. The *body* of the object is composed of luminous molecules and becomes the source of the *lighted* object's substance e.g. the chocolate emanating is the atomic mold of the opaque chocolate substance having a physical existence *verified* (?) by the 5 senses. —The emanating object is an apparition.[16]

The language of this discussion is significant: The heavy "opaque" chocolate, similar to Tzara's ponderous sickening-sweet suet balls of chocolate, becomes "luminous," an "apparition." Tzara's quest for the "lucid" and "bright" seems to have been accomplished by Duchamp's *Chocolate Grinder* and mold.

The work of Salvador Dali spans a much longer period than the two artists discussed above, but we will examine primarily the period of the 1920s and 1930s when he was doing his most engaging Surrealist painting and writing. Dali is not an artist who made specific and intentional use of chocolate imagery, but he can be considered as a contemporary and colleague of Tzara and Duchamp, who may have internalized the same attitudes and content. Certainly in the case of Dali, the visual representation of objects is so photographic that there is no mistaking them, but his dedication to the simulacrum, the specter in the painting, is strong enough to always invite a second or third look. It is in this return that we will find chocolactic overtones.

The writings of Salvador Dali range from provocative poems such as "The Great Masturbator" (1930) to autobiographical works that probe his "inter-uterine memories" as in *The Secret Life of Salvador Dali*.[17] There are occasional references to chocolate, in meaningful situations, but without developing a sense of imagery. In "The Great Masturbator" a lugubrious scene is set by noting the "great silhouette of the chocolate factory fading already into the dusky mists."[18]

In *The Secret Life of Salvador Dali*, the artist is describing what he labels "False Childhood Memories" and recounts an incident of "hypervisuality" that is essentially the sort of déjà vu experience that Marcel Proust felt when he sipped his tea served with madeleine's. In this instance, Dali sees a photograph of a woman raising a cup to her lips, and he recalls being paralyzed by the recognition of a woman seen in an embarrassing childhood encounter where a woman was "parsimoniously lifting a cup of chocolate to her lips."[19] Like the powerful Proustian epiphany, this impacts Dali, and although he does not paint chocolate drinkers, we are well advised to be sensitive to the possibilities of chocolate imagery in his work.

In fact, there are other passages in *The Secret Life* that come close to the spirit of Duchamp's chocolate study. One of these is the tale of "The Manikin with the Sugar Nose." This story relates how a necrophilic king was cured of his aberration when a maiden tricked him by substituting a wax manikin with a sugar nose. When the king "kills" the manikin at the point of his ecstasy, the sugar nose pops into his mouth, and he tastes its sweetness and regrets the assassination. Dali's interpretation of this story dwells on the lifelike properties of the wax and also points out that the "lucid moment of cannibalistic consciousness" when the sugar nose is tasted functions as a bridge to desire, enabling it to pass from death (necrophilia) to the sweetness of life. Dali further compares this transition to the way in which heroines such as his own Gala are able to use sweets as "an 'object-being' of delirium, invented by the passion of one of those women . . . by virtue of the skillful simulacrum of their love, to illuminate moral darkness with the sharp lucidity of 'living madmen.'"[20]

Once again, the sought-after lucidity is produced through a transformation, and Dali adapts some of the methods of Tzara and Duchamp, if not the actual chocolate medium. The wax figure, which has properties very similar to the molded chocolate in Duchamp's image, is also connected to Tzara's excremental imagery since Dali says the king is "a probable cannibalistic copro-necrophile." Meanwhile, the wax manikin is described as being not only the deadest of the king's victims but also "the most life-like, the most softened, desired and 'metaphysical' of all."[21]

There seems little doubt that Dali was capable of envisioning his figures as molded in chocolate. Although he discusses only the inspiration of bread loaves and soft Camembert cheese for his paintings (commonly recognized as the hypersteatopygic buttocks and the melted watches), there are several striking pieces where the smooth extruded forms and rich brown coloration suggest chocolate origins. Gala herself takes on chocolaty hues in some of the later portraits, but none is more striking than the *Soft Self-portrait with Bacon* in which a flaccid mask of the artist is propped up on a pedestal.

Another painting where Dali's figure seems to be made of chocolate is *Sleep*, where again a limp mask is supported by crutches, this time in a vast empty landscape. Dali comments that in it "I express with maximum intensity the anguish induced by empty space" (Plate IV). This refers to the "sentiment of absence and of nothingness"[22] that enveloped him when he first saw the woman drinking chocolate in his childhood memory, a connection Dali suggests by grouping a photo of this painting with other images and photos related to the encounter.

In the examples we have seen of twentieth-century avant-garde art, chocolate is not the food of the gods but is rather a very human substance. It is a body fluid, whether representing solid blood, multicolored excrement, seminal secretions, or erotic flesh. At the same time, it has properties that allow it to make a creative transformation of itself and of those who consume it, helping them attain some degree of desired lucidity. In avant-garde art, chocolate imagery becomes a consciousness-altering drug.

NOTES

1. Hans Bollnger, *Dada in Zurich* (Zurich: Arche, 1985), 40.

2. Tristan Tzara, *Approximate Man and Other Writings*, trans. by Mary Ann Caws (Detroit: Wayne State University Press, 1973), 156.

3. Ibid.

4. Ibid., 171–72.

5. Ibid., 147.

6. Ibid., 151.

7. Ibid., 146.

8. Ibid., 147.

9. Marcel Duchamp, *Salt Seller* (New York: Oxford University Press, 1973), 133.

10. Ibid., 130.

11. Ibid.

12. March Duchamp, *The Green Bag* 1934.

13. Duchamp, *Salt Seller*, 68.

14. Marcel Duchamp, *Notes*, presentation et traduction, Paul Matisse (Paris: Centre National d'art et de culture Georges Pompidou, 1980), Folio 1, #115.

15. Duchamp, *Salt Seller*, 84–85.

16. Ibid., 86.

17. Salvador Dali, *The Secret Life of Salvador Dali* (New York: Dial Press, 1942).

18. Salvador Dali, *Oui* (Paris: Denoel, 1971), 113.

19. Dali, *The Secret Life*, 51.

20. Ibid., 237–40.

21. Ibid., 238.

22. Ibid., 51.

CHAPTER 10

Inside the Pastilles
of the Marquis de Sade

Barbara Lekatsas

Chocolate conquered Europe like an edible form of the noble savage. It was an Aztec Indian version of the Eucharist, an embodiment of deity made available to humans. But more like the nectar of the Greek deities, chocolate had fertility associations, and its aphrodisiac qualities made it quite different from the Christian Eucharist. In an early book entitled *The Indian Nectar*, written in 1662 by H. Stubbe, chocolate is called a cure for "hypochondrial melancholy," and its aphrodisiac use by the Indians is recorded in an account by Bernal Diaz del Castillo, a soldier in Cortez's army. He writes concerning the ritual of drinking it in Montezuma's court:

They brought some in cups of fine gold, with a certain drink made of the cacao itself which they said was effectual to provoke lustful desires toward women . . . then they brought in about fifty jars of good cacao with its froth and they drank it, the women serving them with a great deal of respect and when [Montezuma] did eat, several Indians stood by him and danced before him, Montezuma being much given to pleasure.[1]

Cortez found veritable treasure for a Spain in decline: A sophisticated agricultural economy, silver mines, and slaves. But the Spaniards in their creation of the hacienda, as well as the diseases they brought to Mexico, decimated the Indian population from 25 million to just over a million in less than 100 years, between 1519 and 1605.[2]

It is said that the Indians confounded Quetzalcoatl, their prominent deity and giver of chocolate, with Cortez, and indeed the conquering Spaniards bore many resemblances to the brutal Aztec deities. The worship of Quetzalcoatl ("plumed serpent")[3] included castration and ripping out of the heart. The fertility aspect of the sacrifices cannot be discounted. The victims' hearts were offerings to the sun: Genitals, heart, and cocoa pods are corollary structures, nectaries that secrete and contain vital energizing fluids.[4] Even the practice of using cocoa and other foods as currency to be paid to the treasury is reminiscent of the granaries and store chamber of the Minoan-Mycenian Zeus, where semen offerings were also kept.[5] Originally, chocolate was the beverage of gods, lords, and chieftains. The common man was not allowed to drink it.[6] The exceptions were those to be sacrificed to the gods, although if they did not express joy in becoming food for the gods, their chocolate was mixed with the dry blood of previously sacrificed victims.[7]

The relationship between the religious world of the Aztec Indians and the Marquis de Sade did not escape the notice of Georges Bataille, who wrote in an article entitled "Extinct America":

Continued crime committed in broad daylight for the mere satisfaction of deified nightmares, terrifying phantasms, priests' cannibalistic meals, ceremonial corpses, and streams of blood evoke not so much the historical adventure but rather the debauches of the Marquis de Sade.[8]

For both the Aztecs and Sade, cruelty and war were part of the divine plan. Sade would simply substitute "nature" for divinity. As one of his characters tells the luckless, overly virtuous Justine:

There is no God. Nature sufficeth unto herself; . . . feeble portions of a vile crude matter, upon our death. . . . [W]e are annihilated forever, regardless of what our behavior has been . . . because there is nothing by which Nature is offended. . . . [A]ll men, equally her womb's issue, . . . having acted . . . in accordance with her impulsions . . . will all of them meet . . . the same end and fate.[9]

How like the Aztec lament to their god: "Only as painted figures in your book have we lived here on earth. We were no more than pictures. Rubbed out, erased."[10]

For the European nobility, chocolate was a spoil of war, the fruit of conquest. The ideal of the noble savage existed simultaneously with the reality of European colonization and enslavement. Colonial plantations satisfied aristocratic tastes. Chocolate became a signifier of aristocracy and sexual potency. By the eighteenth century it enjoyed widespread use by the upper castes. Casanova while in Spain complained, "[T]he Spaniards offer visitors chocolate so frequently at all hours that if one accepted it all, one would be choked."[11] An extensive entry on chocolate and its various preparations appears in Diderot's *Encyclopédie*, and books such as that of Dufour in the seventeenth century and Buc'hoz in the eighteenth century, continued the recipes, history, and medicinal prescriptions.[12] In France, chocolate came into use particularly during the reign of Louis XIV. Although introduced by his mother, the Spanish Hapsburg queen, Ann of Austria, it was his wife, a second Spanish Hapsburg queen, Maria Theresa, who was known to consume endless cups. His brother as well, the Duc d'Orleans, according to the Duc de Saint-Simon, drank "copious draughts of chocolate every morning."[13]

The "court of Apollo," as the Versailles of Louis XIV was known, came to dominate Europe in splendor and power, while the aura of the king reached mythical proportions. The whole ritual of genuflection that the Marquis de Sade will take as his primary sexual posture reaches elaborate variety at Versailles. The stifling etiquette surrounding the king was a theater in the service of despotism. The theater gave the people an image of a powerful nobility endowed by God and tradition to rule and to hoard. The hated "droit de chasse" that gave the king the sole right to hunt game was one of many privations that the French Revolution would redress, but the privileges that most alienated the people during the reign of Louis XIV and Louis XV were the sexual excesses of the monarchs, nobility, and clergy. Saint-Simon writes in other anecdotes about the nobility's abuse of privilege and its licentiousness. For instance, the Duc de Vendôme, a colonel of the king, would greet all on his *chaise-percée*. From this position on the privy, he would write his dispatches and see people, offering a view of his backside as he got up to wipe himself. The bishop of Parma was so outraged by this view that he sent a low-born proxy to conduct his business in his place. A clever opportunist, Alberoni, upon seeing this spectacle, exclaimed, "Oh! cullo de angelo," and rushed to embrace the ducal posterior. This worshipful attitude and his ability to make good cheese soups enabled him to attach himself to the Duc de Vendôme and make his fortune.[14]

The erotic exploits of Louis XV have been chronicled in the many memoirs of the period. Queen Marie Leczinska bore him 10 children before she died. At first the popular songs cheered the fecundity of their king, but his alliance with Madame de Pompadour and finally with one of Paris' leading courtesans, Madame du Barry, was sufficient to undo the vested power of monarchy. Jean-Pierre Guicciardi writes in a provocative article entitled "Between the Licit and the Illicit: The Sexuality of the King":

By the eighteenth century, the Kings of France were heirs to a long tradition of veneration earned by their right Christian ancestors from the time of Charlemagne. The tradition and consecration by the church conferred on them almost hallowed awe, even faith in their power to heal the sick by their touch. Such deeply rooted popular myths die hard: Yet the day was coming when the king's mantle of quasi-divinity would easily fall, and it was Louis XV himself, by his manner of life, who unloosed it.[15]

By the time the Marquis de Sade was born in 1740, Louis XV was the subject of public ridicule, and Pompadour was hated not only for her squandering of the public treasury but for her creation of the Parc-au-Cerfs, from where she could procure girls for the king in light of her own frigidity (for which she takes chocolate).[16] Guicciardi writes, "The monarch's sexuality became an unavoidable element in French political thinking."[17]

Chocolate was the drink of the boudoir. It heralded along with the age the sovereignty of the passions. The Goncourt brothers depicted a lady of the eighteenth century rising no earlier than 11 o'clock: "A scratch at the door: May the maid make the fire? Her mistress inquires about the weather, complains of a frightful night, dips into a cup of chocolate."[18] Chocolate had a welcome place in Sade's life and work, restoring the depleted sexual fluids of the libertine. But the debauchery of his life and the fantastic visions of sexual gluttony that dominate his work parallel other forms of noblesse oblige of the time.

A descendant of Petrarch's immortalized beloved heroine Laura, who became the wife of Hugo de Sade, Donatien Alphonse François, the Marquis de Sade was raised in the Château Condé in Paris until he was 4, then by his grand-mother in Avignon. His mother was a lady-in-waiting to the princess de Condé; his father, a marshall to the king and an ambassador to four European courts. When he was 4, his ambitious parents abandoned him to relatives, as they took up a diplomatic post in Cologne. He was educated by his uncle, the Abbé Jacques de Sade, who was noted for a scholarly work he wrote on Petrarch, and by Jesuits. At the age of 14, he entered the Cavalry School of the Royal Guard in Versailles. By the age of 15, he joined the king's infantry regiment. He fought in the Seven Years War. By the time he was 19, he already had a reputation for his debaucheries. At age 20, he received his father's estates. His mother, whose profound indifference to her child mirrors the role that Sade will later attribute to nature in his work, joined a Carmelite convent. Through his father, a marriage to Renée Pélagie de Montreuil only lent method and order to his theatricals, masqued balls, and orgies at the château at La Coste. The first of a series of arrests soon followed. During periods of repentance in between his scandals and between 1767 and 1771, he fathered two sons and a daughter. But even during this period, in 1768 he hired a young woman under false pretenses on Easter Sunday, stripped her, whipped her, made knife incisions on her, and put hot wax, then an astringent, on her wounds. She escaped from the window and reported him to the police. He paid dearly to have the charges dropped. A second incident, however, brought the wrath of the law upon him. Bachaumont writes in his secret memoirs, July 25, 1772:

I am told that Comte de Sade who in 1768 caused a great disorder by his crimes with a prostitute on whom he wanted to test a new cure, has just played in Marseilles a spectacle, at first amusing, later horrible in its consequences. He gave a ball to which he invited many people and for dessert gave them very pretty chocolate pastilles. They were mixed with powdered Spanish fly. Their action is well-known. All who ate them were seized by shameless ardor and lust and started the wildest excesses of love. The festival became an ancient Roman orgy.[19]

A more verifiable account came from the court records. He had given the pastil-les also dipped in anise to four prostitutes procured by his valet Latour. They were supposed to cause winds. He and Latour sodomized each other and also had some form of sex with the young women. But the pastilles in combination with the bloody leather-covered, nail-studded whip that he used to whip and be whipped alarmed the young prostitutes and caused them to bring charges against him. They became violently ill from the pastilles. Although the poisoning charges were later dropped, Sade was sentenced to death and burned in effigy. He fled to Italy with Latour and his sister-in-law, with whom he was having an affair. His mother-in-law had him arrested in Sardinia by power of the *lettre de cachet*.[20] He escaped and returned to La Coste, but his mother-in-law caught up with him in Paris in 1777, where he had returned ironically to pay his last respects to his mother who had just died. For the remainder of his life, he would find himself in various prisons and asylums with brief periods of respite. His wife, accomplice to his debauches, began to visit him in prison in 1781, providing him with linen, chocolate, jams, books, candles, and other items.[21] It was in prison that Sade became a writer.

The work that best characterizes the delirium of the Sadean utopia is *120 Days of Sodom*, written between 1782 and 1785 in the Bastille. Set in the Black Forest in remote Silling Castle during the rein of Louis XIV, 4 seasoned libertines intermarry each others' daughters after disposing of their wives. Based on the obsessive numerology of four and multiples of four, Sade creates an endless theater within a theater of despotism: 4 husband/fathers, 4 daughter/wives, 4 procuresses for women, 4 pimps for men, 4 storytellers, 8 fornicators, 8 little boys, 8 little girls, and 6 comprising the kitchen staff (it is interesting to note that the Aztec religion was also based on the necessity of the number four). Of the 46, 16 will survive the massacre: The 4 masters, the 4 storytellers, 4 fornicators, 1 wife, 3 cooks.

The survivors will return for more. The story is divided into four months. There are four supper parties a week and four different country houses. With each month given to a storyteller whose sexual recountings will be enacted, the violence and filth increase till it culminates in the sexual death orgy of the final month. The libertines, however, allow themselves the greatest refinements in decor and delicacies. But along with the drinking of chocolate and the finest wines and the preparations of the finest food, the libertines also consume vast quantities of urine and copra.

The Duc de Blangis can have up to 55 sexual discharges a day, violate a girl with one hand, and squeeze the life out of a horse with his legs. He had consumed unimaginable quantities of food and could drink up to 30 bottles of wine in one sitting, becoming so overfurious that he had to be tied down. But the narrator adds:

And despite all that would you believe it? A steadfast child might have hurled this giant into a panic. . . . [T]he thought of even the mildest combat but fought on equal terms would send him fleeing to the end of the earth.[22]

The four libertines orchestrate their passions according to laws and statutes. Thus sex is institutionalized in the service of despotism. The Duc says, "[W]e libertines wed women to hold slaves, as wives they are rendered more submissive than mistresses, and you know the value we set upon despotism in the joys we pursue."[23]

Under the first of the statutes, breakfast is served by the little girls "consisting of chocolate, or of roasts cooked in Spanish wine." The dinners are opulent, mirroring those in the court at Versailles:

It began with shellfish soup and hors d'oeuvres composed of twenty dishes; twenty entrees came on next and soon gave way to another twenty lighter entrees made up entirely of breasts of chicken, of assorted game prepared in every possible way. This was offset by a serving of roasts; everything of the rarest imaginable was brought on. Next arrived some cold pastry, soon afterward twenty-six entremets of every description and form. The table was cleared and what had just been removed was replaced by a whole array of cold and hot sugared pastries. Dessert finally appeared: A prodigious number and variety of fruits, though the season was winter, then ices, chocolate, and the liqueurs which were taken at table. As for the wines, they varied with each service.[24]

Once this meal is concluded, the orgy will begin and, with it, additional eating of human waste.

Chocolate will continue as part of the diet of the libertine and his victim also in the novels *Justine* and *Juliette*. In *Justine*, where the virginal heroine will argue on the side of virtue to the titillation of her tormentors, chocolate appears as a disguise for poison and as a restorative. After failing to help the Duc de Brissac kill his mother by poisoning her cup of chocolate, Justine is left among wild dogs. She survives and goes to a Benedictine monastary for succor, where she is beset upon by four libertine monks. The victims in the monastary are allowed the same food as the libertines. They eat four times a day. Chocolate again is on the breakfast menu.[25] Roland Barthes writes:

Sadean chocolate ends up by functioning as the pure sign of this dual alimentary economy. . . . [T]he victim's food is always copious for two libertine reasons: First these victims too must be refreshed . . . and fattened up to furnish vice with fat dimpled "altars"; second, coprophagic passion demands an "abundant, delicate soft food." . . . Thus the function of food in the Sadean city: To restore, to poison, to fatten, to evacuate; everything planned in relation to vice.[26]

Pastille, Bastille: Prisons with their pleasures concealed. Sade's works are parodies of parodies of Voltaire's *Candide*, Diderot's *Religieuse*, Rousseau's *Julie*, and Richardson's *Clarissa*. In his mad quantification, he magnifies and makes repulsive what was exciting and titillating in these works. Vice and virtue are no more than a system of philosophy where virtue exists as a foil for vice. Vice is the experience of sovereignty or despotism. The master can only reveal himself or herself (the female libertines in Sade's works achieve as much power as their male counterparts, proving the success of the philosophy) in relation to a slave. Virtue is the victim of vice, vice the right to silence the opponent by cruelty and violence. The superiority of vice was argued from the point of view of its success. Its flourishing makes it possible to argue against a benevolent God and in favor of predatory nature, where "survival of the fittest" attests to criminality as the plan of nature, for nature reduces all her creations into corpses and waste from which she feeds and procreates. The "Sovereign man," as Georges Bataille was to term the libertine creations of Sade, is only accountable to himself.[27] In this he imitates nature and usurps the position he once gave to God. But the moment of definition can only be experienced in the transition between power and powerlessness, desire and disgust, food and waste product, life and death. Once the victim dies, the master reverts to slave, the masquerade is over, and the ritual must begin again.

By renouncing the mythology of religion, the philosophes of the eighteenth century unleashed the forces of repressed sexuality, bringing to the foreground the sexual basis of power. The king reemerged as a fertility deity to be sacrificed to but also to be sacrificed. Chocolate, the drink of royalty and of sexual potency, the drink of refined gentility, came to Europe mixed with the blood of the colonized Indians. Sovereign privilege exacted at the price of plundering one's subjects led to a passive, isolated ruling class that squandered its wealth.

In this atmosphere of false omnipotence experienced as sexual potency and license, the French aristocracy sealed its doom with the same passivity as had Montezuma and his subjects. Simone de Beauvoir writes:

Scions of a declining class which had once possessed concrete power, [young aristocrats] . . . tried to revive symbolically, in the privacy of the bedchamber, the status for which they were nostalgic: That of the lone and sovereign feudal despot. The orgies of the Duke of Charolais, among others, were bloody and famous. Sade, too, thirsted for this illusion of power.[28]

He found it in prison as a writer and in the consolation that no prison is absolute. For life produces language and death, and both defy the closure of the body and, by extension, the material world. Yet the whole of the physical universe contains its interior counterpart, its granaries, erotic chambers, and chocolate grinders. These orchids and vulvae of life reabsorb us, dress us with other forms of nature, undress us into essence. A lifetime prisoner who grew very fat, Sade in his fantasies got even by becoming the victimizer, the imprisoning body. The Aztec religion was based on a belief in sacrifice as a means of service and submission to the nature gods. Sade, on the other hand, was a misotheist and misogynist. He represented the ruthlessness of a class whose values were totally shaped by the pursuit of position but whose decadence made it impossible to believe in anything but their own appetite. Chocolate became a reified commodity, a fetish item, an excuse for license, and a mark of privilege. Yet all these refinements, copious as they are in the work of Sade, never distract us from the issue at hand, which is the exercise and ritual of power made evident through the evocation of powerlessness; nor do these rituals deflect from the reality of such displays: That the need to display power comes from a heightened sense of powerlessness.

NOTES

1. H. Stubbe, *The Indian Nectar or a Discourse Concerning Chocolate and of the Experience of the Indians by H. Stubbe of the Island of Jamaica in the West Indies* (London, 1662), 1.

2. Stanley J. Stein and Barbara H. Stein, eds., *The Colonial Heritage of Latin America: Essays on Economic Dependence in Perspective* (New York: Oxford University Press, 1970), 37.

3. Burr Cartwright Brundage, *The Fifth Sun, Aztec World* (Austin and London; University of Texas Press, 1979), 102.

4. Fray Diego Duran, *The Aztecs: The History of the Indies in New Spain*, translated with notes by Doris Heyden and Fernando Horcasitas (New York: Orion Press, 1964). See chapter XLIV concerning one of the solemn sacrifices, where 80,400 men were slaughtered over a four-day period.

5. Martin P. Nillson, *The Minoan-Mycenian Religion and Its Survival in Greek Religion* (Lund: C.W.K. Gleerup, 1950), 327.

6. Fray Diego Duran, *Book of the Gods and Rites and the Ancient Calendar*, translated and edited by Fernando Horcasitas and Doris Heyden (University of Oklahoma Press, 1971), 200.

7. Ibid., 132. This drink, which was thought to have intoxicating features, was called *itzpacalatl*, which means "water from washing of the obsidian blades."

8. Georges Bataille, "Extinct America," *October* 36 (1986): 3.

9. Marquis de Sade, *Justine* in *The Marquis de Sade: The Complete Justine, Philosophy of the Bedroom and Other Writings*, compiled and translated by Richard Seaver and Austryn Wainhouse (New York: Grove Press, 1965), 496–97.

10. Brundage, *The Fifth Sun*, 180.

11. Jacques Casanova de Seingalt, "Spanish Passions," in *The Memoirs of Jacques Casanova de Seingalt*, trans. Arthur Machen (New York: G. P. Putnam, 1959), 6: 145.

12. Philippe Sylvestre Dufour, *Traitez nouveaux et curieux du café, du thé et du chocolate ouvrage également nécessaire aux médecins, et à tous ceux qui aiment leur santé* (Lyon: Chez Jean Baptiste Deville, 1688); Pierre Joseph Buc'hoz, *Dissertation sur le cacao, sur la culture et sur les différentes préparations de choco-lat* (Paris: F. J. Desoer, 1787). Both authors wrote other works as well on chocolate.

13. Duc de Saint-Simon, *Memoirs* in *Saint-Simon at Versailles*, edited and translated by Lucy Norton (New York: Harmony Books, 1980), 73.

14. Ibid., 103.

15. Jean-Pierre Guicciardi, "Between the Licit and the Illicit: The Sexuality of the King," *Eighteenth Century Life*, n.s., 3 (1985): 89–90.

16. Stanley Loomis, *Du Barry: A Biography* (New York: J. S. Lippincot, 1959), 17.

17. Guicciardi, "Between the Licit," 92.

18. Edmond de Goncourt and Jules de Goncourt, *The Woman of the Eighteenth Century: Her Life from Birth to Death, Her Love, and Her Philosophy in the Worlds of Salon, Shop, and Street*, trans. Jacques Le Clercq and Ralph Roeder (Westport, Conn.: Hyperion Press, 1981), 70.

19. Cited in Iwan Block, *Marquis de Sade: The Man and His Age*, trans. James Bruce (N.J.: Julian Press, 1931), 174.

20. I am indebted to various biographies for this chapter: *De Sade: A Critical Biography*, by Ronald Hayman (New York: Thomas and Crowell, 1978); *The Revolutionary Ideas of the Marquis de Sade*, by Geoffrey Gorer (London: Wishart and Co., 1934); and *Portrait of de Sade: An Illustrated Biography*, by Walter Lennig (New York: Herder and Herder, 1971).

21. Norman Gear, *The Divine Demon: A Portrait of the Marquis de Sade* (London: Frederick Muller Ltd., 1963), 99, 101.

22. Marquis de Sade, *The 120 Days of Sodom and Other Writings*, compiled and translated by Austryn Wainhouse and Richard Seaver (New York: Grove Press, 1966), 202.

23. Ibid., 192.

24. Ibid., 280.

25. Sade, *Justine* in *The Marquis de Sade*, 522.

26. Roland Barthes, *Sade, Fourier, Loyola*, trans. Richard Miller (New York: Hill and Wang, 1975), 18, 19.

27. See, for instance, "Le Bonheur, l'érotisme et la litterature," *Critique*, nos. 35–36 (1949), where Bataille discusses his view of Sade.

28. Simone de Beauvoir, *Must We Burn Sade?* trans. Annette Michelson (London: Peter Nevill Ltd., 1953), 15.

PART III

Chocolate Commerce and Health

CHAPTER 11

The Role of Chocolate in the American Diet: Nutritional Perspectives

Marion Nestle

Chocolate exemplifies current contradictions in the American food system. It is a favorite and highly promoted food but contains much more fat and sugar than is recommended by public health authorities who, instead, advise greater consumption of fruits, vegetables, and grains, lean meats, and low-fat dairy products as a means to prevent diseases. The contribution of chocolate to overall disease risk is minimal, however, largely because most individuals consume it in small amounts. Individuals who wish to promote dietary health will need to find ways to make eating fruits, vegetables, and grains as profitable and enjoyable as eating chocolates.

The role of chocolate in the American diet can be considered a case study of the contradiction between the nutritional and taste aspects of food intake. From the perspective of taste, chocolate is a highly desirable food; its sensory qualities promote increased consumption. The nutritional perspective is more complex; it includes chocolate both as an element in the global system of food production, marketing, and consumption and as a source of calories, saturated fat, or other substances that may adversely affect health and, therefore, demand decreased consumption.

As an illustration of the dilemma faced by food professionals who wish to produce meals that are healthful but also delicious, this chapter reviews nutritional aspects of chocolate consumption within the context of current dietary recommendations and of the political economy of the U.S. food system. It describes recent trends in production and consumption of chocolate, explains how production of the principal forms of chocolate affects nutritional value, and evaluates claims for the beneficial or deleterious effects of chocolate on specific aspects of health.

DIETARY RECOMMENDATIONS

By definition, an ideal diet contains levels of essential nutrients and energy sufficient to meet physiologic requirements and should be obtained from foods that are available, affordable, and palatable (U.S. Department of Health and Human Services [USDHHS], 1988). From the early years of this century until the mid-1970s, the U.S. Department of Agriculture (USDA) advised the public to achieve the ideal diet by eating specified portions each day from varying numbers of food groups. From 1958 to 1979, for example, the principal format for dietary advice was the USDA's Basic Four, which recommended daily intake of two to four portions from the meat, dairy, fruit and vegetable, and grain groups. Such food groups were designed to encourage consumption of the full range of American agricultural products, and they did not distinguish between foods that varied, for example, in fat or sugar content (U.S. Department of Agriculture [USDA], 1985; Nestle and Porter, 1990).

Beginning in the 1950s, the limitations of food group methods became increasingly apparent. Researchers recognized that the leading causes of death and disability in the United States were chronic diseases related at least in part to dietary factors. They identified linkages between diets that contained excessive energy, fat, saturated fat, cholesterol, salt, and sugar but too little fiber and chronic diseases such as coronary heart disease, certain cancers, and diabetes. This research demonstrated that new recommendations were needed to help the public prevent chronic disease conditions.

Since 1977, recommendations have suggested that the percentage of calories obtained from fat be reduced to 30 percent or less of the total and that carbohydrate calories (especially those from starch) be increased to 55 percent or more. To meet these recommendations, the government advised individuals to eat more fruits, vegetables, and grains and to choose lean meats and dairy products low in fat (U.S. Senate, 1977). To help the public understand this message, the USDA developed a fifth group of "other" foods—fats/sweets/ alcohol—that keep bad "nutritional company," are high in calories but low in essential nutrients and fiber, and are to be eaten only occasionally (USDA, 1979). Within the past few years, the substantial scientific support for such recommendations has been summarized in two major consensus publications, the Public Health Service's *Surgeon General's Report on Nutrition and Health* (USDHHS, 1988) and the National Research Council's *Diet and Health* (National Research Council [NRC], 1989).

Current federal dietary guidance policy is expressed in the *Dietary Guidelines for Americans*, a joint publication of the USDA and the USDHHS. The most recent edition of this document recommends that Americans over the age of two years follow this advice: Eat a variety of foods; balance food intake with physical activity to maintain or improve weight; choose a diet low in fat, saturated fat, and cholesterol; choose a diet with plenty of vegetables, fruits, and grain products; use sugars, sodium, and salt only in moderation; and if you drink alcoholic beverages, do so in moderation (USDA and USDHHS, 1995). This policy reflects the views of many nutritionists that recommendations should be stated in positive terms and that *any* food that supplies calories and essential nutrients should be recognized as contributing to a healthful diet (USDA, 1990). This view denies any distinction between foods considered "good" or "bad" (Hess, 1991). Thus, federal policy does not suggest that foods such as chocolate be prohibited but instead advises that they be consumed in moderation.

CHOCOLATE AS A FOOD

Although chocolate was once considered a perfect food (Fisher, 1971), it now is considered to fall short of ideal largely because of its high fat content and the amounts of sugar added during its processing.

Processing

Chocolate is the semiliquid paste (*chocolate liquor*) made by grinding cocoa beans (nibs) that have been fermented, dried, cleaned, roasted, and separated from their shells (Allerton, 1974; Coe and Coe, 1996; Martin, 1987; Zoumas and Finnegan, 1979). Figure outlines this process.

More than half of the weight of cocoa beans comes from fat—the cocoa butter. This fat has an unusually sharp melting point (89 to 93 degrees Fahrenheit), which is just below body temperature, a fact that explains why chocolate melts in the mouth (Minifie, 1989). Grinding the cocoa beans warms the fat and melts it into chocolate liquor. When the liquor cools, it hardens into *baker's chocolate*. To make *cocoa*, the liquor is pressed to force out some of the cocoa butter; this reduced-fat product is then cooled, dried, and ground into powder.

To make eating chocolate, *extra* cocoa butter is added to the liquor along with a variety of additives, sugars, other sweeteners, milk, and other foods (Rinzler, 1977). These substances are mixed and ground further, often for days, to develop the flavor and texture of the finished chocolate. To ensure quality, every step of these processes must be conducted under precisely defined—but rarely revealed—conditions (Martin, 1987).

In processing, various substances are added to chocolate to alter its color, to enhance its flavor, or to preserve, stabilize, or sweeten it (Rinzler, 1977). Among additives that alter the nutritional value of chocolate are sugars, milk, and nuts. The addition of milk and nuts improves the nutrient content of chocolate to some extent; sugar only contributes energy.

Energy

The major nutritional contribution of chocolate is energy (measured in kilocalories, or kcal). Table 11.1 compares the content of energy and selected nutrients in one ounce of each of the major forms of chocolate—baker's, cocoa,

Figure 11.1
Processing of Cocoa Beans into Chocolate

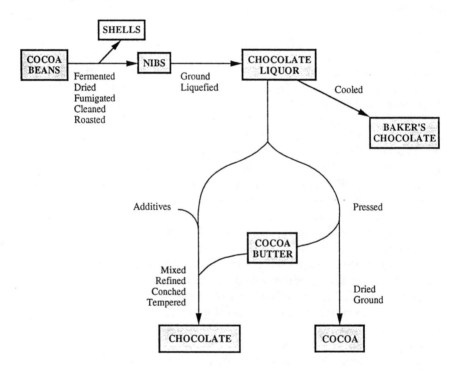

semisweet, and milk chocolate.

One ounce of baker's chocolate (or pure chocolate liquor) contains 148 kilocalories derived from 2.9 grams of protein, 8.0 grams of carbohydrate, and 15.7 grams of fat (USDA, 1991). Cocoa contains less than half the calories of baker's chocolate because some of its fat has been removed. Although semisweet and milk chocolate have less fat than baker's chocolate, their caloric content is similar; the calories from fat have been replaced by those from sugar.

Percentage of Total Calories

Table 11.1 also illustrates the percentage of energy derived from protein, fat, and carbohydrate in the various forms of chocolate. Protein constitutes a relatively small percentage of energy in most chocolates, with cocoa an exception at 16 percent. All forms of chocolate, however, are very high in fat calories; more than half the calories derive from fat in cocoa, semisweet, and milk chocolates, and nearly 90 percent of the calories in baker's chocolate. As noted above, the carbohydrate is mainly sugar; despite its lower amount of fat, milk chocolate remains high in calories because its fat calories have been replaced by those from sugar. Thus, all forms of chocolate are relatively high in proportion of fat; all but baker's chocolate are also high in sugar.

Fats

Because dietary recommendations focus on reduction of total fat, saturated fat, and cholesterol, these substances are of special interest. More than 60 percent of the fatty acids in cocoa butter are saturated (palmitic, 28 percent; stearic, 32 percent), while 35 percent derive from oleic acid, which is monounsaturated (USDA, 1991). Neither stearic nor oleic acids raise blood cholesterol; palmitic acid, however, does (Bonanome and Grundy 1988). Chocolate is a plant food; it only contains cholesterol when milk has been added to it. In general, cocoa butter does not appear to have a significant influence on blood cholesterol levels, perhaps because it is poorly digested (Mitchell et al., 1989).

Vitamins and Minerals

Table 11.1 demonstrates the loss in nutrients that occurs with processing of chocolate liquor into semisweet and milk chocolates. Chocolate liquor contains trace amounts of fat-soluble vitamins such as A and E (not illustrated in the table). It also contains small amounts of water-soluble vitamins such as folate and niacin, and minerals such as calcium, iron, and potassium; these nutrients are concentrated in cocoa but are gradually diluted out when sugar, which is devoid of nutrients, is added. Cocoa contains the highest relative proportion of vitamins and minerals, although the majority of its calories derive from fat and sugar.

Other Natural Substances

Cocoa beans also contain significant amounts of naturally-occurring substances of nutritional concern such as the methylxanthines theobromine and caffeine, tannins, oxalates, phytates, and tyramines. As shown in Table 11.1, cocoa contains especially high levels of theobromine (583 milligrams/ounce); it also is high in phytates (526 milligrams/ounce) and oxalates (623 milligrams/ounce), but most of these substances disappear during chocolate manufacture. One ounce of baker's chocolate contains 58 milligrams of caffeine (USDA, 1991), an amount similar to that found in coffee, tea, and typical carbonated beverages (Pennington, 1989). Milk chocolate contains only about 7 milligrams per ounce (USDA, 1991) but may contribute significantly to the caffeine intake of children (Arbeit et al., 1988). The complexity of chocolate is illustrated by the isolation of at least 387 separate chemicals that contribute to its flavor (Martin, 1987).

DIETARY INTAKE

The amounts of chocolate consumed by individuals and the general population are uncertain. Dietary intake surveys, in which people are asked to identify what they ate within the last 24 hours, are difficult to perform accurately, are often unreliable (Block, 1982; U.S. General Accounting Office [USGAO], 1991), and usually underestimate consumption of foods considered unhealthy (Pao et al., 1989). Thus, it is difficult to assess the validity of national survey data. For example, one study performed in the late 1970s reported that only 8.7 percent of nearly 12,000 respondents ate chocolate on the survey day (Block et al., 1985). Another from the mid-1980s reported that total intake of candy (which amounts to approximately twice the intake of chocolate) among men aged 19 to 50, women aged 19 to 50, and their children aged 1 to 5 was only 4, 5, and 8 grams per day, respectively (USDA, 1985, 1986). The reliability of such data is, at best, uncertain.

One source of corroborative evidence for dietary intake are data on the disappearance of commodities into the food supply. Such data also permit estimation of chocolate consumption. The method involves estimating the amounts of chocolate produced, transported, and imported into the United States, subtracting any amounts exported, and dividing the remainder by the total number of people in the country. The final figure is an estimate of per capita availability of chocolate in the food supply.

Such data indicate that the per capita availability of chocolate confectionery rose from just under 10 pounds per year in 1984 (U.S. Department of Commerce, 1988) to just over 10 pounds in 1989 (U.S. Department of Commerce, 1991), an amount that calculates to about 12 grams per day (less than one-half ounce) for every man, woman, and child in the United States, regardless of age. The amount of cocoa in the U.S. food supply was 5.1 pounds per capita in 1994 (Putnam and Allshouse, 1996). Food availability data, however, usually over-

Table 11.1
Composition of the Principal Forms of Chocolate:
Content of Selected Nutrients and Components per Ounce

TYPE OF CHOCOLATE

	Baker's	Cocoa	Semisweet	Milk
Energy, kcal	148	62	135	145
Protein, g [% kcal]	2.9 [4]	5.7 [16]	1.2 [2]	1.9 [5]
Fat, g [% kcal]	15.7 [87]	4.0 [52]	8.4 [53]	8.6 [52]
Carbohydrate, g [% kcal]	8.0 [10]	15.3 [32]	18.0 [45]	16.7 [43]
Niacin, mg	0.5	0.6	0.1	0.1
Calcium, mg	21	34	9	54
Iron, mg	1.8	3.9	0.9	0.4
Potassium, mg	235	431	174	109
Theobromine	350	583	138	48
Caffeine, mg	58	65	18	7

Note: Data obtained or calculated from USDA (1991).
  g 1 = 1 gram.
  kcal 1 = 1 kilocalorie.
  mg 1 = 1 milligram.
  semi-sweet, and milk chocolate

Table 11.2
Effects of Chocolate on Health: Summary

CONDITION	SUSPECTED CAUSATIVE FACTOR
Supported by controlled research evidence	
Allergies	Proteins similar to those found in legumes
Headaches	Phenylethylamine
Heartburn	Theobromine
Tooth decay	Sugar
Supporting research evidence limited or unavailable	
Acne	Fats
Calcium deficiency	Oxalates, phytates
Heart disease	Fat, saturated fat
Kidney stones	Oxalates
Obesity	Energy (fat)
Digestive disorders in nursing infants	Theobromines or proteins in breast milk
Psychogenic effects, addiction	Methylxanthines, anandamide

Sources: Summarized from Bonanome and Grundy 1988 ; di Tomaso, Beltramo, and Piomelli 1996 ; Fries 1978; Mitchell et al. 1989 ; Murphy and Castell 1988 ; Resman, Blumenthal, and Jusko 1977

estimate actual intake because wastage is not taken into consideration, but they underestimate the average dietary intake of adults (because young infants are included in per capita estimations), and they reveal nothing about the wide range of individual intake levels (USDHHS, 1988).

The few grams of chocolate that apparently constitute average daily intake levels should be considered nutritionally insignificant, but the greater amounts reported as consumed by self-styled "chocoholics" (see, for example, Boynton, 1982; Brody, 1990; Hall, 1991; Virtue, 1990) could well affect health.

HEALTH EFFECTS

Views of the physiologic consequences of chocolate consumption have changed considerably since 1825 when Brillat-Savarin wrote that "people who habitually drink chocolate enjoy unvarying health" (Fisher, 1971). Table 11.2 summarizes current understanding of the effects of chocolate on health. Research on these effects was last reviewed by Fries in 1978, but his conclusions appear to remain valid; they have not been contradicted by the few studies conducted subsequently.

Consumption of chocolate has been demonstrated to induce allergic reactions in the skin, digestive tract, and respiratory system of susceptible individuals, most likely as a result of sensitivity to a protein similar to that in beans and peas. Headaches have been shown to occur in some people who eat chocolate, perhaps in reaction to tyramines (e.g., phenylethylamine), which raise blood pressure.

Consumption of chocolate or theobromine has been observed to impair the function of the muscle at the base of the esophagus (the lower esophageal sphincter) so that stomach contents are permitted to flow into the esophagus and cause heartburn (Murphy and Castell, 1988). Although the sugar in chocolate makes it cariogenic, chocolate candy causes less tooth decay in experimental animals than sugar alone, perhaps because other components in chocolate offer some protection against the action of cariogenic bacteria in the mouth.

In contrast, proposals that chocolate might specifically increase the risk for acne, calcium deficiency, heart disease, kidney stones, or obesity have not been confirmed by scientific studies. Chocolate contributes saturated fats that raise blood cholesterol levels, but meat and dairy foods contribute far more of this type of fat (USDA, 1988). Although theobromine has well-characterized toxic effects (Tarka, 1982), and theobromine from chocolate is incorporated into breast milk (Resman, Blumenthal, and Juskur, 1977), ingestion of chocolate by nursing mothers has not been associated with digestive disturbances in their infants. Despite suggestions that certain chemicals in chocolate might mimic the physiologic and psychogenic effects of marijuana (di Tomaso, Beltramo, and Piomelli, 1996), no controlled scientific studies have yet produced evidence to support popular beliefs that chocolate induces addiction, behavior changes, mood swings, or feelings of love.

The idea that chocolate might improve nutritional intake by promoting increased food consumption has received limited support. Children increase their intake of milk—and its nutrients—when milk is flavored with chocolate (Guthrie, 1977; Garey, Chan, and Parlia, 1990), but they also increase intake of calories from sugar; low-fat chocolate milk contains one-third more calories than regular low-fat milk, virtually all of them from the added sugar (Pennington, 1989).

POLITICAL ECONOMY

The source of chocolate is the bean from the cocoa tree, *Theobroma cacao*. Cocoa trees are grown and the beans harvested in developing countries, but processing of the beans and consumption of chocolate occur mainly in industrialized nations (Allerton, 1974). In the late 1970s, more than 70 percent of the world's cocoa beans were grown in Ghana, Ivory Coast, Brazil, and Nigeria, yet more than 90 percent of the world's chocolate was processed and consumed in the United States and Western Europe (Considine and Considine, 1982). More recently, exports of chocolate to Japan, South Korea, and Taiwan have increased rapidly (Chocolate Manufacturers, 1988).

The United States remains the leading processor of chocolate. In 1986, 268 million pounds of cocoa beans imported at a cost of $279 million were converted in this country to about 2.3 billion pounds of chocolate valued at $4.8 billion (U.S. Department of Commerce, 1987); these amounts increased to 2.6 billion pounds valued at $5.9 billion in 1989 (U.S. Department of Commerce, 1991) and rose to $6.7 billion in 1992 (Corman, 1993).

Since the late 1980s, sales of chocolate have increased at about 3 percent annually, a rate much better than that for most other foods. At least half the sales occur at Easter, Valentine's Day, or Mother's Day, and overall sales led at least one observer to conclude that "few products so relatively overpriced, laden with fat and calories and of little nutritious value have seen such healthy growth" (Corman, 1993, F10).

One reason for this successful marketing is that chocolate manufacturers spend millions of dollars to advertise their products. In 1990, for example, Hershey Foods allocated more than $10 million to promote Peter Paul bars, and nearly $10 million to advertise Reese's. The persistently strong sales of M&M's, Mars Bars, and Snickers may well be due to their advertising budgets, which were $14, $10, and $9 million, respectively, in 1990 ("The Top 100," 1991).

CONCLUSIONS

Despite its apparent status as a most-favored food, chocolate is only a minor component of the diet of most Americans. When eaten in average quantities (less than one-half ounce per day), the contribution of chocolate to total fat and caloric intake is minimal. Chocolate is no higher in calories or lower in content of essential nutrients than other high-fat, high-sugar foods, nor is it directly responsible for very many of the health problems attributed to its consumption. From a nutritional standpoint, chocolate belongs in the "other" group of foods—those that can be eaten occasionally when nutritional needs have been met and extra calories pose no problem.

Of broader nutritional impact is the way chocolate exemplifies contradictions in the dietary intake patterns of Americans and in the overall food system. Although consumers are increasingly aware of issues related to diet and health ("Prevention Index," 1989), their consumption patterns have shown little improvement in recent years. USDA data indicate increasing availability of fats and oils in the food supply (Putnam, 1990), and few Americans consume anywhere near the recommended number of servings of fruits and vegetables each day (Patterson et al., 1990). As already noted, levels of chocolate consumption appear to have remained relatively constant and should not be a source of concern to average consumers. Evaluation of the health impact of high levels of intake must await more accurate and complete data. Given this situation, efforts to increase consumption of fruits, vegetables, and grains should continue to take priority on the national nutrition policy agenda.

Of greater concern are the economic inequalities inherent in the production and marketing of tasty—though not necessarily healthful—foods and in the promulgation of dietary recommendations. U.S. chocolate producers import millions of pounds of cocoa beans from Third World countries, process the beans into billions of pounds of chocolates, spend millions of dollars advertising these products, and sell them for billions more dollars. The government allocates only a small fraction of such sums to programs that advise consumers to eat foods containing less fat and sugar (USDHHS, 1988; NRC 1989; USDA and USDHHS, 1990). Therefore, if Americans are to respond to recommendations of federal and other health agencies to reduce dietary risks for chronic diseases, nutritionists and culinary professionals will need to find ways to make eating fruits, vegetables, and grains as profitable and enjoyable as eating chocolate.

ACKNOWLEDGMENTS

The author thanks Drs. Sharron Dalton, Margaret Hamburg, and Paul Rozin for comments on an earlier draft of this chapter, and Alyce Conrad for preparation of Figure 11.1.

REFERENCES

Allerton, J. 1974. Chocolate and cocoa products. In *Encyclopedia of food technology*, edited by A. H. Johnson and M. S. Peterson. Vol. 2. Westport: AVI. 195–215.
Arbeit, M. L., T. A. Nicklas, and G. C. Frank, 1988. Caffeine intakes of children from a biracial population: The Bogalusa Heart Study. *Journal of the American Dietetic Association* 88: 466–71.

Block, G. 1982. A review of validations of dietary assessment methods. *American Journal of Epidemiology* 115: 492–505.

Block, G., 1982. U.S. General Accounting Office [USGAO] 1991.

Block, G., C. M. Dresser, and A. M. Hartman, 1985. Nutrient sources in the American diet: Quantitative data from the NHANES II survey. II. Macronutrients and fats. *American Journal of Epidemiology* 122: 27–40.

Bonanome, A., and S. M. Grundy, 1988. Effect of dietary stearic acid on plasma cholesterol and lipoprotein levels. *New England Journal of Medicine* 318: 1244–48.

Boynton, S. 1982. *Chocolate: The consuming passion*. New York: Workman.

Brody, L. 1990. *Growing up on the chocolate diet*. New York: Stephen Greene Press/ Pelham Books.

Chocolate Manufacturers Association of the U.S.A. and American Cocoa Research Institute. 1988. *Annual report*. McLean, Va.

Coe, S. D., and M. D. Coe. 1996. *The true history of chocolate*. Thames and Hudson.

Considine, D. M., and G. D. Considine.   1982. *Foods and food production encyclopedia*. New York: Van Nostrand. 317–22.

Corman, L. 1993. America's enduring sweet tooth. *New York Times*, February 21, F10.

di Tomaso, E., M. Beltramo,   and D. Piomelli. 1996. Brain cannabinoids in chocolate. *Nature* 382: 677–78.

Fisher, M. F. K., trans. 1971. *Brillat-Savarin's the physiology of taste or meditations on transcendental gastronomy*. New York: Harcourt Brace Jovanovich.

Fries, J. H. 1978. Chocolate: A review of published reports of allergic and other deleterious effects real or presumed. *Annals of Allergy* 41: 195–219.

Garey, J. G., M. M. Chan, and S. R. Parlia. 1990. Effect of fat content and chocolate flavoring of milk on meal consumption and acceptability by schoolchildren. *Journal of the American Dietetic Association* 90: 719–21.

Guthrie, H. A. 1977. Effect of a flavored milk option in a school lunch program. *Journal of the American Dietetic Association* 71: 35–40.

Hall, T. 1991. The hunt for sweet, low-fat chocolate. *New York Times*, November 6, B6.

Hess, M. A. 1991. Resetting the American table—creating a new alliance of taste and health. *Journal of the American Dietetic Association* 91: 228–30.

Jones, J. J., and J. E. Allshouse. 1996. *Food consumption, prices, and expenditures, 1996, annual data, 1970-94*. USDA Statistical Bulletin Number 928. Washington, D.C.

Martin, R. A. 1987. Chocolate. *Advances in Food Research* 31: 211–342.

Minifie, B. W. 1989. *Chocolate, cocoa and confectionery: Science and technology*. 3 ed. Westport: AVI.

Mitchell, D. C., K. E. McMahon, and C. A. Shively, 1989. Digestibility of cocoa butter and corn oil in human subjects: A preliminary study. *American Journal of Clinical Nutrition* 50: 983-86.

Murphy, D. W., and D. O. Castell. 1988. Chocolate and heartburn: Evidence of increased esophageal acid exposure after chocolate ingestion. *American Journal of Gastroenterology* 83: 633–36.

National Research Council. 1989. *Diet and health: Implications for chronic disease risk*. Washington, D.C.: National Academy Press.

Nestle, M., and D. V. Porter. 1990. Evolution of federal dietary guidance policy: From food adequacy to chronic disease risk. *Caduceus* 6, no. 2: 43–67.

Pao, E. M., K. E. Sykes, and Y. F. Cypel. 1989. *USDA methodological research for large-scale dietary intake surveys, 1975–88.* Home Economics Research Report No. 49. Hyattsville, Md.: HNIS/USDA.

Patterson, B. H., G. Block, and W. F. Rosenberger, 1990. Fruit and vegetables in the American diet: Data from the NHANES II survey. *American Journal of Public Health* 80: 1443–49.

Pennington, J. A. T. 1989. *Bowes and Church's food values of portions commonly used.* 15th ed. New York: Harper and Row.

Prevention index posts highest level in six years. 1989. *CNI Weekly Report,* June 1, 2.

Putnam, J. J. 1990. Food consumption. *National Food Review* July-September, 1–9. Putnam and Allshouse, 1996.

Resman, B. H., H. P. Blumenthal, and W. J. Jusko. 1977. Breast milk distribution of theobromine from chocolate. *Journal of Pediatrics* 91: 477–80.

Rinzler, C. A. 1977. *The book of chocolate.* New York.: St. Martin's Press.

Tarka, S. M. 1982. The toxicology of cocoa and methylxanthines: A review of the literature. *CRC Critical Reviews in Toxicology* no. 9, 4: 275–312.

The top 100 advertisers. 1991. *Advertising Age,* September 25.

U.S. Department of Agriculture. 1979. *Food: The hassle-free guide to a better diet.* Home and Garden Bulletin Number 228. Washington, D.C.: USDA Science and Education Administration.

U.S. Department of Agriculture. 1985. *Nationwide food consumption continuing survey of food intakes by individuals.* NFCS-CSFII Report No. 85-1. Women 19–50 years and their children 1–5 years, 1 day. Hyattsville, Md.: Human Nutrition Information Service.

U.S. Department of Agriculture. 1986. *Nationwide food consumption survey continuing survey of food intakes by individuals.* NFCS-CSFII Report No. 85-3. Men 19–50 years, 1 day. Hyattsville, Md.: Human Nutrition Information Service.

U.S. Department of Agriculture. 1990. *Report of the Dietary Guidelines Advisory Committee on the Dietary Guidelines for Americans, 1990 to the Secretary of Agriculture and the Secretary of Health and Human Services.* Hyattsville, Md.: Human Nutrition Information Service.

U.S. Department of Agriculture. 1991. *Composition of foods: Raw, processed, prepared.* Agriculture Handbook No. 8-19. Hyattsville, Md.: Human Nutrition Information Service.

U.S. Department of Agriculture. 1994. *Nutrient content of the U.S. food supply, 1909–1990.* Home Economic Research Report Number 42. Washington, D.C.: Agricultural Research Service.

U.S. Department of Agriculture and U.S. Department of Health and Human Services. 1995. *Nutrition and your health: Dietary guidelines for Americans.* 4th ed. Washington, D.C.: Government Printing Office.

U.S. Department of Commerce. 1991. *1991 U.S. industrial outlook.* Washington, D.C.: Government Printing Office.

U.S. Department of Commerce, Bureau of the Census, Industry Division. 1987. *Current industrial reports: Confectionery 1986.* MA2OD (86)-1. Washington, D.C.: Government Printing Office.

U.S. Department of Commerce and International Trade Association. 1988. U.S. industrial outlook with new coverage of emerging industries—food. *Confectionery Products* 42: 23-27.

U.S. Department of Health and Human Services. 1988. *The Surgeon General's report on nutrition and health*. Publ. No. (PHS) 88-50210. Washington, D.C.: Government Printing Office.

U.S. Senate, Select Committee on Nutrition and Human Needs. 1977. *Dietary goals for the United States*. 2 ed. Washington, D.C.: Government Printing Office.

Virtue, D. 1990. *Chocoholics dream diet*. New York: Bantam.

Zoumas, B. L., and E. J. Finnegan. 1979. Chocolate and cocoa. In *Kirk-Othmer encyclopedia of chemical technology*. 3d ed. New York: Wiley-Interscience. 6: 1–19.

CHAPTER 12

Bite-Sized Marketing: Candy Bars

Robert M. Rees

This chapter examines a bite-sized portion of modern marketing, the promotion of candy bars. What is proposed is that the best opportunity for a competitive edge in today's market, given the impulsive nature of the purchase, is advertising that literally features the buying process.

If the buying process is featured in the advertising, then the actual in-store experience, the impulsive selection of a candy bar will by itself generate top of mind brand and advertising awareness during the time when such awareness is most desirable. This approach need not be confined to candy bars. In fact, a minor variation was successfully used by Procter & Gamble in its introduction of Charmin. The depiction of a friendly grocery story owner, Mr. Whipple, imploring his customers not to squeeze the Charmin to see how soft it is, was a depiction that was recreated in the mind of the consumer by the actual selection process.

Proctor & Gamble, perhaps without realizing it, had turned the shopping experience into a reminder of its advertising message. This approach can be utilized on behalf of any product that is purchased mostly on impulse and that is in a category where differentiation of benefits is difficult due to the wide array of similar and confusing choices.

When it comes to candy bars, Americans do not lack for a wide array of confusing choices. Of all the chocolate consumed in America, about ten pounds per person per year, nearly half is consumed in the form of candy bars. Only two candy bar manufacturers, M&M/Mars and Hershey with a combined share of 70 percent, dominate the U.S. market. But the market is fragmented among a myriad of individual brands. The leader is M&M/Mars' Snickers with only about eleven percent, followed by M&M's, Reese's Peanut Butter Cups, Kit Kat, Hershey, Milky Way and Twix. The development of candy bars into a hypercompetitive and fragmented industry, one now in the mature stage of its life cycle, has its origins in a long history.

Chocolate had its beginnings as a beverage. The Aztecs consume large quantities of Xocatl, a liquid that resulted when ground cocoa nibs were mixed with water, maize, and spice. (The name Xocatl apparently was derived from the name of an Aztec god, Quetzalcoatl. Appropriately enough, the cacao tree eventually was given the genus name Theobroma, for food of the gods.)

Columbus, on his fourth voyage to the Americas, partook of Xocatl but was not impressed. Seventeen years later, in 1519, Cortez was impressed. He took samples of the new beverage back to Spain, where Xocatl was mispronounced as chocolate.

By the 1600s, chocolate had acquired a certain royal chic. For example, Charles V of Spain enjoyed the new drink. (To make it less bitter, he took to mixing it with cane sugar that came from the Orient.) When 14-year-old Princess Anne of Spain married 14-year-old Louis XIII of France, the young bride chose chocolate as a gift for her betrothed. (The young lovers may have been on to something. Recent evidence suggests that chocolate contains phenylethylamine, a chemical that may account for feelings of happiness and of being in love.)

Chocolate beverages grew in popularity throughout Europe. In 1662, under pressure from chocolate lovers, Cardinal Brancaccio of Rome granted it a dispensation during Lent. "Liquids do not break the fast," ruled the Cardinal.

Cafes serving chocolate drinks flourished in London, and Pepy's Diary of 1664 took special notice of the new fad. By the end of the 17th Century, following its discovery by the mayor of Zurich while he was visiting Belgium, chocolate drink had spread to Switzerland. The British colonies in the Americas, and especially so following the Boston Tea Party, were quick to adopt the chocolate drink. A year before the American declaration of Independence, Thomas Jefferson explained to John Adams and to others that chocolate's superiority for health and nourishment would give it an edge over tea and coffee in the New World. Jefferson turned out to be wrong only in the form of chocolate that would command the allegiance of Americans. That form arrived in 1847 when Fry and Sons in London introduced chocolate as a solid. (Like many discoveries, this one consisted of the obvious. The paste or chocolate liquor from cocoa, the result of removing the cocoa butter, had always hardened into a solid, but it was too bitter and dry to eat. All that Fry and Sons did was to add back some cocoa butter and sugar to the chocolate liquor before it hardened.)

Solid chocolate became an international industry. Henry Nestle of Switzerland saw the potential and began to manufacture not only in Switzerland but in New York. At the end of the 19th century an American candy maker, Milton Snavely Hershey, had entered the fray. (After watching some German chocolate making machinery in action at the Chicago Exposition of 1893, Hershey had concluded that chocolate was here to stay.) Ironically, what helped to firmly establish the food of the gods in the United States was war. After the United States had entered World War I in 1917, the Army Quartermaster ordered that chocolate be dispensed to the troops because it boosted energy and morale. Thousands of soldiers returned home with a sweet tooth provided by Uncle Sam.

The candy bar industry boomed. Between World Wars I and II, more than 30,000 different candy bars were introduced. The Lindy Bar made its appearance just after Lucky Lindy's solo flight across the Atlantic. The Amos 'n' Andy Bar was introduced when a black radio show of the same name hit its peak in 1931.

A man named Frank Mars, using a fluffy nougat center, introduced the Milky Way. The chocolate enrobed candy bar, with a fruit, candy or nut center, became America's unique contribution to confectionery. So big did the candy industry become in America that cocoa became the third largest cash crop after sugar and coffee. Hollywood actress Jean Harlow, in 1935, was able to get millions of movie goers to identify with her lustful appetite simply by popping a few chocolate bon bons into her mouth.

To take advantage of the popularity of sweets, Lucky Strike cigarettes positioned itself as a healthy alternative. The Lucky Strike advertising advised us to, "Reach for a Lucky instead of a sweet." The candy bar was helped along by the new art and technology of packaging. Prewrapped candy and candy bars moved out of confectionery stores (from the Latin confect for to prepare) into grocery stores, drugstores, and even newsstands. (The number of confectionery stores declined from 63,000 in 1929 to less than 14,000 a half century later.) If World War I had given America a sweet tooth, World War II accounted for the spread of the American candy bar around the world. Chocolate bars, cigarettes and nylon stockings became synonymous with Americans bearing gifts. The candy bar, a term that first began to appear in print in the 1940s, had become a ubiquitous part of American life. However, it wasn't until the 1950s and 1960s that candy bars entered into full competitive battle in America.

One major turning point came as recently as 1969 when Hershey, stung by competitive inroads made by M&M/Mars, began to advertise its products. Up until 1969, Hershey had insisted that all it needed was quality, and that everything else would take care of itself. Since that time the advertising and promotional expense for Hershey has grown from 3.7 percent of sales to over ten percent. To keep the competition on the up and up, the Food and Drug Administration entered the fray by defining chocolate. To be called chocolate, the FDA ruled, a product must contain ten percent chocolate liquor or essence, 12 percent whole milk solids and cocoa butter as the fat source. (So called white chocolate is not chocolate at all. It contains cocoa butter but no chocolate liquor.)

By the 1980s, with similar and highly competitive products competing for a saturated market, the industry was confronted with a mature and less profitable market. Most observers isolated four factors that were adversely affecting the per capita growth of candy bars in the early 1980s. First, there had been a swing toward health foods and healthier snacks, the same trend that had impacted on some of the sugar coated breakfast cereals. Second, those with a craving for chocolate were no longer limited to candy. Alternatives, from cookies to ice cream bars to Chocolate covered granola bars, were available. Third, there had been a proliferation of new snack items in new snack food categories, from flavored potato chips to bagged mixtures of nuts, raisins and chocolate chips. Fourth, prices had escalated. During the late 1970s and early 1980s, prices of candy bars increased almost 50 percent. Then, in the mid 1980s, the weakening of the U.S. dollar caused a 36 percent increase in the price of imported chocolate.

The makers of candy bars set about to counter these factors. Rather than fight the trend to health foods, the candy bar industry tried to become part of it. Granola bars appeared in the mid 1970s. The National Confectioners Association hired former Olympic champion Bob Mathias to make appearances on behalf of candy as a snack. In 1984, M&M/Mars sponsored the Olympics on television and ran commercials featuring Snickers as the snack of champions. Larry Bird, retired from his career as a basketball player for the Boston Celtics, was hired to endorse Nestle products.

The candy bar companies also diversified into other forms of chocolate and snacks. M&M/Mars, for example, purchased Dove Bar, a notoriously "sinful" ice cream snack. Hershey attempted to diversify into restaurants, pasta and other types of candy snacks. To counter the consumer resistance to higher prices, the industry increased quantity offered without proportionate price increases. During 1986, for example, Hershey increased its bar weights between 10 percent and 14 percent but increased its wholesale prices by only three (3) cents per bar. The candy bar industry also developed a propensity for new products. During the first 75 years of its existence, Hershey had introduced only 12 new products. In the 1980s, it averaged more than one a year. Twenty percent of Hershey's recent sales have come form new products.

Part of the new marketing for candy bars was new packaging. The regular size individual candy bar, from which had grown the modern candy bar industry, was relegated to less than 40 percent of total volume. Taking its place were multipacks, bagged special sizes, seasonal packages, and giant sizes. As a result of these marketing efforts, the candy bar remained imbedded in American life. Annual sales of candy bars are approaching $4 billion in manufacturers' dollars. But profit margins have declined as competition has increased. Candy bars are in the late mature stage of the product life cycle. The makers of candy bars know that any significant increases in consumption will require new marketing strategies.

The consumer is the best place to look for these new strategies. What most distinguishes the consumers of candy bars is not who they are, but how they behave. In terms of demographics, almost everybody eats candy. Approximately 84 percent of U.S. households consume chocolate, and 72 percent do so more than once a week. (If almost everyone consumes candy, and if from a mental list of 6 to 12 brands that are deemed as acceptable alternatives, the length of the mental menu of acceptable alternatives helps to explain why candy bar buyers almost never purchase the same brand twice in a row). What the candy bar industry hasn't yet recognized is that the actual decision making and purchase process ought to be featured in advertising. The most effective advertising for a candy bar should create awareness that is refreshed and regenerated by the actual buying experience. The more literal and forceful the transference of the buying process into the advertising, the more meaningful and impactful will the advertising become when the consumer goes through the actual buying process.

A television commercial, for example, could feature the anxiety of the consumer who isn't sure which brand of candy bar to select, and who puzzles over the display rack's many choices. The anxiety is relieved when the buyer reminds herself not to panic, and to stick with the best. Or, in a more fanciful and perhaps more memorable mode, the anxiety of the buying process could be resolved when one of the candy bars actually talks to or somehow signals the buyer. Even the names of new candy bars can work to bring closure to the buying process. Names like First Choice and Sure Thing are names that work during the buying process.

The strategy of featuring the buying process in the advertising, and of having the buying process therefore, recreate the advertising in the mind of consumer, offers its greatest reward to whoever uses it first. There is an opportunity for the brand that moves the quickest to become synonymous with the buying process. This won't alter the illustrious history of chocolate, but it will allow a single candy bar to dominate the industry for the first time since the 1920s when Hershey reigned supreme.

CHAPTER 13

Proof That an Entrepreneurial Dream Can Come True ... Through Chocolate

Benneville N. Strohecker

Proof that an entrepreneurial dream can come true is Harbor Sweets, founded in Marblehead, Massachusetts. And the Harbor Sweets dream did indeed come true through chocolate. The catalyst was: A hobby to make the best piece of candy in the world regardless of cost.

I was director of marketing for the Schrafft Candy Company in Charleston, Massachusetts, at the time, and during my 10 years in that position, I served under 12 presidents and three ownerships, all trying to save the $50 million dowager from bankruptcy.

The owners were all similar in that they sent an army of consultants to show us how to turn the company around. The consultants, who were world experts in their field, were ignored because their good advice always required capital or expense, which the owners did not find acceptable. Since the consultants couldn't be fired, they were usually assigned to me to keep them out of the way.

It was after the sixth or seventh year of frustration at Schraffts that I decided to somehow get into my own candy business. With no money, no knowledge of how to make a piece of candy, and no idea of what that piece of candy should be, I had an ambitious objective.

But I had experts to help me. These men were the most respected people in the confectionery field, perhaps in the world. They included Russ Cook, cocoa bean and chocolate expert, whose book *Chocolate Production and Use* is considered by many to be the bible of the industry; George Frederik, cofounder of Russell Stover and former president of Lofts, a name known for quality and innovation during the 1950s and 1960s; and Claude Barnett, author of two books on confectionery technology.

As I got to know and respect these men and others, it occurred to me that what they considered the best piece of candy in the world would be a wonderful testimonial to a product I might pursue. So I asked each of them a highly sophisticated market research question that would have made Yankelovich proud. I asked, "If you could only eat one more piece of candy before you died, what would it be?"

And over the years, I cataloged the answers. The most frequent answer was "a homemade chocolate-covered almond butter crunch, made with a pound of butter to a pound of sugar." The second answer was "a soft, creamy butter-caramel topped with a pecan and dipped in dark chocolate." The purists insisted that "just a piece of smooth, dark, continental chocolate" would be totally sufficient.

All my mentors insisted that what they described couldn't be commercially reproduced because the chocolates could not have preservatives and therefore would not have a sufficiently long shelf life for distribution through traditional candy outlets. And please notice that none of my mentors mentioned anything other than chocolate. Without chocolate, the Harbor Sweets entrepreneurial dream could not have happened.

Recognizing that my candy manufacturing knowledge was nonexistent, I turned to another expert: Fanny Farmer. Her cookbook had a simple recipe for an almond butter crunch, the first product I decided to pursue.[1] The *Farm Journal Cookbook*[2] had another, and someone suggested the best of all: Martin Herrmanns's excellent book *The Art of Making Good Candies at Home*.[3]

During a process of blending the recipes from these books, burning a lot of good ingredients, and asking my famous advisers to critique the results, I finally succeeded in producing an almond butter crunch that pleased all of us.

Now that I had it . . . *what* would I do with it?

I have always been convinced that me-too products weren't much fun, so I wanted differentiation—differentiation in the appearance, the presentation, and perhaps even in the distribution. Serendipity, the most trusted friend of all budding entrepreneurs, came to the rescue. One Sunday afternoon while I was working with my new product, and upon realizing I had run out of dark chocolate, I melted a few ounces of white, cocoa butter "chocolate" that had been given to me by a friend.

The almond butter crunch had become triangular as part of my attempt at differentiation, so when I dipped it into the white chocolate, my son said, "Looks like a sailboat, Dad." His mother, overhearing the remark, exclaimed, "A sweet sloop!" And our entrepreneurial sweet fleet set sail. After dividing the white sail with a mast, dipping the bottom in dark chocolate, then crushed pecans, we wrapped the confection in gold foil to preserve the freshness.

The first red box, hand tied with a gold ribbon, went to a neighbor, then another. Four were donated to a church fair and sold instantly at the outrageously high price of $2.95 for 12 ounces—not even a pound. Considering the fact that I'm a marketer, you'll understand why I simply had to test broader distribution. Rifle shooting with direct mail made sense, so we prepared a simple one-color folder and sent it to the 75 names on our Christmas card list, along with an order form. The simple "Dear Friends—look what we did . . ." approach is still used today.

The results were successful, in fact, overwhelming—not surprising considering that the 75 names on the mailing list included my mother, my sister, aunts, cousins, and old friends. But "overwhelming" to a commuter who can only work nights and weekends caused new problems. In addition to relatives expecting delivery during the rapidly approaching Christmas season, neighbors were increasingly coming to the back door in a tentative approach reminiscent of the speakeasy era, since our back door, next to the Eastern Yacht Club, was not in the commercial district of Marblehead.

I suspect it was at a cocktail party that I expressed my dilemma to Norma Vessot, a neighbor. Norma, out of kindness or pity, volunteered to come in and work for the few hours she had available. She asked another neighbor, and another, until the Christmas crunch was met. By the time we outgrew the cellar, it was not unusual to find combinations of 10 to 15 women and children, cooking, cutting, dipping, foiling, packing, and processing orders, all at minimum wage or less. Why?

Was it the excitement of working in a miniature chocolate factory? It certainly wasn't for fame and riches. One friend of mine, well on his way to becoming the chief executive officer of one of New England's largest law firms, asked his wife, "What is it that attracts all you attractive Marblehead ladies to Ben Strohecker's basement?" "Nick, it's just too difficult to explain" was her mysterious reply.

On St. Patrick's day of 1977, three years after the first Sweet Sloop was consumed, the Schrafft Candy Company forced a spate of increased activity in our new enterprise by separating me from my job at the Schrafft Candy Company. At this time the sales growth was meteoric, the basement was bulging, and it was time for our move to a partially abandoned warehouse in the neighboring seacoast town of Salem. The neighborhood for Harbor Sweets changed dramatically.

The landlord suggested that we reinforce the bars of the windows or at least board up more windows, and he assured us that the fancy Marblehead ladies who worked in our basement would never consider commuting to this unsavory Hispanic neighborhood. We took the bars off the windows, removed the boards, put in glass, and, in effect, said to the neighborhood, "We want to be good neighbors; we trust you want to be good neighbors, too." We've never had an incident; in fact, some of those neighbors are now key employees, and some are supervisors.

The ladies of the basement, without exception, all did come to Salem, and 10 years later, all but 2 are still Harbor Sweets employees. They are part of a workforce of 150. All but a dozen are part-time and seasonal. The mix is precious to us—and more important than the candy.

Ruth Mehrtens Galvin, in her article on chocolate that appeared in *Smithsonian* magazine, described the Harbor Sweets workforce as follows: "There, women of all ages, education and background—the Mayor's wife and the Fire Chief's, college graduates and the retarded, members of the Eastern Yacht Club, Finns, Dominicans, and Vietnamese—work four hour shifts under the motto, 'Love is a quality controller.'"[4]

The employees work in an atmosphere of complete trust. There are no time clocks; each worker keeps his or her own time card and is paid on the basis of what is written on the card. Newcomers usually hand-foil Sweet Sloops but are soon encouraged to switch jobs and try new areas of the 18,000 square foot operation. Employees are carefully selected, and even in the current tight labor market, the company usually works with a full complement.

There are no secrets at Harbor Sweets. All employees meet together five to six times a year to hear about the current financial status of the company, new customers, renovation or expansion plans, and personnel changes. Profit and loss statements are no longer a mystery to the workforce. They learned fast, once they realized that 25 percent of the net profit before taxes is shared with them. They watch the sales growth, now exceeding $2 million, and the debt, which is basically little more than two to three months' seasonal start-up loans.

The six chocolates currently produced reflect the preferences of those Schrafft consultants. The exception is the Periwinkle, a shell-shaped peanut-almond butter crunch in milk chocolate. None of the experts suggested milk chocolate, feeling that the dark variety was perceived to be a better-quality product. But the Metropolitan Opera Company suggested milk chocolate, considering the fact that it is the preference of the majority of Americans, and apparently the same is true of opera lovers.

Since the Met was one of our largest custom customers, our package designer, Roy Parcels of Dixon and Parcels in New York City, suggested that it would be totally appropriate for Harbor Sweets to produce a milk chocolate item—as long as it was the best milk chocolate in the world. The Periwinkle followed.

Custom chocolates—all with a clear Harbor Sweets identity—account for 15 percent of the current $2 million business. Another 35 percent is mail order. (The 75-name mailing list has now expanded to a quarter of a million annually.) The 500 carefully selected gift shops to whom we sell across the nation account for another 35 percent. The Shop at Harbor Sweets is now at $200,000 (one of the Harbor Sweets miracles, considering the fact that it's nearly impossible to find us). Visitors to the little shop on the waterfront now come from all over the world.

Anne Driscoll, author of a *New York Times* article about us, asked us to summarize the reasons why we thought our entrepreneurial dream had come true—through chocolate. The fact that her subheadline read "Chocolate Maker Builds a Staff on Trust" indicates our answer was believable to her.[5]

Trust is the most powerful management tool I've ever known. It is the cornerstone for all Harbor Sweets activities. And trust is reciprocal. The fact that the consumer is willing to pay what in my Schrafft life seemed like outrageous prices for our chocolates indicates that he or she intuitively knows that the value is there and the price is a fair one. The fact that employees suggested a pay cut and the elimination of the bonus one tough fiscal year suggests that the employees trusted our treatment of their compensation. The phenomenon of trust is that if I trust you, and you believe that, you will not betray that trust.

A case could be made, perhaps, that chocolate in itself has the power to assure an entrepreneurial success. Its romantic history with Montezuma, its mystical qualities believed by many to include those of an aphrodisiac, and its use as an ingredient to build the empires of Cadbury, Nestlé, Hershey, and Mars indicate that something unusual is at work here.

The entrepreneurial miracle that is Harbor Sweets strengthens the story, but it helps to prove something equally important. It helps to prove that it is still possible in this country to start a new business in the kitchen, and with practically no capital, with no technical knowledge, in fact, with nothing more than an entrepreneurial dream, it is still possible to build a million-dollar business.

Proof that an entrepreneurial dream can come true . . . through chocolate.

NOTES

1.   Farmer, Fanny Merritt, *The Fanny Farmer Cookbook*. Revised and edited by Marion Cunningham. New York: Alfred A. Knopf, [1914] 1979.

2.   *Homemade Candy by the Food Editors of Farm Journal*. Garden City, NY: Doubleday, 1970.

3.   Martin K. Herrmann, *The Art of Making Good Candies at Home*. Garden City, NY: Doubleday, 1966.

4.   Galvin, Ruth Mehrtens, "Sybaritic to Some, Sinful to Others, but How Sweet It Is." *Smithsonian*, February 1986.

5.   Driscoll, Anne, "Part-Timers Find a Sweet Workplace," *New York Times*, March 20, 1988.

CHAPTER 14

Trends in Chocolate

Barbara Albright

Chocolate has come a long way since its discovery. Cacao and America were discovered around the same time—in the late 1400s. Cocoa beans were discovered by Hernando Cortez, the Spanish conquistador of Mexico. When he was visiting the Aztec emperor Montezuma, he was served the royal drink "chocolatl." At that time, the unsweetened beverage was served in golden goblets and treated like an ambrosia for the gods. In fact, Montezuma served his special cacao drink to nubile Indian maidens as a special love potion. Casanova also used chocolate in his seductions. Since that time, our lust for chocolate has only deepened. I personally think that the addition of sugar to the unsweetened beverage by the Europeans may have gotten us off on the right foot.

As with much of the rest of the specialty foods marketplace, the interest in high-quality chocolate has been growing by leaps and bounds. Whether these foods are called gourmet, fancy, premium, or adult, specialty foods are taking up more and more of the shelf space in grocery stores, as purveyors try to meet the demands of smaller and more discerning market segments. For instance, grocery stores and department stores used to stock only one or maybe two brands of chocolate. Now, across the United States, stores are carrying several types of chocolate or cocoa powder. Rapid expansion has also been seen in chocolate chips and chunks packaging. Van Houten came out with a product that combines both chips and chunks in the same bag. Guittard was first, and Bakers and Nestlé have both come out with larger-sized premium-quality chips. Saco came out with chunks, and now, so has Hershey.

What we've been seeing happening in the chocolate marketplace is similar to what happened to the wine industry several years ago. First, there were jug wines—just like there are lots of different kinds of chocolate bars. Then along came different types of wines, and people became much more aware of them.

Not that they will ever quit drinking the jug wines completely—or ever quit eating M&M's: There is just a bigger selection to choose from. Part of this change is due to the fact that we've been traveling more and have been exposed to a larger selection of items. Basically, Americans have developed a more educated palate, and they are demanding quality. And more American manufacturers are producing higher-quality items.

The company probably most responsible for the introduction of premium chocolate in America is Godiva. Godiva introduced its Belgian-style chocolates to the United States in 1966, and it continues to be the leading manufacturer in the $100 million luxury chocolate market. In 1986, it was estimated that 15 to 20 percent of all the chocolate consumed in the United States was of the *premium* type (though this term is up for discussion). Nestlé, Hershey, M&M/Mars, and Fanny Farmer are now offering their own upscale products. Chocolate boutiques are booming as entrepreneurs go after a piece of the specialty chocolate market with creative new products. Nestlé is even opening up its own boutiques that sell a wide range of its international products.

Right now, the marketplace seems to be making room for a new product segment—quality chocolates at middle premium prices. Consumers have gotten used to higher-quality chocolates, but they need them to be affordable. They want value for their dollar. Madison Avenue, home of many U.S. advertisements, has identified the ultra-consumer. These are consumers who can't afford to splurge across the board. They might drive a BMW, but they might drive it to a discount warehouse. Because of this ultraconsumer who wants value for his or her dollar, we are going to see the market segmented into categories that are focused on premium, best value, economy, and convenience. They are willing to pay for convenience. Campbell's Soup owns Godiva, and it has recently introduced Barringers—an all-American, homier line of chocolate. While Godiva is positioned as "European" with its Euro-style packaging and Euro-style molded chocolates, Barringers is positioned as "American." Godiva sells for about $22 per pound and Barringers sells for about $14 per pound. A former vice president at Godiva started her own line of American chocolates called Claridges, which are being even more mass-marketed. In addition to being sold in department stores, they are found in their own displays in grocery stores. Fanny Farmer, an old American chocolate company, is dusting off its slightly old-school image and is adding upscale touches to its chocolates.

While Europe does seem to have set many of the standards for the industry (as it did in the wine industry), I think that we can expect to see some ingenious American trends applied to our chocolate products of the future. For instance, brownies and chocolate chip cookies are delectable yet uniquely American baked chocolate items. In fact, 50 years after their accidental creation, chocolate chip cookies account for 25 percent of all cookies consumed in the United States. Because of this passion for chocolate, manufacturers are adding chocolate to other cookies as well and more chocolate to chocolate chip cookies in the form of chunks and jumbo-sized chips. Perhaps it is this, the novelty of the American products, that caused the Japanese to purchase $17 million worth of U.S. chocolate last year. There are also several chocolate chip cookie shops in Paris.

After a dramatic increase in consumption of imported chocolates, consumption of imports has dropped substantially in the United States. During this same time, the per person consumption rose to over 11 pounds per person. (It had been at 8.5 pounds per person in 1980.) This increase in consumption indicates that American manufacturers must be doing something right to keep up with our desire to indulge in high-quality chocolate. The Swiss consume well over 20 pounds per person. I do have to say that my staff and I are consuming more than our share of 11 pounds per year, and we are probably skewing these statistics.

During this time of indulgence, premium-quality chocolate seems to be hot on the heels of a couple of other products: Designer ice creams, cookies, mineral waters, and specialty coffees and teas. And it does seem that the next area we are going to see rapidly expanding is that of frozen novelties. Already Americans lead the world in per capita consumption of ice cream, and it seems that our preference is for the super-premium *stuff*. In 1980, frozen novelties earned less than $600 million, but they had shot up to the $1.5 billion (over twice as much) mark in 1986. The introduction of Jell-O pudding pops in 1980–1981 seems to have set off this frozen novelty boom. Then 1984 brought the second generation of pudding pops—and guess what they were dipped in? Chocolate, of course! Because of pudding pops, there have been some new segments that have been developed such as fruit and fruit juice bars. The new frozen novelties are being targeted at adults—not children, as they were in the past.

While Dove Bars had been around as a regional item since 1956, they were formally introduced in 1984 at the specialty foods show, and we all know what's happened since then! They boomed. Dove bars was purchased by M&M/Mars. They produced a new 4-ounce bar in addition to the 6-ounce Dove Bars. Currently, it is test-marketing a frozen Three Musketeers bar, and they have Forever Yours Sundaes and small bite-sized Rondos. This summer our government has allowed the use of Nutrasweet in frozen items, so we are seeing a lot more sugar-free items in the freezer case. There are some new low-calorie sweeteners that we should be seeing soon. Right now, adults can choose from between 3.5 to 5-ounce treats and 1- to 2-ounce bite-size treats for snackers. Small-sized ice cream treats, Rondos, truffles, and Carnation's Bon Bons are indicative of the trends toward convenient, portion-controlled, individual-sized items and toward frozen novelty items that have candy bar–like qualities. In fact, there is a new category being formed that could be called ice cream confections. Hershey's has sundae cups in Reese's Peanut Butter Cup and Mr. Goodbar flavors. Betty Crocker has Goldrush Bars—ice cream coated with caramel, peanuts and milk chocolate.

The sales of frozen novelties are currently at $2 billion and have been growing annually at 15 percent. This category has been growing so rapidly that freezers are overloaded. Lipton has been savvy enough to make its frozen novelties shelf stable. The novelties industry thrives on new product introductions and relies on them for about one third of each year's total sales. Previously, the market was dominated by local and regional products. Now national brands are entering the market, and they are supported by large national advertising budgets. These national brands have already captured two thirds of total annual sales.

You might be wondering how all this can be happening in a country obsessed with good health. If the 1970s were devoted to health and fitness, the 1980s could be called the decade of sweet indulgence. And chances are that we'll be staying home in the 1990s, pampering ourselves. The current prevailing attitude is after we've been "good" all day long—we worked out, didn't drink alcoholic beverages, didn't smoke, ate a prudent meal of grilled fish and vegetables—we want to splurge and reward ourselves for being so good. One of the best ways to do this is with a decadently rich and delicious chocolate or chocolate dessert. Most people feel that if they've eaten moderately during the meal, they can splurge on dessert.

Also, there is no other flavor like chocolate. Cocoa is a complex blend of more than 500 flavor components—nearly 2.5 times as many as those in simpler flavors such as strawberry or lemon. Some of the components contribute only taste. Others, called volatiles contribute aroma as well. Cocoa is a very subtle blend. Food technologists have been able to get close on flavor, but they haven't been able to capture the texture—called "mouth feel"—chocolate's luxurious melt-in-your-mouth quality.

A 1986 Opinion Research Corporation study showed that 84 percent of all U.S. households eat chocolate, and 86 percent of the chocolate eaters enjoy it once a week or more. The Chocolate Manufacturers Association, an industry group in the United States, reports that consumers bought $4.9 billion worth of chocolate in 1986—up 7 percent from 1985. In general, chocolate accounts for 60 percent of candy consumption per person. The present group of 18- to 34-year-olds is now eating 35 percent more candy than previous groups of 18- to 34-year-olds. Surprisingly, this group reports that they are eating more candy than they previously did.

The *New York Times* reported that in a study done by the NPD Group of 2,000 households it found that in the last three years the number of people on diets fell to 19 percent from 27 percent. Of these dieters, MRCA Information Services found that dieters in the later 1980s ate 46 percent more chocolate bars, 59 percent more pretzels, and twice as many croissants as dieters of the early 1980s. In 1986, for the first time in five years, snacking in the home increased. Popular snacking items include ice cream, candy, chips, and popcorn. Quality in these items does seem to be the name of the game. Marketing intelligence services products database of new products measures the frequency of specific items sold. Chocolate desserts alone grew from fewer than a dozen entries in 1982 and climbed to nearly 50 in 1986. The Dancer, Fitzgerald sample new product watch in *Advertising Age* reports that up to half of the dessert listings for products such as cakes, cookies, puddings, and ice cream include the chocolate flavor. Cream desserts quadrupled in number in the same period.

As people trade in their jogging shoes for walking shoes and make a switch from regular aerobics to low-impact aerobics, it's not surprising that curves are back and that the insurance companies have raised the ideal body weights on their charts. If you'll take a look at granola bars, you'll see that the product has made a switch from being a marathon kind of food to being the natural snack choice of couch potatoes. At first, granola bars were positioned as healthy and nutritious snacks because that was what consumers were demanding.

Gradually, this product has evolved from being a natural, grain-based product to becoming a confection. And in most cases, good taste reigns over "natural." First, granola bars had chips added, and recently we're seeing them being enrobed or covered with chocolate. (By the way, coating a filling with chocolate is a very American style of candy bar—the rest of the world either eats their bars plain or with a few nuts in them.) Because of this trend, several grain/ cereal companies that weren't previously in this market segment have been attracted to the confectionery marketplace—Quaker, Ralston, Purina, Kellogg, and General Mills. This group of confections has given us Boppers, Dipps, Whipps, Kudos, Granola Clusters, and Granola Bars.

In the future, we will probably be seeing some more chocolate products that are positioned as healthy—perhaps sweetened with fruit juices. There are several brands of sugar-free chocolate available now—some better than others. It will be interesting to see what products become available as more sweeteners become available. There is also a tofu chocolate bar called the Barat Bar as well as a new line of tofu-based cheesecakes and ice cream sandwiches from Tofutti. Elan is a new superpremium yogurt that is being positioned as a healthful alternative to the high-fat superpremium ice creams. Another soft-serve product, Gise Creme Glace, is 99 percent fat free, has 10 calories per ounce, and contains no salt, sucrose, cholesterol, preservatives, or artificial sweeteners or flavors. As the government allows, Olestra and Simplesse, the two new fat substitutes, will also be added to new products and give consumers some additional items to choose from.

We can also look forward to hearing more about whether or not chocolate raises or lowers blood cholesterol levels. A recent study showed that stearic acid, one of the main fatty acids in cocoa butter, actually lowers blood cholesterol. Right now, cocoa powder is viewed as the most acceptable way for people to consume chocolate in the eyes of the American Heart Association. Another research project that is taking place is studying whether chocolate causes cavities. A group at the Massachusetts Institute of Technology (MIT) has found that one of the tannins in cocoa powder inhibits the activity of the mouth enzyme dextransucrase. This enzyme is a key element in the formation of dental plaque. Without plaque, you don't get dental caries.

Other tidbits that have been in the news about chocolate include: In Switzer- land, they are developing new technology to create a chocolate that won't melt in the heat. Cows are being fed chocolate, and it seems to increase their milk production. Researchers in Pennsylvania are working on developing a stronger cocoa tree so that they can increase production and hopefully lower the cost of chocolate.

Other chocolate trends and products include peanuts or peanut butter and chocolate, a combo that is an all-American favorite. The top three bars in the United States are Snickers, Reese's Peanut Butter Cups, and Peanut M&M's. Snickers has been the number-one seller for awhile now: One out of every eight bars sold is a Snickers. Trombly's is a company that is producing chocolate and peanut butter combinations exclusively—both as spreads and in products. Other companies are marketing extensions of existing lines that are chocolate and peanut butter.

We are seeing more white chocolate line extensions. The West Coast editor of *Chocolatier,* Janice Wald Henderson has recently published a book called *White Chocolate* (Contemporary Books, 1987). White chocolate is being used in a multitude of products, included as chips, as a covering over popcorn, and in sauces. White chocolate desserts are being served around the country. Nestlé saw its Alpine White bar, a white chocolate bar with almonds, catch up with Nestlé Crunch, its best-selling chocolate bar, in only 1.5 years. Nestlé has recently come out with white chocolate baking bars, and their jumbo-sized premium white chocolate chips join Fred's and Guittard in the marketplace with white chocolate chips. In the United States, white chocolate cannot legally be referred to as chocolate because it does not contain the cocoa part of the cocoa bean. White chocolate is made of cocoa butter, milk solids, sugar, and vanilla. Because of this regulation, manufacturers have had to be creative when they name their products. For instance, one of them is the Chocolate Lover's White Chip; another is Vanilla Chips.

As I mentioned earlier, we are seeing, and will probably continue to see, more and more single servings being sold. There are more and more people eating on the run, due in large part to women in the workforce—a trend called "grazing." People are eating for quality sustenance and are not eating as many complete meals. In busy two-income families, often neither partner wants to spend his or her leisure time cooking. And more people are working at home, which leads to more snacking.

Pillsbury did a study of eating habits and calls this new group of people who eat on the run the "chase and grabbits." It found that from 1971 to 1986 the chase and grabbit group grew 136 percent, from 11 percent of the population to 26 percent of the population. In addition to the frozen novelties I mentioned above, some of the products that we've seen that are perfectly suited to this chase and grabbit group include Keebler's Elfin loaves—mini freezer quick breads. The Deer Park Baking Company is producing miniature chocolate chip cookies. At one eightieth of an ounce, one-half inch in diameter, and about one and a half calories, these treats are very munchable and are even being used over ice cream. Pepperidge Farm has individual-serving American Collection frozen desserts, and Spago's Wolfgang Puck has come up with a line of individual-serving high-quality frozen desserts. Frozen chocolate-covered cheesecake bars made by the Sargento Cheese Company are appearing on the market. In addition to chocolate New York–style cheesecake on a stick, Sargento has two bars in popular flavor combinations: Turtle-style cheesecake and grasshopper cheesecake. Heileman's Round 'o Bites are filled donut holes that are sold in resealable bags of 16. They are well suited for munching. After seeing people eat the tops off muffins and throw the rest away, David Lieder-man of David's Cookies is supposedly coming out with Muffin Tops.

We will be seeing more and more microwave desserts—including single-serving products. Sundaes called Hot Scoops claim that they can be microwaved; the hot fudge sauce gets hot, and the ice cream stays frozen. Another product is the microshake—a shake that you can keep in your freezer and then defrost in your microwave. Many of the leading cake mix companies are now adding microwave cake mixes to their lines. Pudding—that all–American favorite—is being put into everything: Cakes, frozen pops, and pies.

The turtle flavor combination, another favorite, is being done in the classic pecan, caramel, and chocolate combination, as well as appearing in other combinations such as macadamia nut, caramel, and white chocolate. The turtle flavor combination has appeared in a brownie mix form. And classic regional American candies should also continue to enjoy popularity. A company called Americandy features candy from every state.

Exotic and tropical foods and flavors are being used in many products. Passion fruit, mango, papaya, macadamia nut, coconut, lime, and ginger are just a few of the popular flavors that are being used.

Liquor and liqueurs are flavoring chocolates as well as being incorporated into desserts. Each state in the United States has different regulations as to how much liquor is allowed in chocolate. Winter's has come up with nonalcoholic liqueur-filled chocolates. Grand Marnier, rum, and coffee-flavored liqueurs have been particularly popular. Liquer-filled or, -flavored chocolates and other confections are sold as part of package deals with flowers and other gift items.

There have been lots of chocolate sauces in a variety of flavor combinations. We've seen at least one company that is packaging all the parts to make a complete sundae. More recently, we've seen chocolate nut butter. While Nutella and other chocolate hazelnut butters have been common in Europe, they are a fairly new product line in the United States. We've seen them done in white chocolate and almond, as well as other flavor combinations.

Cherry and cherry flavor are being found in more products. Some say this is because cherry was a popular flavor during the baby boomers' younger days. Fondness for nostalgic red could also explain why red candies were reintroduced to packages of M&M's. Toffee and caramel are additional flavors that will continue to be popular. And in the United States, we are probably going to be seeing more solid chocolate bars that just have fruits and nuts in them.

Because of chocolate's popularity, we're seeing it being used in or on products. Cookies are being dipped in chocolate, and chocolate cookies are being stirred into ice cream. The mix-in trend will continue as we see that idea being stretched to mix-in cheesecakes and other dessert items.

On packages, we've seen the words *fudgy, double chocolate, premium, ultimate,* and *quality* being used. Products are being positioned as either healthful, fresh and pure, or sinfully decadent. Death by chocolate, double chocolate decadence, and chocolate suicide are just a few of the dessert names that we've seen. We often get asked about the products we've seen—and, oh, the truffles we've seen. Goat cheese? Softball size? Neiman Marcus has white chocolate toothpaste, and there is even a no-calorie chocolate-flavored breath spray. If a sniff is enough, there is a scratch and sniff seven-day dessert diet book with a different dessert to scratch and sniff each day. I've also seen chocolate perfume, shampoo, and soap. In addition to being incorporated into pancake mix, chocolate is being poured over popcorn, gummy bears, and potato chips, and it's being molded into every shape imaginable. I've seen Porsches, a woman's leg, even a chocolate fur coat. Lou-Retta has come out with Buffalo chicken wings complete with a white chocolate dipping sauce, and its most recent addition is white chocolate tortellini. There is even a lobster made of chocolate and filled with pralines.

At least two companies are making chocolate caviar—a larger-sized candy and a smaller size that is meant to be sprinkled over ice cream. Al & Reed's ice cream is made from mashed potatoes. Mrs. Prindable and Paron's are serving up apples that are coated with chocolate and other ingredients, including caramel and nuts. There is also a mousse that is available in an aerosol can, and it comes in both regular and low-calorie versions. Obviously, some of these items are gimmicky, and some are of higher quality than others. After a while, I think that we'll see a shakeout of some of these items. But chocolate, in some form, is here to stay.

PART IV

Chocolate Lore

CHAPTER 15

Cacao: Gift of the New World

Sophie D. Coe

The inhabitants of the Old World first encountered cacao during the fourth voyage of Columbus (1502–4), the only voyage in which he actually landed on the mainland of the New World he had discovered. It was not on the mainland but near an island in the Gulf of Honduras that he came across a Maya trading canoe, a chance meeting that pleased him very much because it gave him a sample of the produce of the country without exposing himself or his men to any risk. It was a huge canoe that they met, eight feet wide and as long as a galley, carrying 25 men and an unspecified quantity of women and children, who were sheltered by a palm leaf roof amidships. After describing their clothing, their wooden swords edged with sharp flint blades, and their maize beer, the chronicler mentions some nuts that they carried on board. "They seemed to hold these nuts at great price; for when they were brought on board the ship together with their goods, I observed that when any of those nuts fell, they all stooped to pick it up, as if an eye had fallen from their heads" (Morrison, 1963, 327).

This should not be read as the Old World's first encounter with chocoholics. The explanation for the respect with which those nuts were treated is much simpler. The Columbus account was using information learned later in Mexico when they say that the nuts were the same as those used as money in Mexico. Thus, the Mayas scrambling around for the nuts under their feet were behaving exactly as Columbus and his men would have done, had someone thrown a handful of coins at their feet. But European coins could not be converted into a variety of tasty and nourishing beverages, nor would they have deteriorated after long storage. This latter quality was considered a great virtue by some of the sixteenth-century moralizers who were always happy to draw edifying lessons from the phenomena coming out of the New World. "Oh happy coin, which gives the human race a smooth and profitable drink, and frees its owners from the darkest plague of avarice, because it can neither be buried nor kept for a long time" (Martir de Anglería, 1944, 393).

The Columbus account does not call the nuts by name, but that is not to be wondered at, because verbal communication between the occupants of the canoe and the Spaniards must have been minimal. By the time Gonzalo Fernandez de Oviedo was traveling in Nicaragua during the second decade of the sixteenth century, he knew what the nuts were called, cacao; he knew how to make them into a drink; and he describes his Italian friend Master Nicolá frying up a mess of fish and eggs in cacao butter (Oviedo, 1959, 117: 272).

We do not know exactly when the word *cacao* was introduced into Spanish, but it is an important clue to the history of cacao and opens to us the long vista of the use and development of cacao among the civilizations of the New World. Cacao did not just happen to be there for the Europeans to pick up and make something of; it was the product of millennia of indigenous experimentation and cultivation.

The word *cacao* is not Mayan. It comes from another language family, Mixe-Zoquean, which is rather marginal today but seems to have contributed many words having to do with civilized life to the languages of Meso-America, as the high culture area of Mexico and Central America is technically called. These words include the terms for paper, writing, and certain maize preparations. It is tempting to think that Mixe-Zoquean was the language of the Olmecs, considered the "mother culture" of that part of the world, and that the Olmecs introduced the growing and consumption of cacao into Meso-America during the second and first millennia B.C. along with the other components of civilized life.

I do not speak of introducing cacao inadvertently. The botanical history of cacao is as complex as its etymology. The greatest concentration of wild species of cacao is found in the Amazon-Orinoco drainage of South America, so that is its most probable hearth of domestication. As far as we know, nobody in South America ever did anything with the seed except nibble at the sweet-sour white coating that surrounds them in their pod and possibly eat a raw seed or two. How *Theobroma cacao*, as Linneaus named it, made its way up the coasts to Meso-America we do not know. The seed loses its germinating power very rapidly, so that a gradual progress is more likely than a single long voyage by missionaries to or from the Olmec.

The first archaeological record for the use of cacao comes from the south coast of Guatemala. An archaeologist digging near Santa Lucia Cotzumalhuapa found a rectangular platform, with ceremonially buried vases full of cacao beans at each corner. He dates his find as going back to the first half of the fifth century A.D. The hot and humid lowlands of the Pacific coast of Guatemala were prime cacao growing areas at the time of the Spanish Conquest, and the province of Soconusco, just to the west, was coveted by the Aztecs for the superb quality of the cacao raised there. In the eighteenth century, Soconusco cacao was considered so fine that it was reserved for the use of the Spanish royal family.

We do not know what language was spoken on the Pacific coast of Guatemala at that time, as uninscribed potsherds do not generally talk. More extensive records of cacao use come to us from the Classic Maya, who lived in southern Mexico, Belize, and parts of Guatemala, Honduras, and El Salvador, between the fourth and ninth centuries A.D. We know about the Classic Maya and their use of cacao because their potsherds do talk. We know about Maya cacao because of one of the most astonishing intellectual breakthroughs of the past 30 years. We know because we can now read Maya hieroglyphic writing. In fact, we can "read" up to 80 percent of the hieroglyphs, read them in the sense of knowing the sounds the signs stand for; what the sounds mean in another matter. But there is a hieroglyph that stands for the sounds "ca-ca-w," and what that meant to the Classic Maya is what it means to us.

The hieroglyph appears on the decorated cylindrical pottery vessels that are part of the tomb furnishings of the Maya elite, along with carved jades, stingray spines, jaguar bones, pearls, and all the other accoutrements of the Maya nobility. The vessels are painted with scenes of warfare, palace life, or Maya gods. Some of them are also inscribed with the name of the owner, and some with the name of the artist. There was a king whose name may have been Cacao, but that reading now seems to be in doubt. We shall have to wait and see. There is no doubt whatever that cacao moved in high circles indeed among the Classic Maya.

Unfortunately, the hieroglyphs do not tell us how the cacao was consumed. For that we must turn from the inscriptions to the paintings on the vases. One of the most famous Maya vases is the one in the Princeton Art Museum, which depicts what seems to be a palace scene, although we know that most of the participants are gods. There is an old gentleman wearing a flowered hat and seated on a throne, two fantastically dressed figures preparing to sacrifice a third, and a bevy of lovely maidens, one of whom holds a cylindrical vessel and pours the liquid from it into another cylindrical vessel at her feet. This same gesture of pouring from one vessel to another shows up in conquest period Aztec manuscripts, labeled as cacao making. The pouring produced the foam, considered the delicacy of delicacies, the sign of quality, and the object of many complicated culinary operations of skimming, reserving, and replacing. I think we may assume that the young lady on the Princeton vase was making a foamy cacao drink and that this was a common occurrence in the palaces of the rulers of the Maya city-states.

We shall probably never know the esoteric recipes the Maya nobility were regaled with. The Classic Maya came to a mysterious end some 650 years before the Spanish Conquest, although there were still plenty of humbler Maya around when the Spaniards arrived. For concrete accounts of elite use of cacao, we must now turn to Spanish eyewitness accounts of the customs of the Aztecs.

It is 1520, and the soldiers of Hernan Cortez are in Tenochtítlan, the present Mexico City, witnessing the meal of the Aztec emperor whom we know as Montezuma but who should correctly be called Motecuhzoma Xocoyotzin "the

Younger." The chronicler is Bernal Díaz del Castillo who was there but wrote long after the fact:

From time to time they brought him, in cup-shaped vessels of pure gold, a certain drink made from cacao which they say he took when he was going to visit his wives, and at the time he took no heed of it, but what I did see was that they brought over fifty great jugs of good cacao frothed up, and he drank of that, and the women served this drink to him with great reverence. (Díaz del Castillo, 1910, 2: 64)

Even in this brief quotation, two preparations of cacao are mentioned, the aphrodisiac and the other one. Motecuhzoma no more used cacao in one way only than we use cacao in one way today.

Given the obviously important place of cacao in Aztec culture, we expect to find qualities of information on it in the great ethnography compiled by the Franciscan Bernardino de Sahagún shortly after the conquest, and indeed, we do. Chapter 13 of Book Eight lists the food of the lords, describing several hundred dishes—a far cry from the usual picture people have of the food of strange tribes, who are usually thought of as eating like the beasts of the field, wolfing down everything edible available. Admittedly, this is the food of the lords; the food of the plebeians was quite a different matter, and the Spaniards were expressing their amazement at how little food the humbler folk consumed. Even Motecuhzoma had puritanical moments when he demanded to eat the hard, rough foods his soldiers ate, rather than the delicate foods of other kings. But when he wanted them, there were many different kinds of cacao available.

Then, stretched out within his house, he finished with his chocolate—blue-green, made of tender cacao; chocolate made with wild honey; chocolate made with flowers, with blue-green vanilla; chili-red chocolate; chocolate with [uitztecol] flowers; pink chocolate; black chocolate; white chocolate. (Dibble and Anderson, Book 8, 39; translated MDC Connors, 1959–1982)

Do not be alarmed at the mention of blue-green chocolate and vanilla. The Aztecs were fond of flowery language, and they ranked colors differently from ourselves. Blue-green was for the Aztecs the color of everything good and desirable. If they had given out paper stars as rewards for their children, their equivalent of our gold star would have been blue-green.

According to Sahagún, cacao, at least in some formulations, was drunk mainly at the end of banquets. The noble women, who ate separately, were not given cacao but a gruel of chian, *Salvia hispanica*, with a top dressing of chili peppers. Perhaps it was the aphrodisiac variety that was denied to the ladies, although it is possible that cacao was completely forbidden for women.

The most common addition to the after-dinner chocolate of the Aztec nobility was *xochinacaztli*, the flower of *Cymbopetalum penduliflorum*, also called the divine ear spice. This is described by Popenoe (1916, 405) as tasting like "black pepper with the addition of a resinous bitterness." Others have said that it tastes rather like nutmeg, although it was replaced with cinnamon by the Spaniards. This was by no means the only possible addition. The one most familiar to us is *tlilxochitl*, the fragrant cured fruit of *Vanilla planifolia*, the vanilla orchid. *Mecaxochitl*, the flower of *Piper amalago*, a New World relative of *Piper nigrum*, the Old World plant that produces black pepper, was another possibility. One could use the flowers of a New World marigold, *Tagetes lucida*, which is not to be confused with the Old World marigold, *Calendula*, or with the strong-smelling *Tagetes* marigold sold for bedding purposes in the springtime. The seeds of *piztle*, *Calocarpum mammosum*, could be added to give the flavor of bitter almonds. The sweet and tasty seeds of *pochotl*, *Ceiba* spp., were mixed in equal parts with cacao beans to make a drink that was said to be extremely fattening. Achiote, *Bixa orellana*, was used for color and flavor and was probably the coloring matter in the red chocolate Sahagún mentioned.

When the Spaniards commented on how little Aztec commoners ate, it is not clear if they meant total consumption or eating as opposed to drinking. A large part of Aztec nourishment came from an endless variety of maize gruels that were drunk rather than eaten. This is a kind of food that is totally alien to us today, having made its last appearance in the chapters of turn-of-the-century cookbooks that dealt with sickroom food. It was perfectly familiar to the sixteenth-century Spaniards, who had their *gachas* and *poleadas* at home and found nothing odd about the Aztec *atolli*.

The base of most Aztec gruels was maize. It could be ground green, ripe, or ripe and toasted. The most common maize preparation and the Aztec staff of life was the tortilla, which was made of maize cooked and soaked in lime water to remove the outer skin, ground into dough, patted into cakes, and toasted. If you did not make your dough into tortillas, you could dilute it with water, cook it, and produce another kind of *atolli*. Ground cacao was added to all these gruels to step them up a bit.

The stress on the use of cacao as elite food is contradicted by the inclusion of cacao among the rations of the Aztec army. These included "toasted grains of maize, maize flour, bean flour, crisp toasted tortillas, tamales baked in the sun, great loads of chilli, cakes of ground cacao, all of this in large quantities" (Duran, 1964, 202).

Cacao followed the Aztecs or young Aztec noblemen, at any rate, to their graves as funerary offerings. In fact, cacao had a strong connection with the divine, being one of the discoveries of the culture hero Quetzalcoatl, along with "jadestone, fine turquoise, and gold, silver, redshell, whiteshell" (Bierhorst, 1984, 27) and the plumes of various birds.

Where did the Aztecs get the cacao that they consumed in such quantity and which was so important to them? The dry and chilly Mexican uplands were hardly the place for growing it. It had to come by trade and as tribute from the hot humid lowland provinces the Aztecs controlled. One of the main sources was the province of Soconusco, already mentioned. Because of their control of this valuable resource, the inhabitants of Soconusco were famous for their wealth and arrogance, and it was no mere pose, for they had beaten back the armies of Motecuhzoma the Elder, an ancestor of Motecuhzoma the Younger, whose chocolate drinking habits were described above. Whether trade or tribute, it is estimated that 980 loads of cacao were received in the Aztec capital every year. A load, what could be carried by a human being, because the Aztecs had no beasts of burden, was three *xiquipiles* (a *xiquipil* was 20 *zontles*, and a *zontle* was 400 cacao beans). Therefore, a load was 24,000 cacao beans. One hundred of these beans could buy you a small cotton mantle; 12 would get you the services of a prostitute if you used the beans as coins instead of consuming them.

If 980 loads of cacao were received yearly, there was either a great deal of it in storage, and it kept better than we have been led to believe, or the account by Herrera y Tordesillas of what might be called the "Great Cacao Bank Robbery of 1520" greatly exaggerates the wealth of Motecuhzoma:

[T]hey [the Spaniards] went into a cacao storage house of Montezuma where there were more than 40,000 loads which were great riches then, and worth more now, because each load is worth forty castellanos. . . . [T]he cacao was in containers so big that six men could not reach around them; they were plastered outside and in and arranged in rows. . . . . [T]hat night they stole six hundred loads and only emptied six containers. (Herrera y Tordesillas, 1601, 1: 280)

Cacao was also available in the great Aztec markets, presumably to anyone who could pay the price, be he noble, merchant, or foreigner. From the text of Sahagún it seems that there were two kinds of cacao sellers, perhaps roughly corresponding to our classification of retail and wholesale. It should be pointed out that there is no gender in Aztec, and making the retail seller female and the wholesale seller male is a modern literary device.

The seller of fine chocolate [is] one who grinds, who provides people with drink, with repasts. She grinds cacao [beans]; she crushes, breaks, pulverizes them. She chooses, selects, separates them. She drenches, soaks, steeps them. She adds water sparingly, conservatively; aerates it, filters it, strains it, pours it back and forth; she makes it form a head, makes it foam; she removes the head, makes it thicken, makes it dry, pours water in, stirs water into it.
     The cacao seller [is] a cacao owner, an owner of cacao fields, an owner of cacao trees; or an importer, a traveler with merchandise, a traveler or retailer who sells in single lots.
     The good cacao seller sells [cacao beans that are] developed, full, round—each one round; firm; each kind selected, chosen. . . .
     The bad cacao seller, [the bad] cacao dealer, the deluder counterfeits cacao. He sells cacao beans which are placed in [hot] ashes, toasted, made full in the fire . . . [with] amaranth seed dough, wax, avocado pits he counterfeits cacao; he covers this over with cacao bean hulls; he places this in the cacao bean shells. (Dibble and Anderson, Book 10, 65)

Despite the deplorable activities of the bad cacao dealer, cacao was an instant hit with the Spanish conquistadors, who seem to have needed only a little urging to try new dishes.

The two Aztecs tasted the different foods and when the Spaniards saw them eating, they too, began to eat turkey, stew, and maize cakes, and enjoy the food with much laughing and sporting. But when the time came to drink the chocolate that had been brought to them, that most highly prized drink of the Indian, they were filled with fear. When the Indians saw that they dared not drink they tasted from all the gourds, and the Spaniards then quenched their thirst with chocolate and realized what a refreshing drink it was. (Duran, 1964, 266)

Indeed, some of the Spaniards became so enthusiastic that they claimed that drinking chocolate prevented snakebite and that one cup of it in the morning was all the food you needed a day, even when traveling. With this sort of publicity, and the added fillip of being a medium of exchange, as well as a commodity, cacao was ready to begin its journey of conquest from the conquered New World to the conquering Old World.

The impression I would like to leave you with at the end of this sketchiest summary of the early history of cacao is of the importance of avoiding the Europe-centered, and rather racist, view that is so tempting when dealing with the achievements of the New World. The New World crops were not just there waiting to be taken to Europe to have something made out of them. They were the products of complex and deeply rooted civilizations that had selected and improved them over the millennia and that utilized them in a multitude of highly sophisticated ways. When I said that cacao was the gift of the New World, I meant that in the field of plant domestication, as in so many other fields, the New World was the equal of the Old.

REFERENCES

Bierhorst, John. *Four Masterworks of American Indian Literature*. Tucson: University of Arizona Press, 1984.

Díaz del Castillo, Bernal. *The True History of the Conquest of New Spain*. London: Hakluyt Society, 1910.

Dibble, C. E., and A.J.O. Anderson, trans. *General History of the Things of New Spain: Florentine Codex*. Santa Fe, New Mex.: School of American Research,1950–82.

Duran, Diego. *The Aztecs: The History of the Indies of New Spain*. New York: Orion Press, 1964.

Herrera y Tordesillas, Antonio. *Historia general de los hechos de los Castellanos*. Madrid: Imprenta Real, 1601.

Martir de Anglería, Pedro. *Décadas del neuvo mundo*. Buenos Aires: Bajel, 1944.

Morrison, Samuel Eliot, trans. *Journals and Other Documents on the Life and Voyages of Christopher Columbus*. New York: Heritage Press, 1963.

Oviedo, Gonzalo Fernandez de. *Historia general y natural de las Indias*. Vol. 117. Biblioteca de Autores Españoles, Madrid: 1959.

Popenoe, Wilson. "Batido and Other Guatemalan Beverages Prepared from Cacao." *American Anthropologist*, N.S., 21: 1916: 405.

CHAPTER 16

The Social and Economic History of Cacao Cultivation in Colonial Soconusco, New Spain

Janine Gasco

When the Spaniards arrived in the province of Soconusco (what is today coastal Chiapas, Mexico) in 1524, they found a thriving cacao industry. At that time the natives of Soconusco were paying an annual tribute to the Aztecs that included over 10,000 pounds of cacao beans (Castillo Farreras 1974; Gasco and Voorhies 1989). Because cacao could only be cultivated in certain hot, lowland regions, the Aztecs, who lived on the high central plateau, had to rely on trade with or tribute from lowland regions to satisfy the demand for cacao. It is likely that the underlying motive for the Aztec conquest of Soconusco in the late 1400s was simply to gain access to the high-quality cacao produced there. The Spaniards apparently took their cue from the Aztecs, because within 25 years of the conquest, the natives of Soconusco were paying tribute to the Spaniards in cacao. For the next 200 hundred years, until the mid-eighteenth century, the Indian inhabitants of Soconusco continued to pay part of their yearly cacao crop in tribute to the Spanish Crown.

PREHISPANIC CACAO CULTIVATION AND USE

Little is known about the origins of cacao cultivation in Middle America. Even less is known about social and economic aspects of cacao cultivation, although we do know that cacao played an important role in the social, economic, and religious spheres of pre-Hispanic Meso-American cultures.

It is frequently argued that *Theobroma cacao* is a native to South America, although there continues to be some disagreement about its exact point of origin (see Coe and Coe 1996; Gómez-Pompa, Flores, and Fernández 1990; Young 1994). Some researchers argue that the Upper Orinoco basin was the original homeland of cacao (Stone 1984, 69), while others point to the upper reaches of the Amazon near the Colombia-Ecuador border (Bergmann 1959, citing Chees-man 1944). Regardless of where *Theobroma cacao* originated, it was only in Middle America that cacao was cultivated prior to the arrival of the Spaniards (Stone 1984, 69).

It is thought that cacao was under cultivation in Middle America by the Late Preclassic period (ca. 600 B.C.–A.D. 300) and perhaps earlier (Coe and Coe 1996, 36ff.). To examine the history of cacao use in Middle America, archaeo-logists have had to rely heavily on depictions of the cacao tree or cacao pods on stone monuments, on pottery, or in painted murals because other, more direct evidence (such as the actual cacao beans themselves) is generally not preserved. Nevertheless, wood, rind, and seeds from cacao trees have been tentatively identified at sites in Belize (McKillop 1994), counterfeit cacao beans were recovered from a cache beneath a temple in southern Guatemala dating to the Early Classic period (ca. A.D. 250–600) (Bove 1993), and cacao residues have been identified from a Classic period (ca. A.D. 250–900) vessel discovered at Rio Azul, Guatemala (Hall et al. 1990). Moreover, recent breakthroughs in the decipherment of Classic period Maya writing has led to the identification of glyphs that refer to cacao (see Coe and Coe 1996, 43ff.). Depictions of cacao include a Late Preclassic stone monument at the Soconusco site of Izapa that appears to have a representation of a cacao pod on it (Lowe, Lee, and Espinosa 1982, 52), a cacao tree on a mural at Teotihuacan from the Early Classic period (ca. A.D. 400–500). Cacao pods appear on sculpture from Classic period sites on the Pacific coastal plain of Guatemala, from El Tajín, Veracruz, and at Chichen Itza in Yucatan; and pottery vessels in the shapes of cacao pods have been reported from Veracruz and coastal Guatemala (Thomp-son 1956: 101–2). Finally, Pre-Columbian and early colonial books or codices produced by Indian scribes and artists sometimes contain depictions of cacao.

While archaeological evidence suggests a long history of cacao use in Meso-America, for more precise information about its production and use, it is useful to turn to early colonial accounts. At the time of the Spanish Conquest, cacao served as a medium of exchange, and it had considerable ritualistic and ceremonial importance. An early Spanish observer noted that there was nothing that could not be bought with cacao beans: One could acquire a rabbit for 10 beans, a slave for 100 beans, and a prostitute for 8 to 10 beans (Oviedo y Váldez 1944, 246).

Cacao also had ritual and ceremonial importance in pre-Hispanic times, and in many areas, it continues to be used in ritual or ceremonial contexts. Cacao has been used as an offering to gods and idols, to decorate altars, to celebrate birth, puberty, and marriage, in agricultural ceremonies, and during sacrificial ceremonies (Thompson 1956, 102–6). Cacao also was (and is) thought to have medicinal qualities (Orellana 1987, 246ff; Oviedo y Váldez 1944, 252–54; Roys 1976, 33, 136, 222; Sahagún, 1964, 155; Thompson 1956, 106–7).

Cacao was consumed in the pre-Hispanic period as a beverage. Typically, the roasted cacao beans were ground and mixed with maize, chile, and achiote (a red coloring), although there were apparently numerous recipes for the beverage (see Coe and Coe 1996, 86ff). The mixture was agitated, producing a froth that was a delicacy (Sahagún 1961, 93). Spaniards found the traditional beverage repulsive. One early observer spoke of it with disgust, arguing that because of the color and texture of the beverage, the Indians were drinking it as if it were blood (Oviedo y Váldez 1944, 247). Another thought it only fit for pigs (Benzoni 1970, 150).

The available evidence indicates that in some areas, consumption of the cacao beverage in the pre-Hispanic period was limited to elites. This may have been true in highland areas like Central Mexico and highland Guatemala, where cacao could not be grown (Sahagún 1961, 93; Orellana 1984, 78). In Yucatan, where it could be grown in small quantities, the beverage was reportedly also consumed by commoners (Tozzer 1941, 90). Perhaps restrictions had more to do with availability than with any widespread custom that it be limited only to elites.

Although there is little evidence regarding the actual mechanics of cacao cultivation in the prehistoric period, the nature of production is mentioned in some early colonial accounts. In some areas the native nobility controlled production. For example, the Tzutujil Maya, a highland Guatemala group, had their own cacao orchards in the Pacific lowlands that were cared for by their retainers (Orellana 1984, 70). In the Yucatan, private ownership of cacao orchards is reported (Tozzer 1941). In other cacao-producing areas like Soconusco, we know only that communities were paying cacao in tribute to foreign powers, but we know nothing about the internal organization of production.

THE COLONIAL PERIOD CACAO INDUSTRY

The arrival of the Spaniards brought about many changes in the cacao industry. One change was that any existing restrictions that limited consumption to elites were eliminated. As a result, even though the native population was dying at a rapid rate due to the introduction of Old World diseases to which it had no immunity, demands for cacao increased, driving up the cacao prices (Torquemada 1969, 620). Eventually, the Spaniards, too, began to consume cacao with a new recipe in which sugar was substituted for maize, and vanilla and cinnamon replaced chile and achiote (Wickizer 1951, 305). By the early seventeenth century, demands for cacao, both in Europe and the Americas, were on the rise.

By the early to mid-seventeenth century, large-scale cacao production was well under way on South American plantations (Arcila Farías 1950; Erneholm 1948, 41ff). The introduction of large quantities of the South American cacaos in the international market resulted in an overall lowering of cacao prices (Gibson 1964, 349). However, the highly desirable but more difficult to grow and increasingly scarce Central American cacaos continued to bring high prices throughout the colonial period.

THE CACAO INDUSTRY IN COLONIAL SOCONUSCO

In the first decades following the conquest, the natives of Soconusco suffered heavy population losses. The population declined from an estimated 80,000 to 90,000 before the conquest to approximately 5,000 people in 1575, a decline of over 90 percent (Gasco 1989b). At the same time, annual tribute payments that had been 200 *cargas* before the conquest (a *carga* of cacao is equal to 24,000 cacao beans and weighs approximately 50 pounds) had been doubled to 400 *cargas* over the same period of time (Gasco 1989a). In other words, the combined effects of population loss and increased tribute meant that per capita tribute payments had increased substantially in the first decades of colonial rule. On the other hand, if the number of cacao trees under cultivation remained roughly the same from pre-Hispanic to early colonial periods, then the number of trees per capita also would have increased by similar proportions. In sum, the first 50 years following the conquest must have seen significant changes in the organization of cacao cultivation in Soconusco and elsewhere.

Cacao continued to be an important product of the Soconusco throughout the colonial period, and the key to understanding how the native population of Soconusco was integrated into the colonial economic system is the cacao industry. Cacao was the most important commodity produced by the inhabitants of Soconusco that linked them with the world economy through both the tribute system and commercial ties with Spanish merchants.

The cacao grown in colonial Soconusco was the superior *criollo* variety, and it was always considered to be of the highest quality (Arcila Farías 1950, 42; Erneholm 1948, 35; MacLeod 1973, 237). The available evidence indicates that in both Guatemalan and Veracruz markets buyers were willing to pay premium prices for Soconusco cacao (Lerdo de Tejada 1967).[1] The high status of Soconusco cacao is further suggested by the fact that some 300 years after the Spanish Conquest the Spanish royal family was still receiving its household chocolate from Soconusco.[2]

While there has not been total agreement about the general organization of cacao production in colonial Soconusco, the evidence indicates that the actual production was controlled primarily by natives (Gasco 1989a). The commercial aspects of the cacao trade, however, were controlled by Spaniards. There are frequent complaints in documents that Spanish merchants were paying Indian cacao producers low prices for their cacao and at the same time charging high prices for the merchandise they brought to the province.

Archaeological evidence from excavations at the predominantly Indian Soconusco town of Ocelocalco, occupied between the late sixteenth century and the mid-eighteenth century, suggests two important changes in socioeconomic organization at Ocelocalco during the course of the colonial period (Gasco

1993). First, there seems to have been a general decline in the use of expensive imported goods at Ocelocalco as the colonial period progressed. Second, there was a decrease in socioeconomic differences among households as the colonial period progressed. That is, differences between rich and poor seem to have decreased later in the colonial period.

To better understand why such changes might have occurred, documents regarding the organization of cacao production in Soconusco communities have been analyzed. The earliest detailed information about the colonial cacao industry in Soconusco comes from the last decades of the sixteenth century. By that time, the demographic situation in Soconusco had stabilized to some extent. The native population had begun to recover, although this was only to be a temporary recovery (Gasco 1989b). By many accounts, the cacao industry was in decline (MacLeod 1973, 68), but at least one observer noted that the natives of Soconusco (as well as those in other cacao-producing areas) were relatively well off economically because of the cacao trade (Pineda 1925, 341–42).

In 1582 a Spanish official, Francisco de Santiago, was sent to the Soconusco to investigate the cacao industry there. Although he presumably visited and reported on all Soconusco towns, only one of his reports, his investigation of Guilocingo (near the modern town of Villa Comaltitlan), is known to have survived.[3] Santiago's report of Guilocingo included a census in which all household members were counted, an inventory of cacao holdings by individual, an evaluation of the fairness of the tribute system, and a revised tribute assessment based on his findings. This document is analyzed in some detail elsewhere (Gasco 1990). Briefly, Santiago reported that Guilocingo was a small town with 46 total residents, including children. Eighteen of Guilocingo's residents were counted as full tributaries and thus eligible to be taxed (a tributary was generally a male head of household). Of these 18 tributaries, 15 owned a cacao orchard. Individual holdings ranged from 200 to 3,200 trees. Santiago's revised tribute assessment raised tribute payments for some community members and lowered payments for others. Although never specifically stated, it is clear from the record that tribute assessments were based on the number of cacao trees an individual had. Moreover, Santiago employed what was basically a regressive tax: The more trees an individual owned, the lower the tribute payments were in number of cacao beans paid per tree. This was presumably an effort to increase production, although we cannot rule out the possibility that the owners of the largest orchards were able to put some pressure on the official. It should also be noted that the owners of the two largest orchards were also community officials.

A much less detailed report of cacao holdings in Guilocingo appears in a 1729 census document.[4] This census lists names and ages of all community members, and it notes whether each family had a house and cacao orchard (number of trees is not specified, however). By 1729, Guilocingo had a total population of only 25 people, and only 3 of 11 households had a cacao orchard.

By 1820–21 the situation in Guilocingo had improved significantly. Not only had the population increased to almost 300 people,[5] but the cacao industry also had been revived. An 1821 census records 63 households,[6] and a second document contains an agricultural survey in which 62 community members who owned cacao trees are named together with the number of cacao trees they owned (trees are classified as either being old, young, or seedlings).[7] This indicates that 98 percent of households now had a cacao orchard. These documents, particularly the more detailed 1582 report and the 1820–21 documents, allow for the identification of several significant changes in the Soconusco cacao industry from the late sixteenth century to the end of the colonial period.

In 1582, 60 years after the Spanish conquest of Soconusco, the ownership of cacao orchards was in the hands of individuals, and individual ownership of cacao orchards continued to be the rule into the nineteenth century. There is no mention of community cacao holdings in any of the documents I have seen. In 1582 the majority of Indian tributaries in Guilocingo did own some cacao trees, but there was a very unequal distribution of trees among community members. Moreover, local political leaders owned the largest orchards, and they may have had some influence in determining tribute rates. There were a total of 15,800 cacao trees under cultivation in the entire community, an average of almost 350 trees per person.

In the first decades of the eighteenth century, both the population and the cacao industry in Guilocingo were in decline. The population reached its lowest point of the colonial period, and a smaller proportion of community members had a cacao orchard than had been the case in the late sixteenth century.

One hundred years later, on the eve of Independence in 1820, the situation in Guilocingo had changed dramatically, both in terms of population size and in the relative well-being of the cacao industry. Almost all households in Guilocingo held some cacao trees. When compared to the 1582 data, the distribution of cacao trees in 1820 was markedly different. First, differences among individuals in terms of the number of trees owned had decreased substantially. Whereas in 1582 the number of trees owned by individuals ranged from 200 to 3,200, in 1820 the number ranged from 10 to 780. A second difference is that the number of cacao trees per capita had declined from approximately 350 in 1582 to approximately 50 in 1820. Thus, there was a much more equitable distribution of cacao trees in the nineteenth century, but there were fewer trees per person.

This kind of change in the per capita ownership of cacao trees, together with a more equitable distribution of trees, fits the kinds of changes seen in the archaeological record remarkably well. The overall decrease in per capita ownership presumably would result in an overall decrease at the community level in consumption of high-cost goods. Similarly, the more equitable distribution of cacao trees seen in the 1820 agricultural survey, when compared to the 1582 distribution, presumably would result in fewer economic differences among households.

These changes may have taken place because of the nature of cacao cultivation in colonial Soconusco (and presumably other cacao-producing areas); specific conditions at this time may have led cacao farmers to prefer smaller orchards. There are frequent reports in colonial documents about yearly fluctuations in the availability of labor, about crop loss to disease and pests, about periodic epidemics that prevent successful harvest, and about natural disasters, including droughts and hurricanes that destroyed the cacao groves. Large orchards may have been much more vulnerable to these unpredictable and uncontrollable forces. In the long run, perhaps it simply was not worth the effort to become a large-scale producer because potential losses were so much greater. On the other hand, small-scale production would have held fewer risks. It must have been relatively easy to become a small-scale producer. All one needed was a few cacao beans and a small parcel of land. We know that population density was always low in colonial Soconusco. There seems to have been little pressure for land. Whereas there were chronic labor shortages in colonial Soconusco, most families in Guilocingo in 1820 had orchards of 300 cacao trees or less. Orchards of this size could almost certainly be cared for relying on only family labor.

In conclusion, 300 years of colonial rule saw dramatic population decline and presumably equally dramatic changes in at least some aspects of the cacao industry in the province of Soconusco. The first major change may have been a marked increase in the average number of cacao trees owned by individuals as a result of the heavy population loss that followed the conquest. Without additional information, it is impossible to determine whether the inequitable distribution of cacao trees recorded in Guilocingo in 1582 was rooted in pre-Hispanic socioeconomic differences or if it was a colonial phenomenon. By the first decades of the eighteenth century the population of Guilocingo, and the community cacao orchards were in decline. Nevertheless, the community did survive, and within less than 100 years (by 1820) the population had increased 10-fold, and the number of cacao trees under cultivation had almost returned to sixteenth-century levels. Whatever the roots of the inequities of the sixteenth-century distribution of cacao trees, by the early nineteenth century, a much more equitable system seems to have been in place.

As a postscript, the cacao industry of Soconusco was to suffer further set-backs in the latter part of the nineteenth century when large-scale coffee cultivation was introduced to the region, and it became the predominant crop (Helbig, 1964; Spenser, 1984). Today there is renewed interest by the Mexican government in reviving the cacao industry, and the people of Soconusco continue to take great pride in the quality of their cacao.

NOTES

1. AGI AG 25, "Certificación de los precios . . . de los tributos reales," 1667–77.

2. AGI AG 850, 1820 letter.

3. AGI Escribania de Camara 331-A, "Provisión a Francisco de Santiago . . ." f. 1527–1545v.

4. AGCAA 3.16 359 4628.

5. Part of the increase was undoubtedly due to the fact that surviving members of at least two nearby towns that had been destroyed or abandoned in the mid-18th century had apparently relocated to Guilocingo (Gerhard, 1993, 171; AGCA A3.16 362 4693).

6. AGCA A1.44 46.547.

7. AGCA A1 313 2188.

REFERENCES

Arcila Farías, Eduardo. 1950. *Comercio entre Venezuela y México en los siglos XVI y XVIII.* Mexico City, Mexico: El Colegio de Mexico.

Benzoni, Gerolomo. 1970. *History of the New World.* Trans. W. H. Smith. New York: Burt Franklin Publishing Co.

Bergmann, J. F. 1959. *The Cultural Geography of Cacao in Aboriginal America and Its Commercialization in Early Guatemala.* Ph.D. diss., University of California, Los Angeles.

Bove, Frederick J. 1993. The Terminal Formative–Early Classic Transition. In *The Balberta Project: The Terminal Formative–Early Classic Transition on the Pacific Coast of Guatemala,* ed. Frederick J. Bove, Sonia Medrana B., Brenda Lou P., and Barbara Arroyo L. University of Pittsburgh Memoirs in Latin American Archaelogy, No. 6. Pittsburgh: University of Pittsburgh, 177–93.

Castillo Farreras, Victor. 1974. Matrícula de tribuots, comentarios, paleografía y versión. *Historia de México,* vols. 27–30.

Coe, Sophie D., and Michael D. Coe. 1996. *The True History of Chocolate.* New York: Thames and Hudson.

Erneholm, Ivor. 1948. *Cacao Production of South America.* Meddelande fran Goteborgs Hogskolas Geografiska Institution 34. Gothenburg, Sweden: C. R. Holmqvists Boktryckeri AB.

Gasco, Janine. 1989a. The Colonial Economy in the Province of Soconusco. In *Ancient Trade and Tribute: Economies of the Soconusco Region of Mesoamerica,* ed. Barbara Voorhies. Salt Lake City: University of Utah Press. 283–303.

Gasco, Janine. 1989b. Una visión de conjunto de la historia demográfica y económica del Soconusco colonial. *Mesoamérica* 18: 371–99.

Gasco, Janine. 1990. Población y economía en el Soconusco durante el siglo XVI: El ejemplo del pueblo de Guilocingo, 1582. *Mesoamérica* 20: 249–65.

Gasco, Janine. 1993. Socioeconomic Change within Native Society in Colonial Soconusco, New Spain. In *Ethnohistory and Archaeology: Approaches to Postcontact Change in the Americas,* ed. J. Daniel Rogers and Samuel Wilson. N.Y.: Plenum Press. 163–180.

Gasco, Janine, and Barbara Voorhies. 1989. The Ultimate Tribute: The Role of the Soconusco as an Aztec Tributary. In *Ancient Trade and Tribute: Economies of the Soconusco Region of Mesoamerica,* ed. Barbara Voorhies. Salt Lake City: University of Utah Press. 48–94.

Gerhard, Peter. 1993. *The Southeast Frontier of New Spain.* Rev. Norman: University of Oklahoma Press.

Gibson, Charles. 1964. *The Aztecs under Spanish Rule: A History of the Indians of the Valley of Mexico 1519–1820.* Stanford: Stanford University Press.

Gómez-Pompa, Arturo, José Salvador Flores, and Mario Aliphat Fernández. 1990. The

Sacred Cacao Groves of the Maya. *Latin American Antiquity* 1, no. 3: 247–57.

Hall, G. D., S. M. Tarka, W. J. Hurst, D. Stuart, and R. E. W. Adams. 1990. Cacao Residues in Ancient Maya Vessels from Rio Azul, Guatemala. *American Antiquity* 55: 138–43.

Helbig, Carlos. 1964. *El Soconusco y su zona cafetalera en Chiapas*. Chiapas, Mexico: Instituto de Ciencias y Artes de Chiapas, Tuxtla Gutierrez.

Lerdo de Tejada, Miguel. 1967. *Comercio exterior de Mexico desde la conquista hasta hoy*. Mexico City: Banco Nacional de Comercio Exterior.

Lowe, Gareth, Thomas A. Lee, and Eduardo Martinez Espinosa. 1982. *Izapa: An Introduction to the Ruins and Monuments*. Papers of the New World Archaeological Foundation, No. 31. Provo: Brigham Young University Press.

MacLeod, Murdo. 1973. *Spanish Central America: A Socioeconomic History, 1520–1720*. Berkeley: University of California Press.

McKillop, Heather. 1994. Ancient Maya Tree Cropping: A Viable Subsistence Adaptation for the Island Maya. *Ancient Mesoamerica* 5: 129–40.

Orellana, Sandra. 1984. *The Tzutujil Maya*. Norman: University of Oklahoma Press.

Orellana, Sandra. 1987. *Indian Medicine in Highland Guatemala*. Albuquerque: University of New Mexico Press.

Oviedo y Váldez, Gonzalo de Fernandez de. 1944. *Historia general y natural de las Indias*. Vol. 2. Asunción, Paraguay: Editorial Guarania.

Pineda, Juan de. 1925 Descripción de la provincia de Guatemala. *Sociedad de Geografía e Historia de Guatemala* 1 no. 4: 327–63.

Roys, Ralph L. 1976. *The Ethno-Botany of the Maya*. Philadelphia: Reprint of original by the Institute for the Study of Human Issues.

Sahagún, Fray Bernardo de. 1961. *Florentine Codex: General History of the Things of New Spain. Book 10—The People*. Trans. Charles Dibble and Arthur J. O. Anderson. Monographs of the School of American Research and the Museum of New Mexico, Santa Fe.

Sahagún, 1964. *Florentine Codex: General History of the Things of New Spain. Book 11—The Earthly Things*. Trans. Charles Dibble and Arthur J. O. Anderson. Monographs of the School of American Research and the Museum of New Mexico, Santa Fe.

Spenser, Daniela. 1984. Soconusco: The Formation of a Coffee Economy in Chiapas. In *Other Mexicos: Essays on Regional Mexican History, 1876–1911*, ed. T. Benjamin and W. McNellie. Albuquerque: University of New Mexico Press. 123–40.

Stone, Doris. 1984. Pre-Columbian Migration of *Theobroma cacao* Linnaeus and *Manihot esculenta* Crantz from Northern South America into Mesoamerica: A Partially Hypothetical View. In *Pre-Columbian Plant Migration*, ed. Doris Stone. Papers of the Peabody Museum of Archaeology and Ethnology, vol. 76. Cambridge: Harvard University Press.

Thompson, J. Eric. 1956. Notes on the Use of Cacao in Middle America. *Notes on Middle American Archaeology and Ethnology*, no. 128: 95–116.

Torquemada, Juan de. 1969. *Monarquía Indiana*. Vol. 2. Mexico City: Biblioteca Porrua.

Tozzer, A. M. 1941. *Landa's relación de las cosas de Yucatan*. Papers of the Peabody Museum, No. 18. Cambridge: Harvard University.

Young, Allen M. 1994. *The Chocolate Tree: A Natural History*. Washington, D.C.: Smithsonian Institution Press.

CHAPTER 17

Chocolate—Its Quality and Flavor (Which Is the World's Best Chocolate?)

Charles S. Telly

For anyone, a most important characteristic of a food item is its flavor. The chocolate industry produces a product that has a unique flavor. Chocolate and its complement, cocoa, are used for flavoring many foods such as milk, puddings, cakes, and ice cream. When sugar is added, it becomes part of our most popular confection. Moreover, chocolate has food value and is generally found in emergency rations.

Although, obviously, chocolate is not one of our most important food products, nor even, perhaps, one of our most important flavors, it is one of civilization's most significant indulgences. It is consequential enough that when the Swedish naturalist Linnaeus classified the flora of the world using Greek and Latin names, he said about the cocoa tree, "The fruit supplies the raw product for a delicious, healthy and nourishing drink."[1] And he gave it a Greek botanical name, *Theobroma*, which means "food of the gods." Such a compliment suggests the significance of chocolate in civilization's recent history.

At first blush, it would seem an easy matter to deal with quality and flavor. One would conjecture that chocolate samples would be obtained, and then the taste test would simply determine the quality and flavor. However, there is much more to the problem than that. As one becomes familiar with chocolate, it becomes obvious that its history has much to do with its acceptance and the kind of chocolate people prefer. Moreover, the production and manufacture of the chocolate beans have to do with quality and taste. Further, the manufacturers sell to "coaters" who create their own different chocolates. And added to this, different regions have been indoctrinated to different kinds of chocolate. Finally, the way chocolate is offered for sale directly affects its quality and taste.

EARLY HISTORY

Many industries can be traced back to the Egyptians or some other ancient civilization of the Old World. But the chocolate industry was born in the New World. Although it developed commercially in Europe, its birthright is of the New World since the cocoa tree originally was found only in Central and South America.

In 1519, when Cortez invaded Mexico, the Spanish found the chocolate drink a favorite of the emperor Montezuma II.[2] Since the court favored the drink, Cortez was impressed with its luxury and mystique. His letter to his king refers to "the divine drink which builds up resistance and fights fatigue. A cup of this precious drink permits a man to walk for a whole day without food."[3] This is an interesting assessment that all of Europe was to later believe about chocolate. That is, that it was religious, healthful, exotic, flavorful, and romantic.

Prescott, in his *Conquest of Mexico*, discusses the luxuriousness of the beverage in Montezuma's court:

[T]he emperor [Montezuma] took no other beverage than the chocolate, a potation of chocolate, flavored with vanilla and other spices, and so prepared as to be reduced to a froth of the consistency of honey which gradually dissolved in the mouth. This beverage, if it so could be called, was served in golden goblets with spoons of the same metal or of tortoise shell finely wrought. The emperor was exceedingly fond of it to judge from the quantity—no less than fifty jars or pitchers being prepared for his own daily consumption. Two thousand more were allowed for that of his household.[4]

On his return to Spain after his first expedition to Mexico in 1528, Cortez introduced the chocolate drink. Charles V's court was so favorably impressed that the Spanish kept this drink a secret for nearly a hundred years. It finally spread all over Europe through the monks who went to France and Germany on church business.

EARLY DEVELOPMENT

The beverage cocoa, which we drink today, is not the same as the chocolate of the early Aztecs and Mayas, nor the early Spanish court's drink, although the drink that spread throughout Europe in the seventeenth and eighteenth centuries was very similar to what Cortez had brought over to Europe.

Today's cocoa was discovered in 1828 in Holland by Conrad van Houten, who developed a process for removing fat from the cocoa bean. This fat was called cocoa butter, and what remained was ground into powder and called "cocoa." This powder would mix much more readily with water and milk because it had a much lower fat content.

The cocoa butter (natural fat) had solidifying qualities that allowed for molded chocolate to be prepared and enjoyed. Solid sweet chocolate was made by adding sugar and cocoa to cocoa butter. Apparently, the English were the first to sell solidified chocolate. The Bristol firm of Fry and Sons introduced "eating chocolate" in 1847.[5]

Milk chocolate was a much later invention of the Swiss, probably by Daniel Peters of Bevey, Geneva, in 1876.[6] He combined milk with solid sweet chocolate, and milk chocolate was the result.

THE COCOA TREE—BOTANY

There are approximately 20 species of *Theobroma* known, but *Theobroma cacao* is commercially the most important. Man-made varieties and natural mixing of the species make identification of the different types difficult. The varieties that have come about from the natural and artificial crossbreeding and seed selection that have gone on over the thousands of years that the cocoa tree has been under cultivation are important. There are fundamentally three distinct types: Criollo, Forastero, and Calabacillo.[7]

Of these three types, most botanists are inclined to include the Calabacillo as a Forastero. If this is the case, then there are in fact only two varieties. These two are discussed because each has a distinct individual flavor and color.[8]

The Criollo beans are large, plump, and white or almost white in color. The Forastero beans are smaller, flatter, and purple or heliotrope in color. The Forastero is the more important commercial type. It constitutes 94 to 95 perent of the world's production. The Criollo and a cross of the Criollo command the rest of the world's production. The Criollo commands a higher price from some manufacturers for inclusion in special flavors and blends. The Forastero is the more popular to grow because it is a very hearty tree and is more resistant to diseases. The Criollo, however, is a more delicate tree and subject to canker and bark diseases. Moreover, the Forastero tree produces more pods and more beans per pod than the Criollo. It becomes obvious that the Forastero has so many advantages over the Criollo that few Criollo trees are raised anymore.[9]

A further characteristic of the cocoa tree is its very narrow range. Basically, the tree grows within 10 degrees of the equator. And consequently, the primary producers in the world, as of 1986–87 October–September production forecasts, are the Ivory Coast, 30.2 percent; Brazil, 18.9 percent; Ghana, 11.8 percent; Malaysia, 7.7 percent; Ecuador, 4.1 percent; Colombia, 2.3 percent; Mexico, 2.1 percent; Indonesia, 2.0 percent; and Venezuela, 0.9 percent.[10]

PRODUCTION OF BEANS—FERMENTATION, DRYING, AND STORAGE AS THEY PERTAIN TO FLAVOR

To obtain good chocolate flavors, the three processes that the beans go through after harvesting—namely fermentation, drying, and storage—need to be accomplished carefully.

It should be obvious that good, sound, healthy trees lead to more pods, and more pods lead to more beans. Like other growing plants, sound cultivation techniques are essential. Moreover, the cocoa tree is very prone to diseases and pests. The conscientious and successful farmer will solve these problems each year for a bountiful crop. Given the cultivation, disease, and pest problems, the essential problem to look at is after the harvest and the methods used to put the beans in condition for sale to the cocoa and chocolate manufacturer. Therefore, the assumption will be made that quality beans are harvested from quality trees that have been carefully husbanded.

Fermentation

Specialist, Bernard W. Minifie makes it very clear that good flavor in the final cocoa and chocolate depends on good fermentation.[11] L. Russell Cook is even stronger in his statements when he says:

[W]hat we recognize as chocolate flavor is absent unless both proper fermenting and roasting are performed. Unfermented cocoa does have a taste, of course, and "acceptable" products are made from it, but the flavor is not that to which we refer when, as consumers, we use the word "chocolate." Even an otherwise "acceptable" flavor is a disappointment if it does not produce the taste anticipated when the confection or food is chosen by the consumer.[12]

When asked, "Why must we ferment the beans?" he answers, "Because the public taste does not accept the unfermented cocoa products as good chocolate."[13] Apparently, there is a market for unfermented beans, but it's very small and will not get bigger because although such beans are cheaper, they just do not have as much chocolate flavor.

How did the idea come about to ferment the beans? No one knows.[14] Probably it was to make it easier to eliminate the pulp from the bean, since if the bean is dried with the pulp still adhering, it becomes "gummy, sticky, and extremely difficult to wash."[15] When the pods are fermented, they easily disintegrate and allow the beans to separate from the pulp.

Arthur W. Knapp explains that if there were no fermentation, and the beans were packed straight from the pod in bags and sent to market, they would decompose and become moldy. Therefore, in order for this not to happen, a farmer would dry the beans. However, then he would find that the dried beans have a tendency to absorb moisture from the air and become sticky and then moldy. But if the beans are fermented, the beans diminish to pulp size, and the character of the bean changes. All of this means the beans dry more easily and arrive after shipping in a more stable state.[16]

The fermentation process is done within 24 hours of the time the beans are taken out of the pod. Once out of the pods, they must be washed and placed in boxes where the fermentation takes place. In one to three days they are transferred to a second box. And then, after one to three days, to a third box for the completion of the fermentation. Each time they are transferred from one box to the other, they are simultaneously turned and aerated.[17] It should be noted at this point that the total time required for fermentation and curing is five to seven days for Forastero varieties and one to three days for Criollo.

Research by Howat, Wadsworth, and Powell shows that three important factors in the fermentation process contribute to food flavor and color in the beans:

1. At the first stages of fermentation, germination must take place because beans that are dead do not give a chocolate flavor.
2. Beans must reach temperatures of 50° C (122° F) for several days after initial germination. Low temperatures of 45° C (115° F) make for too many purple beans rather than brown beans and cause a loss of chocolate flavor.
3. The carbon dioxide that is generated must be removed. This comes about by the turning and aerating when they are moved to different boxes.[18]

Of course, there are many different methods of fermentation. Each method must attempt to make sure that the proper temperatures are reached and that proper aeration is gained. If there is proper fermentation, then the beans, if cut, will be brown or partly purple and cotyledons will be segmented. If the color is salty, and there is a dense structure and the shell adheres firmly, a poor fermentation has been the cause.[19]

Drying

After fermentation the beans go through a drying process. In most countries, the beans are sun dried. However, in certain countries where there is a lot of rain, the beans are dried by machines.

Whichever method is used, the object is to carefully nurture the enzymatic action to its conclusion. This event will be evidenced through the color changes in the bean. The red-brown and yellow-tan colors will deepen, and the beans will continue to lose moisture. Further, there will be a loss of astringency and an overall improvement of flavor, the shell will begin to loosen from the bean, and through shrinking, the cotyledons that are not furrowed will become almost two halves. Drying is accomplished when the moisture content of the bean is about 6 percent.[20] The importance of the drying process is aptly expressed by Cook:

The fact and nature of the observed changes during drying are adequate testimony of the importance of this stage of the art, and indicate the necessity for control of the conditions. Particularly important is that the enzymatic action as evidenced by color changes in the bean be allowed to proceed to conclusion, and not be stopped short either by too early dehydration or high temperature.[21]

Storage

The emphasis has been to show how important it is to have good fermentation and drying. At this stage, transportation and storage become important.

It is important to the farmers to get the beans from their farms to the boats in as short a time as possible. When beans must be stored in buildings, awaiting shipment, high humidity could add moisture and cause molds to develop if the moisture content is over 8 percent. If the moisture content is at 6 to 6.5 percent, then mold will not develop. With this standard, different means can be developed to keep the moisture content low while the beans are in storage waiting to be transferred to the ship.

When in the ship, much damage to the beans can result from condensation. The captain of the ship must see that ventilation is adequate enough so that the moisture content of the beans does not get too high. On arrival at the factory, the beans are usually put through large fumigation chambers and treated with methyl bromide to ensure that no infested beans arrive in the production areas.[22]

COCOA AND CHOCOLATE MANUFACTURE

Preliminary Problems

The chocolate manufacturer has several problems that are relatively clear. These problems must be solved so that a judgment can be made as to flavor and color of the final products. Cook presents the variables common in the beans that arrive:

1. Beans may be harvested while immature, or they may be overripe.
2. Too little or too much fermentation, with many variations in between may be present. Even mechanical fermentation may yield differences because of lack of control and/or differences in what growers judge to be good or poor.
3. The presence, degree, and kind of mold in cocoa beans will affect the finished product, even though no living mold is by then present.
4. Infestation cannot be completely avoided and thus influences the flavor of the beans.
5. Seasonal and regional variations in climate alter the precise characteristics of cocoa beans, including flavor and color, and will affect the results of the application of any given procedure for fermenting and curing. Seldom will a grower vary handling for any such reason; habits become too fixed.
6. Moisture content of the beans when they are bagged will affect the possibility of mold. Moreover, there are aging changes that go on during storage. These changes may be good or bad, but they are variables, nonetheless. Further, the degree of bitterness is another factor.
7. Age is an important factor, and there is no way a buyer can tell the age of the beans.[23]

(Figure 17.1) shows the process of chocolate manufacture and of cocoa, which is part of the same process.

Figure 17.1
Chocolate Manufacturing Flow Sheet

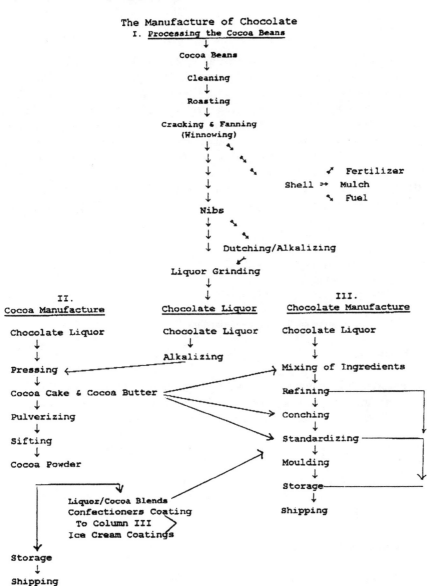

Cleaning

The first step is to remove all foreign matter that may have gotten into the bag as it was packed on the plantation or when it was shipped and stored. Debris removal is accomplished with screens, magnets, and air streams.

Roasting

Cook makes it quite clear that roasting is an art. The artisan must be very careful to roast the beans in such a manner that the proper flavor is achieved. There are three basic problems in roasting. The first concerns the characteristics of the lot being handled. Since all cocoa beans are different, each lot is different and the particular roasting must take this into consideration. Second, beans require different roasts for different purposes. Fondant coatings require a specific roast. Nib-Dutch cocoas use a higher roast. Natural process cocoa powders can be made from different roasts. And third, different kinds of beans require different roasts. The Criollo type beans require low temperature. Various Forastero types require varying temperatures in the roast.[24] The changes that occur in roasting are basically:

1. The development of the aroma and flavor of chocolate.
2. Evaporation of sharp-tasting acids.
3. Reduction of bitterness.
4. Darkening of beans to a deep brown.
5. Reduction of moisture content.
6. Loosening of the shell from the cotyledons.[25]

Winnowing

This process is simply separating the cocoa beans from the shells. First, the shells are broken by rollers. Then through various machine processes, the cotyledon pieces, called "nibs," are separated from the shells.

Liquor Grinding

In this next process the nibs are ground at the melting point of cocoa butter, which causes the mass to flow freely in a thin stream. The product that results is called *chocolate liquor*.

Cocoa Bean Blending

Cook contents that "it is rare that any chocolate or cocoa product is formulated with only one type or growth of cocoa beans."[26] Cook maintains that although there are other times in the process that blending could occur, it is at this stage when blending of the cocoa beans is best. Whatever formula is desired, the mix of beans is best at the point when the chocolate liquor is produced.

Dutch Processing (or Alkalizing)

Fermented cocoa beans as received from the producers are acidic. In alkalizing cocoa, Food and Drug Administration (FDA) Standards of Identity allow a maximum of 3 percent anhydrous potassium carbonate or an alkaline equivalent based on roasted nib weight. Several methods of Dutch processing are in common use, a technique discovered by the Dutch. The result of Dutch processing is a milder flavor and often a darker color. The milder flavor is preferred by some, not by others.[27]

Cocoa Pressing—Juncture Between
Cocoa and Chocolate

So far, both cocoa and chocolate have gone through the same process. At this point in the process, there is a separation and each takes a different route.

The following is a brief description of the process for cocoa making (see Figure 17.1, *left* side). Cocoa presses receive the chocolate liquor, which has been heated to 200° F to 215° F. The hot liquor is put into these pots under pressure and the cocoa butter is separated from the cocoa. The result is cocoa butter separated from hard cocoa cakes.[28]

Cocoa Cakes—Pulverizing and Sifting

The remaining cocoa cakes are cooled. Then they are pulverized into cocoa powder.

Chocolate Making

The blending of various chocolate liquors takes place, according to the formula established, in the mixing kettle. Added to the chocolate formula now made are refined sugar, cocoa butter, milk (if milk chocolate), and any flavoring materials. The fat content of the chocolate paste ranges from 25 percent to 30 percent. At the lower range are coarse chocolates, confectionery coatings, oil coatings for ice cream novelties, and so on. At the upper range are the smooth products with high chocolate content.[29]

Refining

In refining, the particle sizes of the ingredients are reduced. The chocolate goes through a five-roller refiner, which reduces particle size by crushing and sheering. As the chocolate goes through each roller, the solids are gradually reduced as they go through progressively smaller openings.

Conching

Conching came about because individuals wanted chocolate with a "smoother" and "richer" flavor. "The process of conching is primarily one of flavor development by removing the undesirable volatile acidic components remaining after fermentation and by the chemical changes that take place in the flavoring components in the chocolate mix."[30] Thus, a machine was developed to push the chocolate to and fro with a heavy roller. There is no general agreement as to how the conch produces the effects, but it is known that if the process is continued for a certain amount of time—from hours to days—changes occur that give the chocolate a more "mellow" and "finished" taste and a "velvet touch in the mouth."

It used to be true that long conching times produced better results. But now, with many different styles of conching machines, satisfactory results can be obtained in much less time. In any case, conching is expensive because of the additional production time and the cost of the machines.[31]

Because conching is expensive, not all chocolates are conched. The less expensive candies, cookies, and ice cream novelties do not get the same treatment.

Aging

The deliberate aging of high-quality dark chocolate to increase taste quality has been practiced for some time. The problem is, How long should aging occur? All agree that a few days to a couple of weeks is necessary. But different palates disagree as to the effects of longer periods of time.

Milk chocolate is different because it came into widespread popularity later. While many assume aging does not improve taste, it does, in fact, improve with aging of several days. Continued controversy surrounds whether, after the first week, a three- to four-week aging period continues to improve taste.[32]

THE CHOCOLATE INDUSTRY— MANUFACTURERS AND "COATERS"

It is interesting to note that the chocolate industry is not made up of "chocolate factories" that produce chocolates for the consumer. In fact, the usual local chocolate factory in a particular town will generally "produce" only the chocolates for candy boxes or peanut clusters or bonbons, and so on. Those who actually import the cocoa beans and manufacture the chocolate may not even be familiar names to the public since they only manufacture chocolate for the "coaters." It is the coaters who buy from the chocolate manufacturers that put coatings on all kinds of nuts and fillings to "produce" chocolates in their "factories" for their consumers. Thus, the industry is divided into manufacturers of chocolate and chocolate coaters."[33]

The early chocolate makers who started as manufacturers stayed manufacturers and were coaters as well. Thus, Swiss companies such as Nestlé, Suchard, Lindt, Tobler, and Callier began as manufacturers and coaters with their special consumer candies and continued as both. Some British and American firms share the same historical background and are manufacturers and coaters. Thus, the British firms of Cadbury and Perugina and the American firms of Hershey and Ghirardelli maintain the Swiss tradition of doing both.

However, many small candy makers do only coating in their factories and buy from large wholesale manufacturers of chocolate. Some chocolatiers such as Godiva, Cornela Toisond'Or, and Kron are just coaters who buy from manufacturers. Many of the best American candies are coated with Callebaut chocolate from Belgium, with Lindt from Switzerland, or with Nestlé made in America from Swiss formulas. American manufacturers who sell coatings are Guittard, Van Leer, Bloomer, Ambrosia, Merckens, and Wilbur. These American manufacturers sell to coaters who merchandise their own wares to the consumers.[34]

Many of the coaters who have small, medium, or even large factories produce chocolates, bonbons, turtles, and the like, boxed under famous brand names for New York, Chicago, and Boston firms that neither coat nor package their "exclusive" candies. The large department stores make up the name, determine the flavors and quality and packaging, and market the goods as their own famous brands—the "finest chocolates made." Therefore, many marketers are not manufacturers but coaters of chocolate made by manufacturers to their specifications. The best known examples are Godiva, Fanny Farmer, Kron, and Candy Cupboard.

QUALITY CHOCOLATES IN THE UNITED STATES

The best way to describe a chocolate lover and his or her taste is to quote from *The Chocolate Bible* by Adrianne Marcus. Two friends, who are devoted chocolate lovers, decided to obtain the chocolates they desired. Their trip was a journey to realize their chocolate fantasies and to find the "ultimate chocolate dream." Their goal was to find those places in this vast America where the exquisite chocolates were made. They drove across the United States with a huge cooler in the trunk of their automobile where the chocolates would be stored. It was a six-week trip in which they could see, taste, and bring some chocolates home with them. They had been informed by the large manufacturers of chocolate that there would be specific differences between the West Coast chocolate they were accustomed to consuming and the Eastern chocolate. Their information was that the Westerner preferred the lighter, milkier chocolate candies and the Easterner preferred the darker, even bittersweet chocolates. Their experiences from West to East and back again confirmed the manufacturer's conclusions. Chocolate is regional and each region has different preferences. The Westerner does prefer lighter, milkier chocolate and the

Easterner the darker and more bittersweet chocolates.

The history books on chocolate described an America where each town had their individual candy makers. In the early days the candy industry had grown very rapidly and spread across the country. However, many of the old, hand dipped candies by small shop keepers were, in fact, things of the past. Mass produced commercial, inexpensive candy bars had taken their toll. The two found that there are, in fact, fewer small shops throughout the country. However, the places that remain are fine quality places that maintain the old hand dipped, hand made, and hand crafted product. Some of these places produce such large quantities of chocolates that they are more than regional candy makers. Their products are sold in department stores throughout the country. The small shops and the large shops continue to practice the art of chocolate making. The emphasis is on art. They each make every effort to make exquisite distinctive candies.

The two tourists found that in spite of the mass produced candies crowding out the artistically produced brands, the distinctively produced candies were such artistic achievements that they are certain to continue to exist. They described the different places in Los Angeles where Swiss chocolates are made and further, the Edelweiss chocolates that have fruit in the middle surrounded by delightful chocolate. In addition, in Salt Lake City, which prides itself on the number of individual artistic chocolate shops, more specifically, where the two brothers, C. Kay and Paul Cummings, have separate chocolate stores that compete with each other in rival artistic delights. Moreover, they singled out Vermillion, Ohio, and Lititz, Pennsylvania where distinctive chocolates are produced. Each town has the splendid chocolates that characterize the best art in chocolate making in their areas. And, our two searchers were very taken by candies that are mass produced, such as Critchley's mints in New Jersey, Godiva from Dowington, Pennsylvania, and Harbor Sweets in Marblehead, Massachusetts. Each of these mass produced candies are shipped all over the U.S.

They concluded their journey with these words:

And we were lucky enough to enjoy it; to have our chocolate and eat it also. As to the question that comes up time after time, which places make the best, it depends on what you want. That is not a diplomatic answer, that is the answer. Somewhere ahead of you, on the road you did not expect to take, in a town or city in America, there is a chocolate candy you have been looking for. Your chocolate heart's desire.[35]

Our author proceeds to describe the "great" chocolate candies, from California in the West to New York in the East; then she describes the great chocolate candies of Europe.

It is interesting to note that as she describes the "different zones" for candy— Fanny Farmer in the East, Fanny May in the Midwest, and See's in the West— that each one of these "fine candies" is not made in its own chocolate factory.

Each company is a coater who buys its candies from other manufacturers. Even in Europe, where more candies are manufactured and coated by the same firm, many of the smaller firms and even some larger ones are only coaters and not manufacturers.

Some rather interesting conclusions can be drawn from *The Chocolate Bible*:

1. Different regions have different tastes in chocolate.
2. Although there were more manufacturers of chocolate in the past, now most chocolate "makers" are coaters, not manufacturers.
3. The main difference in the chocolates was the insides, not the coatings of the chocolates.
4. The best candy depends on your own taste. And probably a great deal has to do with what region you come from and, thus, the kind of chocolate you are used to eating. That, of course, is the "best."
5. Europe is not much different, and all that pertains to chocolates is the same there as here. There are, however, perhaps a few more manufacturers who also are coaters, which makes sense historically, since the Europeans performed the initial chocolate research.

A PRELIMINARY ANALYSIS OF FLAVOR IN CHOCOLATE

A Rational Analysis

The question is, Is the consumer more interested in product or price? Surely he or she wants a delectable piece of chocolate, and price does not influence him or her. But in a rational world, it does have a dramatic influence. Ergo, it is probably a little bit of both for the rational consumer.

Candy makers must think in terms of both product and price. They want to make sure that the consumer has a chocolate delight, but at the same time, they know that price is crucial for the sale of the product and for their profits.

For the consumer, the next thought that runs through his or her mind is the smoothness of the chocolate. However, smoothness is a relative characteristic and difficult to measure, especially if we are dealing with two relatively smooth chocolates. Moreover, the chocolate smoothness may be smothered, or at least influenced, by the penetrating tastes of the center filling. Such a disguise may negate or at least render neutral the smoother chocolate.

How about the color? Many who sell chocolate try to deal with eye appeal and make the color of the dark chocolate very dark and the light chocolate very light. This may help in the appeal of the package, but many people assume that dark chocolate is bitter and the light is sweet, and they will hesitate to buy where the package has much dark chocolate in it.

So what must the buyer do? Most buyers will rationally try to buy the best chocolate for the least price. And most sellers will try to sell the best chocolate for the least price.

A Nonrational Analysis of Flavor
in Chocolate

In fact, people do not really know what good chocolate is. Most of what has been written in this chapter about the cocoa tree and its harvesting few chocolate eaters know. Nor do they know the historical background. Furthermore, they do not know about the different grades of chocolate and conching, which adds to the quality and taste.

Adrianne Marcus, the chocolate addict who traveled across the United States and then later across Europe in search of quality chocolate, is a person who appreciates chocolate but doesn't necessarily know quality chocolate. As she tells us, in the end, it only has to do with what you yourself like. She did not know that most chocolate is not manufactured by the coaters. She did not even know that many retailers are not even coaters but buy the chocolates from coaters who make them to their specifications. But after she found out some of these facts, it did not really matter as long as the chocolate was of good quality to *her taste*.

AN ANALYSIS OF FLAVOR IN CHOCOLATE

The foregoing account shows quite clearly that chocolate has a unique flavor and is an indulgence of the modern world.

In planting a crop of cocoa trees, those planted are 95 percent the most hearty, but not necessarily the best, cocoa bean trees. However, perhaps given the economics of depending on less hearty trees that produce less yield, the planting of the most hearty trees is the most economically practical.

Fermentation is the next problem, and it is a difficult process to control for the best results. Nonetheless, the planters and harvesters are depended on to do as good a job as possible.

Once at the manufacturing plant, several problems arise, but they are effectively and practically taken care of by mixing the cocoa beans that are received. Further, the conching process is very important, yet the length of time and different methods leave many questions about conching.

Manufacturers have their own formulas for making different qualities of chocolate. Purchasers can buy from them whatever grades they wish if they are prepared to pay the price. Further, buyers can ask for various mixes, any of which can be put together by the manufacturer for a price. Moreover, coaters may mix different qualities of chocolates that they buy from the manufacturers to make their own blends of chocolates. Thus, numerous chocolate variations are possible with many different grades and qualities.

And there are historical consequences. When the original experimenters with chocolates came up with their formulas, they developed them and sold them regionally. As a result, people believe that their particular home area produces the best chocolates and what the rest of the world produces is "good" but not as good as Nestlé or Cadbury or Hershey or whichever brand they are used to as the prime chocolate taste.

Added to all of the above is advertising, which psychologically suggests the best taste to millions of people who are willing to believe the company who knows how to advertise best. And there is packaging. Good packaging can convince people that an expensive product with fine packaging, and a carefully contrived name, is consequently quality candy.

The point is that there are clearly different grades and qualities of chocolate. But it is difficult, once one goes into the smoother and more flavorful chocolates to tell which is the best, especially since advertising and ethnocentricity and a taste everyone has grown up with challenge the most discriminating connoisseur of chocolate.

Ergo, in the end, except for obvious lack of smoothness and flavor, the "better" grades and qualities of chocolate whether more expensive or not, depend primarily on an individual's taste test.

CONCLUSION

Chocolate is, indeed, the food of the gods, but determining quality is an elusive pursuit. Many variables in chocolate's early planting, harvesting, and manufacturing make it difficult to pursue a rational way of arriving at real quality, especially when ethnocentricity, history, and advertising add to the influence on each idiosyncratic consumer.

The best chocolate flavor in the world is, thus, without a doubt, the elixir of that person who has found it and is satisfied with the knowledge and glorious taste.

NOTES

1. Marcia Morton and Frederic Morton, *Chocolate: An Illustrated History* (New York: Crown Publishers, 1986), 33.

2. Ibid., 4.

3. Ibid., 6.

4. Donald G. Mitchell, *The Chocolate Industry*, American Industries No. 17 (Boston, Mass.: Bellman Publishing Company, 1951), 10.

5. Ibid., 50.

6. Bernard W. Minifie, *Chocolate, Cocoa and Confectionery: Science and Technology* (Westport, Conn.: AVI Publishing Company, 1970), 3.

7. H. R. Jensen, *The Chemistry, Flavoring and Manufacture of Chocolate Confectionery and Cocoa* (Philadelphia: Blakiston's Son & Co., Inc., 1931), 4–5.

8. Ibid., 5.

9. Ibid.

10. Dr. Arthur Stevenson, *Cocoa: A Fundamental Report, E. F. Hutton Futures Division Research*, July 5, 1987, 15.

11. Bernard W. Minifie, *Chocolate, Cocoa and Confectionery: Science and Technology*, 2d. ed. (Westport, Conn.: AVI Publishing Company, 1980), 3.

12. L. Russell Cook, *Chocolate Production and Use* (New York: Magazines for Industry, Inc., 1963), 26.

13. Ibid.

14. Ibid., 28.

15. Ibid.

16. Arthur W. Knapp, *The Cocoa and Chocolate Industry: The Tree, the Bean, the Beverage* (London: Sir Isaac Pitman & Sons, 1923), 56–57.

17. Cook, *Chocolate Production*, 32.

18. Minifie, *Chocolate*, 1980, 13.

19. Ibid.

20. Cook, *Chocolate Production*, 36.

21. Ibid.

22. Minifie, *Chocolate*, 1980, 15–16.

23. Cook, *Chocolate Production*, 127–28.

24. Ibid., 132–34.

25. Ibid., 137.

26. Ibid., 144.

27. Mitchell, *The Chocolate Industry*, 23–24.

28. Ibid., 20.

29. Ibid., 21–22; Minifie, *Chocolate*, 1980, 105–26.

30. R. Lees and E. B. Jackson, *Sugar Confectionery and Chocolate Manufacture* (Great Britain: Leonard Hill Books, 1973), 136.

31. Ibid., 136–39.

32. Ibid., 173–174.

33. Dudley Anderson, interview with owner of Betty Dixon Candies, Jamestown, NY., April 30, 1988.

34. Morton and Morton, *Chocolate*, 141.

35. Adrianne Marcus, *The Chocolate Bible* (New York: G. P. Putnam and Sons, 1979), 45–48.

REFERENCES

Anderson, Dudley. Interview with owner of Betty Dixon Candies. Jamestown, NY., April 30, 1988.

Bixler, Raymond W. *The West Africa Story*. New York: Vantage Press, 1972.

Boynton, Sandra. *Chocolate: The Consuming Passion*. New York: Workman Publishing, 1982.

Cook, L. Russell. *Chocolate Production and Use*. New York: Magazines for Industry, Inc., 1963.

Finch, Robert. *A World-Wide Business*. Birmingham, England: Cadbury Brothers Ltd., 1948.

Gannon College—Pulakos Candies. *Short Course in Retail Candy Making—Syllabus*. Associated Retail Confectioners of North America, 2d Annual, Erie, Pa. July 9–29, 1967.

Gott, Philip P., and L. F. van Houton. *All about Candy and Chocolate: A Comprehensive Study of the Candy and Chocolate Industry*. Chicago: National Confectioners Association, 1958.

Henderson, Janice Walk. *White Chocolate*. Chicago, Ill.: Contemporary Books, Inc., 1987.

Jensen, H. R. *The Chemistry, Flavoring and Manufacture of Chocolate Confectionery and Cocoa*. Philadelphia: P. Blakiston's Son & Co., Inc., 1931.

Johnson, W. H. *Cocoa: Its Cultivation and Preparation*. London: John Murray Publishers, 1912.

Knapp, Arthur W. *The Cocoa and Chocolate Industry: The Tree, the Bean, the Beverage*. London: Sir Isaac Pitman & Sons, 1923.

Knapp, Arthur W. *Cocoa and Chocolate: Their History from Plantation to Consumer*. London: Chapman & Hall, Ltd., 1920.

Kolpas, Norman. *The Chocolate Lovers' Companion*. New York: Aladin Books: 1977.

Lees, R., and E. B. Jackson. *Sugar Confectionery and Chocolate Manufacture*. Great Britain: Leonard Hill Books, 1973.

Long, Eula. *Chocolate from Mayan to Modern*. New York: Aladin Books, 1950.

Marcus, Adrianne. *The Chocolate Bible*. New York: G. P. Putnam and Sons, 1979.

Minifie, Bernard W. *Chocolate, Cocoa and Confectionery: Science and Technology*. Westport, Conn.: AVI Publishing Company, 1970.

Minifie, Bernard W. *Chocolate, Cocoa and Confectionary: Science and Technology*. 2d ed. Westport, Conn.: AVI Publishing Company, 1980.

Mitchell, Donald G. *The Chocolate Industry*. American Industries No. 17. Boston, Mass.: Bellman Publishing Company, 1951.

Montgomery, E. G., and Alice M. Taylor. *World Trade in Cocoa*. Industrial Series No. 71, Department of Commerce, Foodstuff Division. Washington, D.C.: U.S. Government Printing Office, 1947.

Morton, Marcia, and Frederic Morton. *Chocolate: An Illustrated History*. New York: Crown Publishers, 1986.

Okali, C., and P.L.N.A. Addy. *Economics of Cocoa Production and Marketing with Special Reference to Ghana*. An Annotated Bibliography. Institute of Statistical, Social and Economic Research, University of Ghana, 1974.

Richmond, Walter L. *Candy Production: Methods and Formulas*. Chicago, Ill.: The Manufacturing Confectioner, 1948.

Rigby, W. O. *Rigby's Reliable Candy Teacher*. 2d ed. Topeka, Kans.: Rigby Publishing Company, 1945.

Rinzler, Carole Ann. *The Book of Chocolate*. New York: St. Martin's Press, 1977.

Simmon, John, ed. *Cocoa Production: Economic and Botanical Perspectives*. New York: Praeger Publishers, 1976.

Smaridge, Norah. *The World of Chocolate*. New York: Julian Messner, 1969.

Stevenson, Arthur. *Cocoa: A Fundamental Report. E. F. Hutton Futures Division Research*, July 1987, 15.

The Story of Chocolate. Chocolate Manufacturers Association, 1960.

Wieland, Henry. *Cocoa and Chocolate Processing 1972*. Park Ridge, N.J.: Noyes Data Corporation, 1972.

Zipperer, Paul. *The Manufacture of Chocolate and Other Cacao Preparations*. 2d ed. Berlin: W. Verlag von M. Krayn, 1902.

CHAPTER 18

Location Factors in Cocoa Growing and the Chocolate Industry

John E. Ullmann

The cocoa and chocolate industries have established themselves in locations far from the original habitat of the cacao tree. As with natural rubber and other tropical crops indigenous to the Western Hemisphere, cocoa production was largely transferred to Africa and Southeast Asia. In contrast to other such products, cocoa growing started there with small-scale growers. The circumstances of this shift are explored in the context of industrial location practice.

The same approach is used in analyzing the chocolate industry. Spain once had a dominant role, but that was soon eclipsed by France, Britain, Switzerland, Holland, Belgium, and Austria. Chocolate is made in all major industrial countries, but only a few have become major exporters of top products. The original locations of the major firms were concentrated in the homes of their founders, but this condition was not to last, as greater scale, mergers, consolidations, and some eclipses changed the industry drastically. In both cocoa growing and chocolate manufacture, what had started on a small scale thus became large, concentrated, and globalized.

THE DETERMINANTS OF LOCATION

This study deals with two quite different location problems. Cocoa growing is an agricultural operation, whereas chocolate production is part of manufacturing. From earliest human history, climate has been the main deciding factor in what could be grown where. Temperatures, rainfall, and soil types were the specific variables. It is also true, however, that as soon as agriculture expanded in scale, moved beyond the subsistence level, and received infusions of science, technology, and capital, it had to pay attention to some of the same factors as industry. One of the most important was transportation, which often became decisive when required to handle large volumes of bulk commodities of low specific value, as well as perishable.

Although knowledge of agricultural practice is ancient, beginning in the nineteenth century, science showed ways of changing fertility and, at least in some cases, coping with plant disease and pests. The later effort has a checkered record, not only in its failures in major problem areas but in its more general impacts on the environment. Natural and man-made problems in agriculture strike with particular force at countries that depend on single crops, especially when the crop is not indigenous but transplanted.

The impact of technology and capital together with often inadequate scientific knowledge nevertheless fostered a belief that within broad climatic restrictions, anything could be grown anywhere. Other factors, most notably (some would say "notoriously") labor, could then be made a decisive element in settling on a location. Much of the economic development of the colonial empires was shaped by such decisions. The Third World today lives with the consequences, but especially given the record of many of its governments, it would be much too facile to view these problems as yet another transgression by the erstwhile colonial powers and today's industrial countries. This is especially so with cocoa, because its establishment in West Africa was mainly due to native initiative, rather than imposition by the colonial powers.

This study deals with the transfer of cocoa growing from the Western Hemisphere to West Africa, as well as with the location factors in chocolate production. The latter show the much greater flexibility of industrial plant location. While it is not true that anything can be made anywhere, it is true that a great deal of discretion exists.

The classic formulation of the location problems is that manufacturing must be able to take advantage of at least one of the principal input factors. These are locally available raw materials including, in some cases, cheap energy, labor of the skill required, and markets for the product. The development of transportation facilities and machinery that began in the nineteenth century meant that many industries could be started in given places for other reasons, not the least of which was where the founders lived. This turns out to have been an important location criterion in chocolate manufacture (Ullmann and Gluck, 1980, 40–56).

THE TRANSFER OF COCOA GROWING

The cacao tree (*Theobroma cacao*) is native to tropical America, and its early uses ranged from southern Mexico to Peru and Ecuador. Venezuela was an important early source of cocoa for Europe. Until the end of the eighteenth century, a drink made of ground chocolate rather than cocoa powder was the principal product, and Spain accounted for a large part of its market. As the Spanish empire in South America declined and then disintegrated in the early nineteenth century, Spain looked to the development of other colonial territories, among them the island of Fernando Po off the west coast of Africa. After its discovery in the fifteenth century, it had been a Portuguese possession like the nearby islands of São Tomé and Principe but was ceded to Spain in 1778.

It later became a British base that was used after the international agreements of 1807 for the interdiction of the Atlantic slave trade. After a protracted time of mixed sovereignty, the island became an undisputed Spanish possession in 1844. By then, the growing of cacao trees had been established there in a modest way; these limited operations were to prove central to the establishment of cocoa growing on the African mainland.

The cacao tree requires a mean shade temperature of about 80° F, an evenly distributed rainfall of 50 to 150 inches a year, and a deep and rich, porous soil. It must also be protected from the wind. These conditions are found in some areas of the Tropics in America, Africa, and Asia between about 20 degrees north and south of the equator, but the requirements of rainfall, soil depth and wind protection restrict locations in practice.

The Gold Coast, now Ghana, became the main grower and accounted for up to 50 percent of the world crop for most of the twentieth century until the 1970s, when it lost first place to the Ivory Coast (Brooke, 1988). The story of how the crop got its start toward the end of the nineteenth century is not only instructive because it resulted in a drastic reorientation of the world supply; rather, it also was a true case of individual native enterprise that contrasted sharply with such other contemporary changes as the tranfer of rubber growing to Southeast Asia and central Africa.

The export of seedlings of the rubber tree (*Hevea brasiliensis*) had been strictly forbidden by the Brazilian and other South American governments, but as demand for rubber products grew following the invention of vulcanization, a sufficiently large number of seedlings was smuggled out of Brazil in 1876 by Sir Henry Wickham in what was probably the biggest cloak and dagger operation in the history of botany. The plants eventually became the basis for the rubber plantations of today's Malaysia and Indonesia.

The Gold Coast also saw some rubber development, but significant cultivation was short-lived and was soon supplanted by cocoa. In that it was fortunate, because the exploitation of rubber by traditional forest cultivation was to result in some of the worst excesses of colonialist exploitation on record. The revelations of the British journalist Sir Roger Casement of conditions in the rubber camps of the then-Belgian Congo, and in the operations of the Anglo-Peruvian Amazon Company along the Putumayo River in Peru, created major scandals in the first decade of this century.

The contrast between this and the establishment of cocoa growing in West Africa could not be more marked. In 1857, a few cacao seedlings had first been brought from Surinam (then Dutch Guyana) to the Gold Coast by the so-called Basel Missionaries, that is a group from Switzerland where, as noted later, some of the pioneering work in its chocolate industry was then being done. The industry did not take hold until 1879, however when Tetteh Quashie, a blacksmith from the Ga tribe, brought more seedlings from Fernando Po and successfully cultivated them in the Akuapem area, realizing his first crop in 1883. Local farmers bought his first crop and used this as seed for their own plantings.

William Brandford Griffith, a British governor also promoted the industry, having brought seedlings from São Tomé, started a nursery, and distributed more seedlings to the farmers. The Basel Missionaries also remained active, established tree nurseries of their own and also distributed seeds. By 1895, the cocoa industry had spread to the entire Gold Coast Protectorate, including the Northern Ashanti territory around its capital of Kumasi (Reynolds, 1974, 179).

Cacao trees do not bear fruit for their first four or five years, so that all this represented quite a risk. It is all the more remarkable that the whole pioneering development was directed toward, and largely run by, local farmers. Cocoa cultivation in the early years was, as one report puts it,

very much a matter of trial and error; and this can be a costly process on a large scale as more recent experiments in tropical agriculture have shown. A further point in favor of the small plot was the ease with which local inhabitants could apply for [tribal] grants of land. . . . At first, a man would require only as much land as he could cultivate with the help of his family, though he might clear new farms as his skill and capital increased. This did not mean that every farmer produced on a small scale; but even the wealthiest were more likely to have series of farms, often in different places, in different stages of bearing than one large scale holding. (Kimble, 1963, 35)

Where insufficient land was available, cooperatives called "companies" were formed that migrated to areas where they could apply for suitable land. In addition to what could be described as "tribal peasants," a long-established class of traders and craftsmen centered in the Akuapem area and was crucial to the development of the burgeoning cocoa industry. Many of them had taken to Christianity and, in part through contact with missionaries, had an early appreciation of the market possibilities of cocoa (Reynolds, 1974, 180–85).

In short, the model contrasted sharply with the huge rubber estates that were then being established in Southeast Asia and certainly with the great landholdings of the Latin American *latifundias* in the native habitat of the cacao plant.

Nevertheless, cocoa growing had a profound effect on land tenure. At the same time as cocoa, palm oil was also being developed by native initiatives as an export crop in the Akuapem and Krobo areas. These two crops required fixed, rather than shifting cultivation and land rotation as traditionally practiced. The native merchants and traders not only furnished credit and supplies to the farmers; they soon conducted their export trade directly with foreign trading partners, rather than going through colonial authorities. Their initial prosperity gave way to a slump after they had overreached themselves in the 1860s and was followed by a brief period of recovery. But from the 1890s onward, multinational corporations like Unilever managed to achieve a dominant role in the economy of the Gold Coast that lasted until independence and well beyond (Reynolds, 1974, 190).

Cocoa marketing, however, remained to a considerable degree in native hands, with the "companies" described earlier taking on an important role with assistance from the colonial government. However, whenever there was a buyer's market, large purchasers, including major chocolate manufacturers, had decisive influence on the country's economy.

The development of cocoa growing was encouraged by the colonial adminis-tration not only in direct ways, as Governor Griffith had done, but by such infrastructure projects as railroad construction. Lines were built inland from the ports of Accra and Takoradi to Kumasi, which gave the Gold Coast an east-west connection of sorts. A branch from the Takoradi line was intended as an east-west cutoff south of Kumasi, but that was not completed until the 1950s (Salkield, 1952).

The A-shaped network of today's Ghana Railways thus differs somewhat from much of colonial railroad building, which was designed to bring minerals and produce from inland areas to the coast; internal, cross-country communications were more limited. To this day, the short A-line in Ghana and another only slightly longer one in Nigeria are the only lines in West Africa that do not simply run from the coast to some inland railhead (Thomas Cook, 1987, map 25). Even so, cocoa growing in the large region between the coast and the cross connection took hold without any reliance on rail transportation at all (Munro, 1976, 101).

The lines to Kumasi were crucial to cocoa growing, but they had been built by the colonial power for other reasons besides service to farmers. From 1807 to 1830 and intermittently until 1874, there had been savage wars in the Ashanti territories so that access was perceived as a military necessity. The wars had mainly started, one regrets to say, because of the economic dislocation that followed the suppression of the slave trade. It had provided the Ashantis, as well as coastal rulers like the kings of Dahomey and Benin, with lucrative incomes; their role in the slave trade is commonly forgotten in accounts about it that portray it almost exclusively as a white crime. The Ashanti wars, in fact, were started to provide security for the British naval bases on the coast that enforced the blockade against the slave trade after 1807 (Ransford, 1971, 264–65; see also Edgerton, 1995).

The discovery of gold in the Ashanti regions and early success with kola nut cultivation helped create a new economic base, but there was real political conflict as the powers of the traditional rulers waned in favor of the new merchant class. In fact, memories of early tribal conflicts related to the slave trade bedevil the political life of West Africa to this day. In fall 1995, Nigeria and Ghana, among others, were trying to mediate what had become almost per-petual civil wars in Sierra Leone and Liberia.

One more economic development of the time deserves mention: The exploita-tion of the region's timber resources was getting under way. Clearing of forests provided much-needed agricultural land, especially in view of the conflicts between fixed and shifting agriculture noted above. It eventually was to wreak ecological havoc in all of West Africa and serve as a dreadful example of the exclusive destruction of tropical forests.

In the early days, however, in addition to the long familiar and prized ebony, European furniture makers especially welcomed an alternative source of mahogany, a variant of which grows in Africa, and such other forest products as a soft and easily worked wood called *obeche*. With mahogany, incidentally, the American tropics to which it is native were faced with yet another case of African competition, just as with cocoa and rubber.

Finally, in order to diversify the economies of its colonies, as well as meeting a need of the time immediately after World War II, the British government promoted the so-called Ground Nuts Scheme in its African colonies, designed to expand greatly the growing of ground nuts (peanuts) for their oil and protein. That eventually turned into one of the major fiascos of foreign aid and "top-down" economic development; not the least of its troubles was a total misjudgment of the market. When it started, there was a major shortage of edible oils and fats, but that was among the first to disappear in postwar recovery, and there has been an almost unbroken glut ever since.

A detailed history of the cocoa industry is beyond the scope of this chapter. However, two problems have sharply affected not only its scope but its location. The first is the melancholy fact that cacao trees are much given to plant diseases and crop failures. Extensive hybridization has expanded the limited genetic endowment of the original plantings, but even so, finding species with pest resistance has often proved difficult. In the 1940s, a virus disease called swollen shoot had spread so widely that it was feared the industry would be wiped out. Swollen shoot was spread by mealybugs; it cut the yield of affected trees and eventually killed them. Wholesale cutting and destruction of the sick trees proved the only remedy (Kay, 1972, 238–77, esp. 272–76). Richard Wright, the novelist, who had settled in Ghana, also wrote of those troubled times (Wright, 1954, 304).

Black pod is another disease; in *The Money Game*, Adam Smith (1967, 255–69) gives an account of the vicissitudes of traders in cocoa futures who had to try to balance good and bad news with respect to rain, diseases, and the West African civil wars of the 1960s. The tone is humorous, but actually, West Africa has had a set of Third World miseries that rank among the world's worst. They make up the second very real set of problems that affect the cocoa industry.

First, there are the demographic pressures that have led to land and food shortages. From being self-sufficient, most West African countries are now large food importers. Export crops have dislocated agriculture further; one result has been a population explosion in the capital cities. It is the political situation as such, however, that has been most alarming.

Thus, Nigeria, another cocoa producer, had its Biafra civil war, one of the worst in Africa, and a succession of military juntas that have brought it close to bankruptcy notwithstanding its oil riches. Extortion and banditry are rife, beginning for travelers with arrival at Lagos airport and the ride into the city; the country is also a major center of the international drug trade.

Fernando Po and a small mainland enclave called Rio Muni made up Spanish Guinea; it still was a cocoa producer, though no longer a major center of the industry. After independence as Equatorial Guinea in 1968, it fell under the sway of perhaps the worst of all African tyrannies, that of Nguemo Masie. By the time he was overthrown and shot in 1979, he had managed to murder or drive out over one third of the population. It remains one of the major African horror stories to the present day. In 1976, Nigeria threatened military intervention to protect its citizens who had gone to work the cocoa plantations.

In 1957, the Gold Coast turned into Ghana with Kwame Nkrumah as its charismatic leader. Nkrumah thought of himself as a leader of the Third World and beyond and eventually styled himself Osajefo (the Redeemer). In 1962, he convened a large and prestigious conference on world peace in Accra. A somewhat sour note was struck, however, by the delivery at the same time of three minesweepers while, as participants could not help noticing, the harbor of Accra was so inadequate as to need barges for bringing in almost everything. More directly, no attempt had been made to promote any local processing of cocoa beans, rather than shipping them as a crop. Nkrumah was overthrown by the army in 1966 and took refuge in Guinea, another, though minor, cocoa producer. He was cordially received by its dictator Sekou Touré, who during his long rule (until 1984) was responsible for more than his own share of horrors. Ghana has had a succession of army regimes ever since Nkrumah's overthrow and ethnic strife, of which the last example was a clash in February 1993 in the old Ashanti lands in which a thousand people were killed.

The principal exception to these miseries is the Ivory Coast, once a French colony that was ruled by the same civilian president, Felix Houphouet-Boigny, from its independence in 1960 to his death in December 1993. It has managed to avoid the militarist turmoil of its neighbors, and as noted before, its development policies enabled it in the 1970s to overtake Ghana as the world's largest cocoa producer. It is also the largest rubber grower in Africa and third in cotton, both crops that were nonexistent at the time of independence. The country had long been an exporter of cocoa, coffee, and timber, but as a result of overcutting for the latter and the new crops, the forest cover has been reduced from 50 percent in 1960 to the present 3 percent, making the country one of the world's worst destroyers of the rain forest.

Like most African countries, the Ivory Coast is a one-party state. It has had its share of questionable practices, notably the building of the world's largest Roman Catholic cathedral (larger than St. Peter's in Rome) in Yamoussoukro, Houphouet-Boigny's birthplace. It was once visited by Pope John Paul II, who tactfully refrained from commenting on the wisdom of the project.

From its early times as a popular initiative, the cocoa industry has moved toward larger-scale operations even though still widely dispersed at its sources. Beyond this, it shares not only in the vicissitudes of commodity fluctuations but in the broader troubles of the region that became its center.

THE CHOCOLATE INDUSTRY

Chocolate originated in Spain, which first substituted sugar for the ground pepper and other spices in the ancestral concoction favored by the Aztecs. It remained a Spanish monopoly and secret until the seventeenth century when, according to one authoritative source, it was brought successively to France, Italy, Holland, England, Germany, and Switzerland, largely by refugees of Jewish origins ("Schokolade," 1973). As is common in declining societies, the governments of Spain and neighboring Portugal had turned nasty; the Inquisition was in full cry, and conversion to Catholicism was no longer enough. This time the Marranos—the Jewish converts—were attacked not only for insufficient religious zeal, as in the fifteenth century, but for racial reasons; *limpieza de sangre*—purity of the blood—had become the watchword, and the whole process had turned into a murderous extortion racket that drove those in danger to seek a better life elsewhere (Roth, 1959, 74–98).

Spanish Jesuits also helped spread knowledge of chocolate. The order had come under increasing attack for its political activities, which, in South America especially, had overtones of what is now called liberation theology. As a result, it was persecuted in Spain and expelled entirely in 1766 (Condon, 1982; see also Madariaga, 1963, 205–60 who identifies the treatment by the government and church of Marranos, Jesuits, and Freemasons as a major factor in the end of the Spanish empire).

Chocolate was a very expensive luxury at first; in the 1650s, solid chocolate for turning into drinks cost from 10 to 15 shillings a pound in London. The French *Grande Encyclopédie*, published around 1900, also says that chocolate in the seventeenth century was only for *les grandes fortunes* and was highly prized. It then delivers itself of an obiter dictum that departs markedly from the bland neutralism one normally expects from such sources:

[Chocolate], however, did not have the success of coffee which has the property of stimulating the cerebral functions, whereas chocolate induces doing nothing [*porte au farniente*], a property which makes it highly appreciated by the peoples of the South [*Méridionaux*] and above all, by the Spaniards. ("Chocolat," 1900)

The article cited dismisses the role of Anne of Austria and Maria Theresa of Spain, consorts, respectively, of Louis XIII and Louis XIV, in popularizing chocolate; Condon (1982) gives the former credit.

The famous Marquise de Sévigné was a prominent consumer of chocolate when it first became fashionable in Paris but complained that "*il me rabêtit*"—it makes me act silly. By the eighteenth century, chocolate manufacture had benefited from relatively low prices for cocoa and sugar as cultivation expanded, even though it had not reached anything like its scope and extent in the nineteenth century.

The main problem was not so much a lack of formulas for making chocolate;

those seemed to be widely available. The trouble was the difficulty in manufacture. Handwork was still universal. Cocoa beans had to be laboriously hulled by hand, cracked, roasted, and then ground by mortar and pestle; sugar came in solid sugar loaves that also had to be smashed and then ground. The first German chocolate factory established by Count Schaumburg-Lippe with Portuguese assistance in 1765, and its contemporaries, relied on this kind of hard and tedious handwork. Even in 1819, the shop of M. Pelletier in Paris recorded the typical output per worker as only 12 to 14 pounds a day. Chocolate was also laced with some alarming ingredients in those days, such as a pinch of iodine ("Chocolat," 1900). In addition to such tips on recipes, the *Encyclopédie* article cited has many illustrations of the by then quite sophisticated chocolate machinery of the late nineteenth century.

What changed the situation was a spate of inventions in machinery unique in history. As K. R. Gilbert (1958, 417–41) puts it, "In 1775 the machine tools at the disposal of industry had scarcely advanced beyond those of the Middle Ages: By 1850 the majority of modern machine tools had been invented." Machine tools, in turn, could make other kinds of machinery with the precision they required, and specialized machinery was soon devised for all the major manufacturing industries. Energy requirements also were crucial in the early times to eliminate the manual crushing and grinding. By the end of the eighteenth century, water power was being used in a few suitable locations, but by the 1840s, steam began to furnish both machine drives and process heat.

Chocolate manufacture had essentially started in a multitude of small shops, but the availability of steam power suggested larger facilities, and chocolate manufacturers felt able, as well as compelled, to concentrate on process design and new machinery; better equipment became almost as important as better recipes. Thus, countries prominent in machine design found their talents in that area crucial to commercial success.

For example, Rudolf Lindt, the cofounder of Lindt & Spruengli of Switzerland, invented the "conching" process, a heating and kneading process that improved the smoothness of chocolate and removed bitter aftertastes. It soon led to the Swiss practice of adding more cocoa butter rather than cocoa power, which gives Swiss chocolate its distinctive melting characteristics and taste in contrast, for instance, to chocolate made in the United States (Condon, 1982). Lindt & Spruengli is still a leader in process development.

The constant interaction of product and process design continues today; machines for making chocolates and chocolate bars, and then packaging them, are prominent examples of advanced high-speed mechanical processing. Moreover, the necessary materials handling is also automatic, thus making for an increasingly automated continuous production system. Before then, even after the early machinery, chocolate manufacture had been highly labor-intensive, especially for filling and packaging operations.

The foregoing record shows the highly diffused origins of chocolate manufacture. A multitude of small enterprises sprung up all over Western

Europe that, aided by the burgeoning talents in machine design, speedily eclipsed early centers of the industry in Italy and especially in Spain. Many of them were in big cities and thus started up near their markets as well as a labor supply, but this was not invariably the case. Rather, many enterprises successful to this day were simply established where the founders had their origins, either in or near towns that were small, at least at the time, or in the country.

The Swiss producers are cases in point. Lindt was from Bern, but when he joined the Zurich firm of David Spruengli, founded in 1846, they set up shop in Kilchberg, a Zurich suburb where the firm is still located. It was similar with Tobler, whose founder Jean Tobler set up a factory in his hometown of Bern that employed 50 people. It is still there, employing 500. Suchard, whose founder was from Neuchâtel, has its plant there; Tobler merged with it in 1976.

The first Swiss factory was that of F. L. Cailler in Vevey. It is now a subsidiary of Nestlé that makes no chocolate in Switzerland under its name. Nestlé itself started in 1866 as a merger of the small chocolate factory of Henri Nestlé with the Anglo Swiss Condensed Milk Company. The headquarters of this giant multinational corporation are in Vevey.

Cadbury's in Britain had its origins in the Birmingham area. In 1861, George Cadbury and his brother Richard inherited from their parents a small chocolate business with only 12 employees and built it into one of the world's largest. In 1879 they founded Bournville, a garden village for their employees, which was to become a model for such other developments later, notably that of Hershey, Pennsylvania.

When I visited Bournville in 1939, it contrasted sharply with the slums of the rest of the industrial Midlands; the plant itself was an island of modernity among the archaic factories with famous names (such as the bicycle maker BSA) that were typical of the area. Bournville still stands out amid today's industrial decay of its region. The rather distant second largest British chocolate producer was Rowntree's of York, also established in the founders' native town.

The Hershey development is an even more impressive example. Milton S. Hershey, the founder, was born in Derry Township near Harrisburg but first established himself in Chicago, where he became a successful manufacturer of caramels. He sold that business and with the proceeds returned to his home grounds, where he built his chocolate factory and, in 1903, founded the village of Hershey for his employees. It was in a rural area that is remote from major population centers even today. To improve the inadequate transportation facilities, Hershey built an interurban electric railway to Harrisburg with other branches; it became a key link in the trolley system that then ran all the way from Philadelphia to west of Harrisburg. Its main line ran until 1946 (Hilton and Due, 1960, 296–97).

Hershey also built an electric interurban line to connect the port of Havana with Central Hershey, a new community it founded amid the huge Cuban sugar properties it first acquired in 1913 and with the city of Matanzas. It was nationalized in 1960 and apparently still runs in part with its original equipment;

thus, it is the last survivor of what had once been a major form of transportation in the United States (Hilton and Due, 1961, 223n; Middleton, 1961, 356–66).

Our last example in a real sense harks back to the original diffusion of knowledge of chocolate manufacture. When Hitler annexed Austria in 1938, there were three major chocolate manufacturers, Victor Schmidt & Söhne, Heller, and Küfferle. There was also a smaller but upscale producer, Altmann & Kühne, which was noted not only for the high quality of its chocolates but also for its imaginative packaging design.

Heller and Altmann & Kühne had Jewish owners. The former went into eclipse but was reestablished after the war. Meanwhile, some executives had managed to reach Israel, where they started to make one of Heller's non-chocolate specialties, the jam-filled hard candies known as Viennese candy. Altmann & Kühne had a store in New York on Fifth Avenue until the early 1950s. In 1938, some of its former executives started Barton's Candy Corporation, which eventually had some 3,000 outlets for its "Continental Chocolates" with packaging much like that of Altmann & Kühne. Once again, the places where the owners had settled became the location of their businesses.

Although there remain some small, independent, "boutique"-type makers of chocolate products, such as Godiva of Belgium and Teuscher of Lucerne, Switzerland, the decentralization of the industry was not to last. In more recent times, the dominant factor in it has been a wave of mergers, consolidations, and liquidations that has created almost kaleidoscopic shifts in its cast of characters. Cadbury, now Cadbury-Schweppes, and Nestlé are diversified giant multinationals. In addition to Cailler, Nestlé owns several famous European chocolate manufacturers, such as Côte d'Or of Belgium and Sarotti, the largest maker in Germany and, most recently, the main producer in the Czech Republic.

Rowntree absorbed Mackintosh, an old Scottish candy maker in May 1988; Suchard owned 29.9 percent of Rowntree, and Nestlé made a buyout offer of almost $4 billion, having meanwhile acquired 14.7 percent of the stock. Nestlé prevailed in the takeover battle; there was great concern in York, which, though a major tourist attraction, is located in the deeply distressed industrial northeast of England. There were demonstrations demanding to "Keep Rowntree's British" —almost as if it were a national treasure about to be bought by foreigners.

To add to the complexity, Kit Kat chocolate wafers, Rowntree's best-known product, are made in the United States by H. B. Reese, a division of Hershey's, which is Nestlé's biggest competitor. In 1988, Hershey's also purchased the U.S. candy business of Cadbury-Schweppes.

In 1990, Jacobs Suchard, a product of further mergers, was acquired by the Philip Morris Companies for $4.2 billion. Philip Morris had merged with Kraft-General Foods in 1985. Although its later acquisitions concentrated on the erstwhile cigarette and tobacco monopolies of the formerly Communist countries, in 1993 it also bought Terry's, another company with roots in York and the main Bulgarian producer (Moody's, 1995, 4093).

Barton's began to lose money in 1978 and was acquired by American Safety

Razor Co. in 1981. Its retail operations were closed, and the company exists only in vestigial form. True to the industrial shifts and declines that were then besetting American manufacturing in general, some of its most popular chocolate products had for some time been made in Israel and Switzerland.

Finally, in a Long Island example, Mason, Au & Magenheimer, the makers of Mason Mints, had moved from their ancestral Brooklyn to Carle Place and, after some years there, were taken over by a company that found the real estate more valuable than the factory. When the asset stripping had been done, it had turned into a shopping center. Sadly enough, not many years before, a major survey by the executive secretary of the Nassau County Planning Commission had shown that plant location even *within* Long Island had a strong correlation with where the chief executives of the firms lived (Stonier, 1964).

It is necessary, therefore, to end this chapter on a not-very encouraging note. Both cocoa growing and the chocolate industry had polycentric and diverse origins, but agglomeration and concentration became their lot whether through multinational corporations or government-prompted cartels. In such circumstances, individuals may not fare too well; most announcements of mergers and acquisitions seem to include prospective layoffs, often on a large scale. There is no intent here to sentimentalize a bucolic past that very likely never was, nor to put down the time-honored practice of seeking one's fortune far afield. Still, it is regrettable that in all too many places and circumstances entrepreneurs and especially workers can no longer take it for granted that they can stay and make a living in the old hometown or ancestral lands.

REFERENCES

Brooke, J. 1988. "Ivory Coast: African Success Story Built on Rich Farms and Stable Politics." *New York Times*, April 26, 1900.

"Chocolat," 1900. *Grande Encyclopédie*. Paris: H. Lamirault. 11: 191.

Condon, R. 1982. "Swiss Chocolate." *Gourmet*, November, 20 ff.

Edgerton, R. B. 1995. *The Fall of the Asante Empire*. New York: Free Press.

Gilbert, K. R. 1958. "Machine Tool." In *A History of Technology*, ed. C. Singer, New York: Oxford University Press. 4: 417–41.

Hilton, G. W., and J. F. Due. 1960. *The Electric Interurban Railways in America*. Stanford, Calif.: Stanford University Press.

Kay, G. B., ed. 1972. *The Political Economy of Colonialism in Ghana*. Cambridge, England: Cambridge University Press.

Kimble, D. 1963. *A Political History of Ghana*. Oxford: Clarendon Press.

Madariaga, S. de. 1963. *The Fall of the Spanish American Empire*. New York: Collier.

Middleton, D. W. 1961. *The Interurban Era*. Milwaukee: Kalmbach.

Munro, J. F. 1976. *Africa and the International Economy*. London: Dent.

Ransford, O. 1971. *The Slave Trade*. London: John Murray.

Reynolds, E. 1974. *Trade and Economic Change on the Gold Coast, 1807–1874*. New York: Longman, Inc.

Roth, C. 1959. *A History of the Marranos*. New York: Meridian Books.

Salkield, W. H. 1952. "Gold Coast Railway." *Railway Gazette Overseas Railways*.

"Schokolade." 1973. *Brockhaus Enzyklopedie*. Wiesbaden: Brockhaus. 16: 801.

Smith, Adam. 1967. In *The Money Game*. New York: Random House.

Stonier, C. E., ed. 1964. *Industrial Location Principles and Their Role in Site Selection on Long Island*. Hempstead, N.Y.: Hofstra Yearbooks of Business.

Thomas Cook 1987 International Timetable. Peterborough, England: Thomas Cook, 1987, Map 25.

Ullmann, J. E., and S. E. Gluck. 1980. *Manufacturing Management*. Columbus, Ohio: Transwin.

Wright, R. 1954. *Black Power*. New York: Harper.

CHAPTER 19

Chocolatissimo!

Alex Szogyi

Foods of predilection: caviar, truffles, saffron, chocolate, raspberries, pome-granates, chocolate, oysters, clams, chocolate, coffee, champagne, chocolate. Chocolate, always chocolate. The one saving grace, the one absolute, the one serious perfection.

The eminent chocolate specialist Judith Olney once came to the experimental kitchen, De Gustibus, at Macy's, New York, and before demonstrating the virtues of chocolate, placed her hands securely on her provocative hips, stating with characteristic bravura: "I never met a man who was as good as a piece of chocolate!" This could lead to Maye West's dictum: "It's not the men in my life; it's the life in my men." From these pronunciamentos, it is easy to segue into the realization that chocolate is symbolic not only of pleasurable food but also of pleasurable lovemaking. The chocoholic searches for a feeling of satiation, and in a world in which sexuality has become a synonym for suicide, both moral and physical, chocolate still remains a viable way to serendipity without dangerous surrender.

History affords to many examples of this efficacious surrender. Josephine made Napoleon a chocolate rhapsody of a cake, pure chocolate augmented only with some essence of raspberry, shaped in a lingot, as if it were expensive gold. The most celebrated Martian stimulants are basil, capers, and legendary chocolates. Casanova, who filled chocolate with spanish fly, drank it instead of champagne. Madame DuBarry, Louis XV's mistress, gave chocolate to all her lovers.

For chocolate inspires physical and verbal desires. In an ad for Godiva Chocolatier, called "Claus and Effect," one sees the inspired figure of a chocolate santa.

Do you believe in Santa Claus? You will as Godiva's milk chocolate Santa disappears before your eyes. You'll savor every moment of his whimsical existence. And if you truly believe, you'll be rewarded with other Godiva chocolate fantasies—with luscious fillings that'll make you kringle with joy. This holiday, share the gift of Godiva. It's always a claus for celebration.

Chocolate is thus often personified as decadent pleasure. Joanna Preuss, a raunchy food writer, featured the following in a piece on decadent desserts:

When the mood strikes me—and it happens often enough, then I seek pure, unrestrained decadent pleasure. For the seduction to be complete, the object of my affections will be a combination of caramel with nuts, or fruit with chocolate. The texture must be at least partially crunch or crisp, and the dessert must be beautiful to behold. Like love, temptation is often sparked at first sight.

Then she provides the particulars for an orange-chocolate *dacquoise*, a piquant contrast of acidity and sweetness.

In my orange-chocolate dacquoise, the bright orange segments half-robed in bittersweet chocolate, placed like spikes on top, tempt the eye while giving an important clue to the flavors married within. Sight alone seems to say the dessert will be delicious. A variety of textures also adds sensual pleasure to the palate. A mousse-like chocolate buttercream is predictably smooth. Put it between layers of cake, however delicious, and you have unmitigated softness. But buffered by firm almond meringues, the buttercream offers a stimulating interplay. Appearance and texture, however, only draw us to the dessert. It is the discovery of flavors, full of complexities and nuances, which brings satisfaction of taste.

But where did all this chocolate frenzy originate? The Mexicans made the most of chocolate. Mole sauce was supposedly created by nuns in a convent in the Mexican city of Puebla. The dish, to be served to a visiting bishop for Sunday dinner, was originally made with turkey, a native bird. The peppery sauce was conventionally Mexican, but at the last moment, the cooks grated in some bitter chocolate. Carol Ann Rinzler (1977) in her book on chocolate waxes enthusiastically: "Like wine, chocolate has mythological roots that are mixed with religion."[1] She regrets that chocolate is rarely taken seriously. She insists that it is food for the most philosophical gourmet.

The year 1519 seems to be chocolate's watershed year, when the Spanish explorer Hernando Cortez first tasted it at the court of the Aztec emperor Montezuma. Before that, all is conjecture, myth, and circumstantial evidence. The first cocoa trees probably grew wild in the Amazon or Orinoco valleys more than 4,000 years ago. The Mayans took it with them to the Yucatan when they migrated there in the seventh century A.D. The derivation of the word *chocolate* is certainly Aztec/Mayan. It comes from *chocolatl*, which is what the Indians called the cold, bitter drink they made by mixing ground cocoa beans with liquid. But from there, conjecture still prevails. Is it a combination of two

Mayan words, *choco* (warm) and *latl* (beverage)? But since chocolate was usually served cold, beware. Another possibility is that *latl* means water and that *choco* describes the sound made when the ground beans were mixed with the liquid, whirled in an earthenware golden cup with a wooden implement called the *molinet*. The *molinet*, which looked something like a child's wooden hammer, made the drink frothy (from there to the egg cream, New York's vintage Lower East Side drink, might only be a hop, skip, and a jump: Could the seltzer bottle be Mexican in spirit)? And *choco* might mean froth or foam. At any rate, legend has it that *chocolatl* was an intoxicating drink, but this has never been completely verified.

Chocolatl went alcoholic early on. The Indian *chocolatl* was made by mixing the ground beans with fermented corn mash or with wine instead of water and drunk in intoxicating quantities. At Montezuma's court, more than 2,000 cups of *chocolatl* were poured each and every day. The emperor himself drank 50 of them and may well have believed that every single cup was blessed by the Aztec god Quetzalcoatl. (How fortunate that the notion of cholesterol was as yet unknown. Imagine mass cholesterol hysteria among the Aztecs!)

The myth went wild. In Mexico at the start of the planting season, the Itza Indians are said to have sacrificed a prisoner to Tonacxatecutli, the goddess of food, and Calchiutucue, the goddess of water. Prisoners were given cups of *chocolatl* in the belief that it would turn their hearts to chocolate. Then the heart was torn from the body and offered to the goddesses. (Imagine what could be done with Baci today!) In Nicaragua, the gods were more beneficent. The cocoa farmers attempted to placate Quetzalcoatl (the god of the moon) and ensured the fertility of the crop by abstaining from sexual activity for at least two weeks before sowing the seeds. Hence, the notion of abstinence and the sensual power of chocolate began a long time ago, indeed.

The Spanish conquistadors were not impressed by all of this. They only were moved by the fact that cocoa beans were used for money. Hence, the first modern philosophical chocolate questions: Where was Christopher Columbus in 1502 when he became the first European to see and taste chocolate? Was he in Nicaragua? Was the chocolate brought to his ship by Indians who rode out to greet him? Columbus didn't bring any home, the rotter. Seventeen years later, Cortez was unimpressed with the taste of chocolatl but fascinated by the gold cups in which the drink was served and the use of cocoa beans as money. The tribute from Montezuma's defeated enemies included chests of cocoa beans and ground chocolate, among other booty. Cortez immediately established a cocoa plantation under the Spanish flag to grow money for the king. The Spanish enjoyed the monopoly on chocolate for a good long time. Until the eighteenth century, almost all the chocolate used in Europe passed through Spanish hands. Chocolate eating was invented in the nineteenth century, and a distinction was drawn between cocoa or hot chocolate (the liquid) and chocolate as solid food. All chocolate meant drinking chocolate, some variation or other on the basic drink *chocolatl*. Money always meant counterfeit money. Some Indians hollowed out the cocoa bean shells and filled them with dirt, reserving the valuable beans for themselves.

Chocolate was always somehow a secret pleasure. The Spanish drank chocolate made by monks in monasteries, and they drank it in secret. And they hoarded their supplies. In 1606, an Italian gentleman named Antonio Carletti was said to be the first person to carry chocolate from Spain into Italy. From there, it made its way into the Austrian courts, and from that point on, chocolate traveled thanks to a spate of royal marriages. Anne of Austria married Louis XIII of France and took her chocolate with her. Spain's Maria Theresa, a passionate devotee, took her chocolate to France as well, when she was betrothed to Louis XIV. A royal chocolate maker was appointed, and the drink became the rage. In Mexico, chocolate was served to the ladies in church. When one bishop forbade the practice, the ladies took themselves to another church, and the offending clergyman, it was rumored, later died of a cup of poisoned chocolate. A fearful scandal resulted.

The bishop of Rome declared in 1662 that "liquidum non frangit jejunum"— liquids including chocolate do not break the fast. Chocolates were thought of as a medicine, as a panacea for all human ills, the domain of the apothecaries and not the confectioners. Thomas Gage in A New Survey of the West Indies (1648) explained that drinking five cups of chocolate every day for 12 years had turned him into a tower of good health. Many Europeans thought of chocolate as an aphrodisiac. Casanova and the Marquis de Sade turned chocolate into a sexual stimulant and a means to aphrodisiacal power. Caffeine and theobromine, the stimulant in chocolate, can produce an irritating, diuretic effect. Pepper was usually added to chocolate and caused an irritation similar to that of the aphrodisiac catharis. However, it has never been confirmed that chocolate definitely significantly raised the population of Western Europe.

Chocolate eventually triumphed. In 1780, the first machine-ground chocolate is reported to have been produced in a factory near Barcelona. And that, as we know, is always the beginning of the end.

The Mexicans smoothed their chocolate by rubbing it with stone trollers in stone troughs. The Swiss adapted the principle and invented refiners that smoothed the chocolate liquor by passing it between porcelain discs or by rubbing it against itself in a procedure called conching. They produced a smooth chocolate that had a particularly mellow flavor. As we can readily see, chocolate has always been sexually oriented. Rubbing produces the best effect.

In Judith Olney's Entertainments (1981), she produces the ultimate dinner for the purpose of seduction. She sets the scene with the seducer-cook's offer of richly inflaming, elegant I-cared-enough-to-do-this-for-you dishes. The menu contains as many aphrodisiacs as are available: caviar, eggs, pepper, cayenne, spices, nuts, seafood, and of course, chocolate. Alcohol is kept to a minimum, which, "as we know, promoteth desire but taketh away the performance there of." The white chocolate mousse with bittersweet chocolate sauces provides a contrast of chocolate savoir faire. A good cigar is included—even for the woman. The Philippines make a great cigarillo called Mahaba Regaliz. The deep brown paper wrapper is redolent of chocolate.

Inevitably, it is Brillat-Savarin who codifies for the French and for the modern cultist the ultimate aesthetic of any food. In his Physiology of Taste (1826), Brillat-Savarin stars chocolate. He understood that the men who first assaulted the frontiers of America were driven by the hunger for gold. Cocoa was among their truest treasures. "We have come to think of chocolate as the mixture which results from roasting together the cocoa paste and not chocolate. And when we add the delicious perfume of vanilla to the mixture of sugar, cocoa and cinnamon, we achieve the nec plus ultra of perfection in which such a concoction may be carried" (109). It is through the creation of chocolate that we perceive that a new perfection has been achieved.

Brillat-Savarin always psychs out the true aesthetic meaning of all these phenomena:

The Spanish ladies of the New World are madly addicted to chocolate to such a point that, not content to drink it several times each day, they each have it served to them in church. This sensuality has often brought down upon them the wrath of their bishops but the latter have ended by closing their eyes to the sin, and the Reverend Father Escobar whose spiritual reasoning was as subtle as his moral doctrine was accommodating, issued a formal declaration that chocolate made with water was not contrary to the rules of fast days.[2]

Chocolate's strong flavor was appreciated by women and especially by monks. Thus, we are to understand the profound connection between monks and women: This could be the subject of a feminist doctoral thesis which they might pay to suppress. The various ambassadors from Spain to Paris also helped make chocolate fashionable, and at the beginning of the Regency, it was more commonly known than coffee, since it was drunk as a pleasant ailment, while coffee was still thought of as a luxurious and rare beverage.

It was also Brillat-Savarin who stated most categorically that with time and experience, these two sublime teachers, it has been shown as proof positive that carefully prepared chocolate is as healthful a food as it is pleasant; that it is nourishing and easily digested; and that it does not cause the same harmful effects to feminine beauty that are blamed on coffee. On the contrary, it is a remedy helpful to people who must do a great deal of mental work; to those who labor in the pulpit or the courtroom; and especially, to travelers. It has produced good results in cases of chronic illness and has even been used as the last resort in diseases of the pylorus. Brillat-Savarin goes as far as to say that few substances contain more nourishing particles for a like weight: all of which makes it completely assimilable. When people complain they cannot digest chocolate or insist that it digests too quickly, he feels they have only themselves to blame and that the chocolate they eat is of inferior quality, for good, well-made chocolate can be assimilated by any stomach that can still digest even feebly.

His recommendations can be personally experimented with:

When you have breakfasted well and fully, if you will drink a big cup of chocolate at the end, you will have digested the whole perfectly three hours later and you will be able to dine. . . . Because of my scientific enthusiasm and the sheer force of my eloquence, I have persuaded a number of ladies to try this although they were convinced it would kill them, they have always found themselves in fine shape indeed, and have not forgotten to give the Professor his rightful due.[3]

Brillat-Savarin can even become a bit pedantic about his belief in chocolate:

People who habitually drink chocolate enjoy unvarying health and are least attacked by a host of little illnesses which can destroy the true joy of living; their physical weight is almost stationary, and he bestows all these good feelings on men, as well. Very well, then, if any man has drunk a little too deeply from the cup of physical pleasure, if he has spent too much time at his desk that should have been spent asleep, if his fine spirits have temporarily become dulled, if he finds the air too damp, the minutes too slow and the atmosphere too heavy to withstand: if he is obsessed by a fixed idea which bars him from any freedom of thought: if he is any of these poor creatures, we say, let him be given a good pint of amber-flavored chocolate, in the proportion of sixty to seventy-two grains of amber to a pound and marvels will be performed.[4]

His remarks on chocolate end with a comment made to him by Madame d'Atrestel, superior of the Convent of the Visitation at Belley, some 50 years previously:

Whenever you want to have a really good cup of chocolate, make it the day before in a porcelain coffee pot and let it set. The night's rest will concentrate it and give it a velvety quality which will make it better. Our good God cannot possibly take offense at this little refinement since he himself is everything that is most perfect.[5]

As a way of ending this little excursion into chocolate lore and lasciviousness, it would, I think, be appropriate to share the thoughts of Maida Heatter (1980), the chairperson of the board of the Chocolate Lovers Association of the World. She started as a Brownie and worked her way up.

We understand each other, chocolate and I. My husband says that I can hear chocolate. . . . Chocolate is a magnet. Word of a special chocolate cake at a certain restaurant draws people for hundreds of miles. People send from around the world when they hear of a chocolate dessert they can buy by mail. When a magazine wants to increase its circulation they simply have to use a cover photograph of a mouth-watering, three layer chocolate cake. . . . For many years we have fed the sea gulls stale bread and crackers. When I made too many brownies once I decided to try them on the gulls. I have never seen them so excited—they were frantic; they have never come as close, nor grabbed the food as hungrily; they fought with each other over every crumb. Then they sat in the bay for hours waiting for more. Gulls will be gulls.[6]

The finest chocolate taste in a New York restaurant can now be had at Restaurant Bouley, 165 Duane Street, where Chef David Bouley presents a chocolate soufflé that could easily bring back Brillat-Savarin from the other world. Antoine Bouterin, chef of his own restaurant, Bouterin, produces soufflés every bit as enticing.

This conference has proven that erudite people who go to conferences will interrupt their busy lives and gravitate to Hofstra without ever thinking of reevaluating a great literary figure or a president. And if we were to discover that George Sand loved Chopin because his name began with *cho*, this could launch yet another memorable conference. Let us end this happy moment with the thought inscribed on my little cup here: "Promise me anything, but give me chocolate." Let us imbibe.

NOTES

1. Carol Ann Rinzler, *The Book of Chocolate*, 3–5, 17.
2. Jean-Anthelme Brillat-Savarin, *The Physiology of Taste*, 107.
3. Ibid., 109.
4. Ibid., 109–10.
5. Ibid., 113.
6. Maida Heatter, *Maida Heatter's Book of Great Chocolate Desserts*, ix–x.

REFERENCES

Beranbaum, Rose Levy. *The Cake Bible*. N.Y.: William Morrow, 1988.

Boynton, Sandra. *Chocolate: The Consuming Passion*. N.Y.: Workman Publishing, 1982.

Brillat-Savarin, Jean-Anthelme. *Physiologie du goût* (Physiology of taste). Paris: Michel Guibert, 1826.

Heatter, Maida. *Maida Heatter's Book of Great Chocolate Desserts*. N.Y.: Alfred A. Knopf, 1980.

Jolly, Martine. *Le Chocolat*. N.Y.: Pantheon Books, 1985.

Olney, Judith. *Entertainments*. N.Y.: Barron's, 1981.

Rinzler, Carol Ann. *The Book of Chocolate*. N.Y.: St. Martin's Press, 1977.

CHAPTER 20

Chocolate Recipes

Compiled by Alex Szogyi

However much scientific and historical truth the world of chocolate has motivated our scholars, we still know deep down that chocolate is an irresistible taste. Brillat-Savarin assured the world that chocolate was one of the most worthwhile pleasures of life. Although some still feel guilty about the amount of chocolate they consume, we know that the positive factors far outweigh any negative results. Chocoholics were given more than their due at the conference's chocolate banquet. Herewith are recipes for some of the dishes our guests consumed and also some of the favorite recipes of one of our speakers, Lucille Fillin, who unfortunately departed this world soon after the conference. We dedicate them to her memory.

LUCILLE'S RECIPES

Here are some popular everyday chocolate recipes from Lucille Fillin.

Chocolate Mousse or Pots-de-Creme
4 servings

In a double boiler with a *low flame*, combine
    1 cup chocolate bits
    1 ½ cups cream
Melt, stirring until chocolate bits are melted.
In a separate bowl, combine
    2 whole eggs plus
    2 yolks
Add to the double boiler, mix well, and add
    1 teaspoon vanilla or
    2 teaspoons Jamaica Rum
Boil for about 10 minutes, but keep the flame low.

When you taste the mixture and all is dissolved, pour into 8 custard cups or soufflé-dishes and chill. When ready to serve, add a few teaspoons of whipped heavy cream (do not use "pasteurized cream") that has been beaten with a little confectioner's sugar and vanilla. For a nice decorative touch, put a candied violet on top.

This keeps well in the freezer, but add the whipped cream when ready to serve.

Chocolate Icing
to make about 2 cups unwhipped icing

½ pound semisweet chocolate (Baker's)
½ pound unsalted butter, softened

Melt the chocolate in the top of a double boiler over hot water. When the chocolate is soft, add the butter. Swirl the butter and chocolate until they are completely dissolved and all lumps have disappeared. Let the icing cool slightly before pouring it over the cake.

The icing is easily spread by using a rubber spatula or an artist's palette knife (available in art supply stores). Decorate with fresh walnut halves.

Chocolate Pudding from the Young New Yorkers Cookbook
Vanilla or Chocolate Pudding
Double this for 8

Mix together in saucepan
3 tablespoons cornstarch (dissolve in 2 teaspoons milk)
¼ cup sugar
A few grains of salt
Stir in gradually
2 cups of milk
Boil for one minute.
Add: one teaspoon of vanilla.
Variation: For chocolate pudding, add 2 tablespoons sugar
and 3 tablepoons cocoa to cornstarch.
Yield: 4 servings.
Standards: Smooth cornstarch thoroughly cooked, chilled.

My Mother's Chocolate Cake

Grease two 9-inch layer pans and line each with a sheet of buttered waxed
paper.
Sift and measure:
2 cups flour
Resift the flour with
2 teaspoons baking powder
½ teaspoon salt
In a separate bowl, beat
½ cup butter
1 teaspoon vanilla
Add in small amounts and continue beating until soft and fluffy
1 cup sugar
Beat well and add
2 eggs
Add sifted dry ingredients alternating with
⅜ cup of milk
Pour into greased pans.

Bake in a moderate oven (375° F). Cupcakes—20 minutes; layers—25 minutes. When done, spread strawberry or apricot jam between the layers and top
with chocolate icing. *Yield*: Two 9-inch layers or 16 cupcakes. *Standards*:
Evenly browned, rounded on top; fine, even grain; crumb, moist and tender;
delicate flavor.

BANQUET RECIPES

Cincinnati Chili
serves 4 (or 8 over spaghetti)

1 tablespoon olive oil
2 medium onions, finely chopped
4 cloves garlic (optional),
  finely minced
2 pounds lean ground beef
4 cups beef broth
1 15-ounce can tomato sauce
1 teaspoon ground allspice
3 tablespoons chili powder
½ teaspoon cayenne, or more
  if you wish it hotter

1 teaspoon cumin seeds,
  freshly roasted in a small
  skillet and ground
1 teaspoon flour
1 bay leaf
¼ teaspoon ground cloves
2 tablespoons white or cider
  vinegar
½ ounce unsweetened chocolate
  salt, if desired
  spaghetti, chopped onions,
  cheese, and oyster crackers—
  selection as desired

In a covered medium (4-quart) saucepan, sweat onions and garlic in oil over medium flame until soft and translucent, about 8 minutes. With a slotted spoon, lift out the onions and garlic and set aside.

Drop meat into the saucepan and cook over medium-high heat until all the redness is gone and the meat is a light brown, about 6 minutes. Break up the clumps of meat with a wooden spoon to ensure that it is cooked thoroughly. Add the cooked onion and garlic to the meat and stir well to mix. Add the beef broth, tomato sauce, and allspice. Cook over low heat, barely simmering, for about one half hour.

Make a thin paste with the chili powder, cayenne, freshly ground cumin, 1 teaspoon flour, and about 2 tablespoons water. The chili puree or paste in this form makes it easier to control the amount of hot stuff to be added. Begin with 2 tablespoons of the chili paste mixed into the saucepan; stir to blend it well. Taste. Add more by the single tablespoon until the desired seasoning is reached.

Add bay leaf, ground cloves, vinegar, chocolate, and salt.

Cover and cook over low heat for at least 1 hour. Some Cincinnati cooks let the pot simmer for up to 3 hours. But don't let it turn into a solid before adding more beef stock or water.

Taste and test one more time and correct seasoning to suit the tongue and the occasion. Serve chili in heated bowls—and pass saltines. Or, as in Cincinnati, layer spaghetti, chili, onions, cheese, and oyster crackers.

Chocolate Bread (German Dark Rye Bread)

3 cups sifted all-purpose flour	⅓ cup molasses
2 envelopes active dry yeast	2 tablespoons butter or
¼ cup cocoa powder	margarine
1 tablespoon caraway seed	1 tablespoon sugar
2 cups water	1 tablespoon salt
	3 to 3½ cups rye flour

In large mixer bowl, combine the all-purpose flour, yeast, cocoa powder, and caraway seed till well blended. In saucepan, combine water, molasses, butter or margarine, sugar, and salt; heat till just warm, stirring occasionally to melt butter. Add to dry mixture in mixer bowl. Beat at low speed with electric mixer for ½ minute, scraping sides of bowl constantly. Beat 3 minutes at high speed. By hand, stir in enough rye flour to make a soft dough. Turn onto floured surface; knead till smooth, about 5 minutes. *Cover*; let rest 20 minutes. Punch down and divide dough in half. Shape each half into a round loaf; place on greased baking sheets or in two 8-inch pie plates. Brush surface of loaves with a little cooking oil. Slash tops of loaves with sharp knife. Let rise till double, 45 to 60 minutes. Bake in 400° F oven for 25 to 30 minutes.

Chicken Mole
serves 8

4 pounds chicken breasts, halved	2 tablespoons olive oil
Oil for frying	7 tablespoons mild chili powder
2 garlic cloves, minced	¼ teaspoon each: cumin, cloves,
1 medium onion, sliced	cinnamon, coriander seeds,
1 small tortilla, cut into strips	anise, sugar
¼ cup raisins	¾ teaspoon salt
¼ cup blanched almonds	1 ounce unsweetened chocolate, melted
1 tablespoon sesame seeds	3 cups chicken broth ½ pound tomatoes,
	peeled and seeded

Brown the chicken on all sides in hot oil; set aside. Blend the next 8 ingredients to a smooth paste. Add chili powder, seasonings, and melted chocolate. Heat olive oil in a large frying pan; fry the above sauce 5 minutes, lowering the heat as soon as sauce is in the pan; stir to prevent burning. Stir in the broth, add chicken, and cover pan; simmer over low heat 30 minutes or until tender.

Index

About the Editor and Contributors

BARBARA ALBRIGHT is the former editor in chief of *Chocolatier* magazine and has held various positions in food and communications. Currently she writes a monthly column for the Associated Press and is a contributing editor for *Familyfun* in addition to working on several book projects. She was the editor of a special publication entitled *The Good Housekeeping Editors Entertain*. She is also a registered dietitian and has a master's degree from Boston University in nutrition communications. She is a member of the Chocolate Lovers Hall of Fame.

DIANE BARTHEL-BOUCHIER received her doctorate from Harvard University and is currently professor of sociology at the State University of New York at Stony Brook. Bouchier has also taught at Boston College and the University of Essex and worked as a research associate at the Martin Centre for Architectural and Urban Studies, Cambridge University, England. She is author of *Amana: From Pietiet Sect to American Community* (1984), *Putting on Appearances: Gender and Advertising* (1988), and *Historic Preservation: Collective Memory and Historical Identity* (1996).

SOPHIE D. COE was an anthropologist and food historian. Born in Pasadena, California in 1933, she received her A.B. degree from Radcliffe College in 1955 and her Ph.D. from Harvard University in 1964. From 1984 until her death in 1994, she was an active participant in the Oxford Symposium on Food and Cookery and a frequent contributor to *Petits Propos Culinaires*. For a number of years her principal research interest was in the native cuisines of the pre-Columbian civilizations; two books were based on this research: *America's First Cuisines* (1994) and *The True History of Chocolate*, with Michael D. Coe (1996).

CATHERINE S. ELLIOTT is an economist and an educator. She received her Ph.D. from the University of Michigan and is currently teaching at New College, the honors college of the State University System of Florida. While originally schooled as a theoretical microeconomist, she now enjoys working in the fields of behavioral economics and socioeconomics—drawing on other disciplines and noneconomic factors to help explain actual behavior. This interdisciplinary approach to studying decision making allows her to investigate such questions as: What is rational choice? Why do I do what I do when I know I'll regret it later? And of course: Can chocolate cure irrationality? She has published two books and numerous journal articles and has won awards for both teaching and research.

ROBERT FYNE is an associate professor of English at Kean College, New Jersey, where he teaches film and literature courses. He is the author of *The Hollywood Propaganda of World War II*, a study of over 300 motion pictures produced during the global conflict that glorified the achievements of the American fighting man while vilifying all members of the Axis Pact. Some of his reviews and essays have appeared in *Historical Journal of Film, Radio, and Television, Social Science Journal, Film Library Quarterly, New Guard, Film Library Quarterly, Journal of Popular Film and Television, Alaska Quarterly Review,* and *Christian Century*. He is also the book review editor of *Film & History*.

JANINE GASCO received her Ph.D. in anthropology from the University of California at Santa Barbara in 1987. She has taught at the University of Minneapolis, the State University of New York at Albany, the University of California at Irvine, and California State University at Los Angeles. Currently, she is adjunct assistant professer at Occidental College and research associate at the Institute of Archaeology at the University of California, Los Angeles. She has conducted archaeological and historical research on the late prehistoric and colonial indigenous societies of southern Mexico and Guatemala, and her particular interest is in the history of cacao cultivation in these areas.

ANNE K. KALER is a professor of English at Gwynedd-Mercy College. She earned her doctorate from Temple University in Shakespeare and fiction, her master's degree from the University of Pennsylvania, and her bachelor's degree from Catholic University of America in speech and drama. Her publications include *The Picara: From Hera to Fantasy Heroine* and articles in *The Culture of Celebrations, Heroines of Popular Culture,* and Andrew Greeley's World, in addition to many journals. She has presented papers at Hofstra's conferences on van Gogh and Anglo-Irish literature as well as at other professional conferences.

KAREN S. KUBENA is professor of nutrition on the Faculty of Nutrition, Texas A&M University in College Station. Her degrees were earned at the

University of Wisconsin at Madison (B.S.), Mississippi State University in Starkville (M.S.), and Texas A&M University (Ph.D.). A registered dietitian, she has served as director for dietetics education programs at Texas A&M and was section leader of the Human Nutrition Section, Department of Animal Science, at Texas A&M until 1995. At that time, she assumed the position of associate dean for academic programs for the College of Agriculture and Life Sciences. A member of the board of editors for the *Journal of the American Dietetic Association and Magnesium Research*, her current research interests include dietary assessment and nutrition through the life cycle.

WENDALL A. LANDMANN, professor emeritus, retired in the late 1980s after a career in which he was recognized as an authority on protein metabolism. After completing degrees at the University of Illinois and Purdue University, his first area of research was meat science, in conjunction with which he held positions at the Argonne National Laboratory in Lemont, Illinois, and the American Meat Institute Foundation, Chicago. In 1964, he joined the faculty of Texas A&M University as professor of biochemistry and biophysics and of animal science. During the 1970s, he served as head, Department of Biochemistry and Biophysics. It was at this time that he became interested in nutrition, which was reflected in a new research direction of protein metabolism in humans.

BARBARA LEKATSAS holds a Ph.D. in comparative literature from New York University. She is also twice a recipient of the Fulbright grant. She is the author of *Persephone, Cross-cultural Communications* (1986), and the *Howard L. and Muriel Weingrow Collection of Avant-garde Art and Literature at Hofstra University: An Annotated Bibliography* (Greenwood Press, 1985).

WILLIAM ALEX MCINTOSH received his Ph.D. in sociology from Iowa State in 1975. He is a full professor in both the Departments of Rural Sociology and Sociology. He is also a member of the Faculty of Nutrition as well as of the Centre for Food Safety. His current projects include investigations of how parental relationships with adolescents affect those adolescents' risk of coronary heart disease through their effects on lipid status and body fat status. He has recently published articles on adolescent cardiovascular intake in journals such as the *Journal of the American Dietetic Association, Applied Social Science Review*, and *Wellness Perspectives*. His book *Sociologies of Food and Nutrition* was published in August 1996.

MARION NESTLE, who received a Ph.D. in molecular biology from the University of California at Berkeley and a master's in public health nutrition from the same institution, has been professor and chair of the Department of Nutrition and Food Studies at New York University since fall 1988. She held prior positions at Brandeis University, the University of California at San Francisco School of Medicine and the U.S. Public Health Service. She was managing editor of the 1988 *Surgeon General's Report on Nutrition and Health* and is the author of *Nutrition in Clinical Practice*. Her research focuses on food and nutrition policy issues, particularly those that influence the development and acceptance of federal dietary recommendations.

ROBERT M. REES received his bachelor's degree at Stanford University and graduate degrees from the University of California at Berkeley and Columbia University. He has attended special sessions on American history at Harvard University. Rees is on the faculty at the University of Hawaii and teaches in American Studies and in the College of Business Administration. He also is moderator of a weekly TV show in Honolulu, *Island Issues*, and a regular contributor to *Honolulu Weekly* and to *Honolulu Magazine*.

DAVID W. SEAMAN holds a Ph.D. from Stanford University. He is a professor of French and chair of the Department of Foreign Languages at Georgia Southern University. He is the author of the book *Concrete Poetry in France* (1981) and has published numerous articles on the avant-garde, literature, culture, and the arts. He was a Fulbright professor in Morocco and pursues the study of the literature and culture of the Maghreb. Sculptor, poet, filmmaker, and videographer, he is actively involved with the Lettristes avant-garde group. He is an experienced wine maker and a cook specializing in French and exotic cuisines.

ELANA ROSE STARR is a film publicist. In addition, she teaches film courses in Villanova University's Communication Arts Department. An abiding love of chocolate (preferably the dark variety) notwithstanding, her main area of interest is the cinematic representation of "outsiders," particularly in mainstream Hollywood films.

LARRY M. STARR, a Ph.D. and professor at Villanova University, teaches undergraduate courses in health/medical psychology and industrial/organizational psychology and graduate courses in administrative decision making and literature and psychology. He is chief executive officer for SOS Technologies, a Philadelphia area emergency care training and consulting company. For Oxygen Therapy Institute, a Detroit-based international medical manufacturing and distribution company, he is director of medical education and research.

BENNEVILLE N. STROHECKER, founder and chief executive officer of Harbor Sweets in Salem, Massachusetts, is a living testament to the power of trust and commitment to a dream. What started as a hobby to make the "best chocolates in the world regardless of price" has grown into a nationally acclaimed $3 million handmade chocolate company. Along the way, Strohecker has become recognized not only for his extraordinary product but for his inspiring management style. The development of the Sweet Sloop, Harbor

Sweet's signature candy, is in many ways a foreshadowing of the story of Harbor Sweets, the company. It tells of Strohecker's creativity, attention to detail, insistence on quality, and trust—not only in his instincts, but in others.

ALEX SZOGYI is professor of French and comparative literature at Hunter College/City University of New York. He is a founding member of the Friends of George Sand at Hofstra University and has published extensively on her works for theater and novels. He was one of the translators of her auto-biography, *L'Histoire de Ma Vie*. He has been restaurant reviewer of the Village Voice and cookbook editor for many culinary mazagines over the years. He was twice decorated by the French Government (Officier dans l'ordre des Palmes Académiques) and is distinguished alumnus of Brooklyn College. He has translated 53 plays from many languages. His Guggenheim Fellowship (1962) made it possible for him to be the only American ever to have translated all of the plays of Anton Chekhov. His study of Molière, *Molière Abstrait* (Paris, Nizet, 1985), led to his being invited to Bernard Pivot's *Apostrophes*, one of the very few Americans to have had this honor.

CHARLES S. TELLY is professor of management in the Department of Business Administration at the State University of New York at Fredonia. He is a Williams College graduate with a B.A. in philosophy and history. His M.A. in philosophy is from the University of Arizona. His Ph.D. is from the University of Washington at Seattle. He also has a J.D. degree in law from the University of Buffalo and an LL.M. and J.S.D. degrees from Columbia University Law School. He has taught at the Business Colleges at the University of Washington, University of New Mexico, and University of Utah and the Law Schools at the University of Dayton, Wake Forest University, and Oklahoma City University. His articles and theories are directed toward the corporation both as to how it functions and as to its legal nature.

JOHN E. ULLMANN is professor emeritus of management in the School of Business of Hofstra University. An industrial engineer, he is the author of 30 books and monographs and over a hundred articles on technical and industrial innovation and development. His books include *The Anatomy of Industrial Decline, The Prospects of American Industrial Recovery, Social Costs in Modern Society* and *The Suburban Economic Network*.

ERDMUTE WENZEL WHITE teaches French, comparative literature, and film studies at Purdue University. She has taught as a visiting professor at the University of Hamburg, Germany. Her research concerns the affiliation of poets, painters, and musicians, the avant-garde and intermedia texts. She is a collector of first editions and manuscripts pertaining to concrete poetry, Dada, and Fluxus. Her publications include work on Vassily Kandinsky, Tom Phillips, Fernando Pessoa, Oswald de Andrade, and Paual Wühr. She has completed a book-length manuscript with the working title *The Magic Bishop: Hugo Ball, Dada Poet*.

HAROLD E. YUKER is Mervyn Schloss Distinguished Professor of Psychology and director of the Center for the Study of Attitudes toward Persons with Disabilities at Hofstra University. His major interest is in attitude research. He and his colleagues developed the "Attitudes toward Disabled Persons Scale," which is the most used measure of its kind. His research has resulted in the publication of many articles, several research monographs, and an edited book, *Attitudes toward Persons with Disabilities*, published in 1988. He is a fellow of the Division of Rehabilitation Psychology of the American Psychological Association, and in 1991 he received the Roger Barker Distinguished Research Award from them.